Doing
Psychology
Experiments
Third Edition

Doing Psychology Experiments

Third Edition

David W. Martin

New Mexico State University

Brooks/Cole Publishing Company
Pacific Grove, California

Consulting Editor: Roger Kirk

Printed in the United States of America
10 9 8 7 6 5 4 3 2

Library of Congress Cataloging-in-Publication Data
Martin, David W., [date]
  Doing psychology experiments / David W. Martin. — 3rd ed.
    p.   cm.
  Includes bibliographical references and index.
  ISBN 0-534-14490-X
    1. Psychology, Experimental.   2. Psychology—Research.   I. Title.
BF181.M315   1990
150'.724—dc20   90-44823
                                                                            CIP

Sponsoring Editor: *Phillip L. Curson*
Project Development Editor: *Marlene Chamberlain*
Editorial Assistant: *Heather L. Riedl*
Production Editor: *Ben Greensfelder*
Manuscript Editor: *Lieselotte Hoffman*
Permissions Editor: *Carline Haga*
Interior Design: *Vernon T. Boes*
Cover Design: *Katherine Minerva*
Art Coordinator: *Lisa Torri*
Interior Illustration: *Kevin East*
Typesetting: *Graphic Typesetting Service*
Cover Printing: *Phoenix Color Corporation*
Printing and Binding: *The Maple Press, Inc.*

This book is dedicated to:

My father, Daniel W. Martin,
>   who taught me logical thinking,

My high school teacher Doris Mitchell,
>   who showed me that teachers can care.

My undergraduate professor Harve E. Rawson,
>   who introduced me to psychology,

My graduate professor the late George E. Briggs,
>   who best demonstrated experimental rigor,

And all of my students,
>   from whom I am continually learning to teach.

Preface to the Third Edition

Doing Psychology Experiments has now been on the market for 15 years and it still seems to be fulfilling its original function: to teach students with little or no background in experimentation how to do simple experiments in psychology. Throughout the three editions of the book I have tried to keep the writing style informal and friendly. Although scientific results are usually reported in an objective and impersonal style, I believe that doing experiments is a highly personal experience. The experimenter reviews the literature and forms a view of the body of knowledge. The experimenter creates the theories and hypotheses for testing. The experimenter decides which variables to manipulate and which to measure. The experimenter interprets the results and determines how the body of knowledge has been advanced. The experimenter is personally involved in the process of experimentation and I believe that the best way to teach new experimenters about this process is through a personal book.

Now for a few words about what this book does and does not do. It provides enough information so that a student with no experimental background will be able to design, execute, interpret, and report simple psychological experiments. While the book has most often been used for undergraduate courses in experimental methods, it has also been used along with other books for other purposes. Several colleges use it for the laboratory section of introductory psychology courses. It is sometimes used in conjunction with a statistics book or a content book for experimental courses having those orientations. It is frequently adopted for undergraduate content courses (ranging from deviant behavior to consumer psychology) when the professor requires experiments to be done and the students have little experimental background. I have talked with many users, both professors and students. They report that the book can be used successfully as a stand-alone supplement. In fact, in my own experimental methods course, I assign chapters before lecturing on the material, give a little quiz to encourage the students to read the material prior to class, and then spend lecture time clarifying points where necessary, but mostly discussing experimental proposals and problems. The book does a good job of bringing a diverse set of students up to the same level so that class time can be used for more creative interaction. Although the book is often used as a supplemental text and may appear physically smaller than some others on the market, it nevertheless does discuss most of the important concepts from experimental methods. I have attempted to provide comprehensive coverage of the area and some recent research indicates that the attempt has been success-ful.* Authors of textbooks representing many areas of psychology were asked to rate the importance of terms and concepts from their subfields. Of the top 100 ranked terms in the methods/statistics area, 33 emphasized statistics or psychometric testing. Of the remaining 67 that emphasized methods, this book discusses all but 6. Four of those terms are discussed at a conceptual level but using alternative terminology. Only two terms, both with ranks in the 90s, are not represented in this book. I believe that this evidence confirms the claim that the book does provide a comprehensive coverage of experimental methods.

What this book does not do is teach students much about the content and current findings in the various areas of experimental psychology. Many of the examples I use are contrived; they illustrate the methods being discussed, but in many cases they are not real and certainly will not give students a representative coverage of the content of experimental psychology. The book also does not teach students much about the intricacies of complex experimental design and statistical analysis. I have tried to keep it simple. Although I do discuss the rationale behind descriptive and inferential statistics, the actual statistical operations presented in the appendix are admittedly cookbookish.

The third edition has a few new features. Chapter 12 provides some thoughts on how to know when an experiment is ready to go. Over the years of teaching experimental methods, I have discovered that many of the details of doing an experiment that are obvious to an experienced experimenter often elude new experimenters. This chapter was written to provide a final check for students before they launch their experiments. Because the world is changing so rapidly in the areas of animal research and science fraud, the chapters on being fair with subjects and with science required considerable updating. Reviewers also offered many, more minor suggestions for improving all the chapters. Several new tables and figures have been added that should help clarify the text. Yet the length has been only marginally increased. For those who have used previous editions, I hope you like the changes. For new users, I hope you like the book.

I would like to thank New Mexico State University for providing me with the resources to write the third edition. My editor at Brooks/Cole, Phil Curson, plied me with various incentives to induce me to get on with the third edition. I would also like to thank Ben Greensfelder, Vernon Boes, Kath Minerva, Heather Riedl, and Liese Hoffman for additional editorial and design assistance. I am also grateful to the following manuscript reviewers: Eve Bhumitra, Adelphi University; Richard Deni, Rider College; Susan E. Dutch, Westfield State College, Westfield, Massachusetts; Jennifer Gille, University of California, Santa Cruz; Michele Y. Martel, Northeast Missouri State University; Michael F. Shaughnessy, Eastern New Mexico State Uni-

---

*Boneau, C. A. (1990). Psychological literacy: A first approximation. *American Psychologist, 45,* 891–900.

versity; Randolph A. Smith, Ouachita Baptist University, Arkadelphia, Arkansas; and particularly Richard A. King, University of North Carolina at Chapel Hill, who provided extensive valuable comments. Finally, I would like to thank the students who have used and will use this book, students in my class who, by their performance, have told me where I have succeeded and failed, and the many students from around the country who recognize me at meetings and let me know they liked the book.

David W. Martin

Contents

Doing
Psychology
Experiments
Third Edition

1
How to Make Orderly Observations

Direct, intuitive observation, accompanied by questioning, imagination, or creative intervention, is a limited and misleading prescientific technique.[*]

The perversity of animate subjects has, of necessity, whelped a remarkable degree of experimental sophistication in the behavioral sciences.[†]

This book is meant to teach you how to do experiments in the science of psychology. Aside from the fact that learning to do this is required of psychology majors at many colleges, why would you want to know how to do psychological experimentation? One reason could be because you plan to become a psychologist, a scientist studying human and, sometimes, animal behavior. The experimental method is one of the major research tools for collecting data to build the scientific body of knowledge in psychology. I will briefly discuss some of the other tools in this book, but most of the book is concerned with how to do experiments.

Even if you do not plan to become a psychologist, learning about the use of experimentation in psychology can help you become a well-educated person and can provide you with useful skills that generalize to a number of careers. For example, suppose you go into the banking business and work your way up to being a vice president. Obviously, some of what you learn in psychology courses can help you succeed because you know something about human relations. However, what you know about experimentation can also help. Your boss calls you in and says, "You know, we have just installed all these automatic tellers in our banks. Trouble is that only a few of our customers are using them. We spent a lot of money on these newfangled machines, but for some reason the customers don't like to use them. I want you to figure out why and make whatever changes are necessary to get them to use the machines."

You will see as you read this book that carrying out such an assignment, while not a formal experiment, requires most of the skills needed for doing a psychology experiment. First, you must form several hypotheses about why the automatic tellers are not being used: Do the customers feel depersonalized interacting with a machine? Are they intimidated? Do they not know how to use them? Do they feel less safe carrying their money around

[*]Monte, C. F. (1975). *Psychology's scientific endeavor.* New York: Praeger, p. 63.
[†]Roscoe, S. N. (1980). *Aviation Psychology.* Ames: Iowa State University Press, p. 273.

without the security of another person present? As a second step, some sort of data must be collected to narrow down the possible hypotheses: perhaps by doing interviews or using a questionnaire. Then you would probably want to make a manipulation to see whether you can change the customer's behavior: perhaps offering an educational program, if knowledge is a problem; perhaps giving prizes, if motivation is a problem; perhaps increasing privacy, if security is a problem. Finally, you would want to measure behavior to see whether it changes with your manipulation and to determine whether any change in behavior was meaningful. Although your boss never asked you to do a psychology experiment, you have carried out most of the steps required to do one. Most employment settings require the solving of people problems, and the skills you learn from this book should make you a better people-problem solver.

Over and above these practical reasons for learning to do psychology experiments, I hope that part of the reason you want to learn these skills is just because it's fun! We are all curious about the world around us. We want to know why things happen as they do. Humans invented science in order to better understand their world.* Science is an attempt to approach this discovery process in an orderly way. Early in life I found out that, for me, experimentation was the most intriguing tool of science because it leads to the discovery of new relationships that have never before been known. Then when I learned about the science of psychology, I further discovered that this powerful tool could be used to understand what I considered to be the most interesting subject matter of all, human behavior.

Most people are very curious about their own behavior and the behavior of others. That is why we watch soap operas, gossip behind people's backs, fantasize, and read the *National Enquirer* in the grocery line—to speculate about human behavior. The use of experimentation in psychology allows us to check our speculations. What a thrill it was during my first course in experimental psychology to find scientific relationships that nobody else had ever seen. Even after years of doing experiments, my heart beats a little stronger when I get that first look at the results of a new experiment. My colleagues probably get tired of my running to their offices to show them the exciting new discoveries as they unfold in my lab. I hope that you feel the same excitement when you do your research. Although there are more serious reasons for doing the science of psychology, may you always continue to appreciate the fun of experimentation.

Psychology as a Science

Psychologists do go about their business much like scientists in other scientific fields. In their search for an understanding of human behavior, psychologists attempt to (1) establish relationships between circumstances and

---

*And, in the case of astronomy, other worlds as well.

behaviors and (2) fit these relationships into an orderly body of knowledge. In this book we will deal primarily with the first activity, although we will touch on the second activity in Chapters 10 and 11.

What kind of a relationship is acceptable to us as scientists? When we can demonstrate that one event is related to a second event in some predictable way, then we have a statement that will fit into the scientific body of knowledge. At least one of these events must be a measurable behavior. Here we can make a distinction among the sciences. The behavior of major concern to us as psychologists is human behavior (and sometimes animal behavior). And this is where we run into one of our first problems—a problem that haunts psychologists but not physical scientists. Humans are variable. We humans often cannot repeat a response precisely even if we wish to, and in some cases we may not wish to. In terms of variability, physical scientists typically have it easier than psychologists.

A physicist measuring the coefficient of friction for a wooden block might measure the time it takes the block to slide down an inclined plane. Although the times might vary from trial to trial, such variability would be relatively small. The physicist would not be making too great an error to consider the variability a minor nuisance and measure the time for only one trial. However, a psychologist who wants to measure the time it takes a human to press a button in response to a light would be making a considerably greater error by ignoring human variability. Although it is unlikely that our physicist's block will be a little slow on certain trials because it had its mind on other things, wasn't ready, or was blinking or asleep, a human subject can experience these and many other problems.

In addition to variability among trials, variability among human subjects must also be taken into account by psychologists. Our physicist could construct another block of the same size, weight, and surface finish as the original and repeat the experiment. The psychologist, however, cannot re-create human subjects. Humans seldom have exactly the same genetic background (identical twins being an exception), and they never have exactly the same environmental background. For this reason, in responding to the light, typically one subject's fastest response is considerably slower than another subject's slowest response. Thus, as psychologists we have to deal not only with one person's variability from trial to trial but also with the variability among humans.*

One way to handle variability is to use statistical techniques. Many psychology students learn to do this by taking a statistics class early in their course work. Because this is not a statistics text, we will not spend much time considering statistical solutions. The topic is briefly mentioned in Chapter 9, where interpreting the results of experiments is discussed, and in Appendix A, where simple statistical operations are demonstrated. A second way

---

*You can see why some psychologists decide to use animals as subjects. Whereas psychologists can breed animals with similar genetic characteristics and rear them in similar boxes, it would be frowned upon if they tried to do the same thing with humans. Your friends may say "All men are animals" or "All women are alike," but don't believe them!

to handle variability is to control it as much as possible in the design of your research. This book is written to help you do good research, which is a simple way of saying "Know where the variability is, and be able to account for it."

The Experimental Method

We as scientists establish relationships between events, but these events are not always behaviors. In fact, when we do an experiment, or use the **experimental method,** the relationship of interest is between a set of circumstances and a behavior. A physicist wants to know the time it takes a block to slide down a plane when the plane is at a particular angle, with a particular surface, and at a particular temperature. A psychologist wants to know the time it takes a person to press a button when the light is a particular intensity, a particular color, and in a particular place. Both scientists are attempting to establish relationships between a set of circumstances and a behavior. These relationships are scientific facts, the building blocks with which we build our science.

Unfortunately, designing an experiment to establish such a relationship is not always easy. Ideally, we would like to specify exhaustively and precisely a particular set of circumstances and then measure all the behaviors taking place under those circumstances. We could then say that, whenever this set of circumstances recurred, the same behaviors would result. However, if we could list *all* the circumstances, we would have a unique set. In our reaction-time experiment, we would list not only the intensity and color of the light but also the temperature and humidity of the room, who the experimenter was, who the subjects were, what their ages were, how much

Circumstances   Behaviors

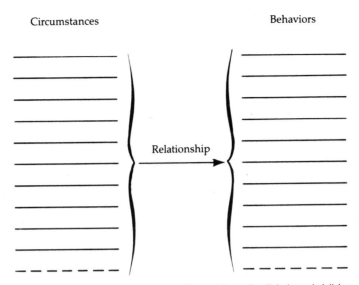

Relationship

Figure 1-1. A diagram representing the attempt by scientists to establish a relationship between a set of circumstances and measurable behaviors.

sleep each had had the night before, what they had eaten for lunch, and so on. In other words, we would have a unique set of circumstances that would never be repeated.

Thus, we are caught in a dilemma. On the one hand, we want to build our science on statements of precise relationships between circumstances and behaviors. On the other hand, if we could, we would end up with an infinite number of statements, one for each unique set of circumstances. We would never be able to predict behavior from circumstances, because we would not have seen those particular circumstances before. How do we resolve this paradox?

Figure 1-1 diagrams the situation. The lines on the left represent the conditions in a unique set of circumstances. The lines on the right represent the potential behaviors that could be measured (such as speed of response, strength of response, brain-wave activity, and blood pressure). Both of these lists are potentially of infinite length. The arrow indicates the possibility of a relationship between the circumstances and the behaviors.

To resolve the paradox, scientists have had to make a compromise. They have chosen to specify only a general set of circumstances rather than every possible condition in a unique combination of circumstances.

Variables

Independent Variables

At least one circumstance is of major interest in an experiment (for example, light intensity in a reaction-time experiment). We call this circumstance an **independent variable.** The best way to remember this name is to recall that the variable is independent of the subjects' behavior. As experimenters, we choose two or more levels of this circumstance to present, and nothing the subject does can change the levels of the independent variable. For example, if our independent variable is light intensity, we might select high and low intensity as our two levels and observe our subject's behavior under both circumstances.

Dependent Variables

Once we have chosen the independent variable, we will want to measure a subject's behavior in response to manipulations of that variable. We call the behavior we choose to measure the **dependent variable,** because it is dependent on what the subject does.* In the reaction-time experiment, for example, we want to find out whether a relationship exists between light intensity and time to respond. Thus, our dependent variable is the time from the onset of the light until the subject depresses a button. It is sometimes useful to make a statement about the expected nature of the relationship. Such a statement is called a **hypothesis.** In the example, we might hypothesize that the more intense the light, the quicker the response will be. The outcome of the experiment will determine whether the hypothesis is supported and becomes part of the scientific body of knowledge or whether it is refuted.

In some cases the hypothesis is softer and more uncertain, particularly when you simply wonder what would happen to a behavior if the independent variable were manipulated. In this case, the hypothesis is simply a question. How does crowding affect aggression? Does marking your first guess or thinking longer lead to better grades on multiple-choice tests? Are politicians who smile in their campaign posters more or less likely to be elected than those who don't? Answers to hypotheses such as these can also add to the scientific body of knowledge.

Control Variables

So far, we have chosen one circumstance to manipulate (the independent variable). However, other circumstances in an experiment will need to be accounted for in some way. One possibility is to control them, thus making them into **control variables.** We can control such circumstances by seeing that they do not vary from a single level. For example, in our reaction-time experiment, we might require that the lighting conditions in the room be constant, all subjects be right-handed, the temperature be constant, and so on. Ideally, all circumstances other than the independent variable would stay constant throughout an experiment. We would then know that any

---

*I believe that it is easier to remember the term this way, although the word **dependent** really refers to the behavior being potentially dependent on the levels of the independent variable.

change in the dependent variable must be due to changes in the independent variable brought about by the experimenter.

The concept of control is an important one for experimentation and makes the experiment distinct from other forms of research that will be discussed later in this chapter. In the experiments that you do, most of the variables will be set as control variables. As an experimenter, you will want to be sure that you have indeed achieved complete command of the control variables in your experiment. Control in experimentation is critical to the experimental method. That is why psychologists go to considerable expense to build special environments in which sound, light, and temperature are controlled and to use special equipment that ensures that stimulus characteristics are consistent and responses are carefully measured.

However, even though control variables will usually outnumber all other variables in your experiments, you should realize that, especially in psychology, not all variables will be assigned as control variables. First, it is impossible to control all the variables. Not only is it impossible to control many genetic and environmental conditions, but it is impossible to force cooperative attitudes, attentional states, metabolic rates, and many other situational factors on our human subjects.

Second, we really do not wish to control all the variables in an experiment, for we put ourselves back in the box we were trying to extricate ourselves from; we create a unique set of circumstances. If we could control all variables while manipulating the independent variable, the relationship established by the experiment would hold in only one case—when all variables were set at exactly the levels established for control. In other words, we could not *generalize* the experimental result to any other situation. As a rule of thumb, the more highly controlled the experiment, the less generally applicable the results.

Suppose, for example, that General Nosedive from the U.S. Air Force came to you and said, "Say, I understand you ran an experiment on reaction time. Tell me how intense I should make the fire-warning light in the F-111 so that my pilots will respond within half a second." Having conducted a well-controlled experiment, you reply, "Sir, if you can guarantee that the pilot is a 19-year-old college sophomore with an IQ of 115, sitting in an air-conditioned, 10-foot-by-15-foot room, with no distracting sounds and nothing else to do, and if you always give a warning signal one second before the light comes on, then I might be able to give you an answer." You can probably imagine the general's reply. The moral of the story is—if you want to generalize the results of your experiment, do not control all the variables.

Confounding Variables

Having established that we do not want to control all the circumstances, what can we do with the remaining circumstances in our experiment? One possibility is to let them vary. However, because our goal is to make a clear-cut statement about the effect of the independent variable on the dependent variable, we must be careful that none of these other factors also vary with the independent variable. Any circumstance that changes systematically as the independent variable is manipulated is called a **confounding variable.**

Suppose, for example, that we used three different light intensities in our reaction-time experiment: a low-intensity light for the first 20 trials, a medium-intensity light for the next 20, and a high-intensity light for the last 20. If we reported that "subjects respond more quickly the more intense the light," someone else could say "No, subjects respond more quickly after practice." In fact, we could both be correct, or either one of us could be incorrect! The problem is that we have unintentionally *confounded* the experiment with a variable that changes systematically with the independent variable.

An experimenter can record the most sophisticated measurements, do the finest statistical test, and write up the results with the style of Hemingway, yet a confounding variable can make the whole effort worthless. A feud between Coca-Cola and Pepsi-Cola illustrates the type of confusion that can be caused in this manner (Staff, 1976). Pepsi pitted its cola against Coke in a drinkers' test in which subjects who said they were Coke drinkers drank Coke from a glass marked Q and Pepsi from a glass marked M. More than half of the subjects reportedly chose the glass containing Pepsi as their favorite. Coke officials countered by conducting their own preference test—not of colas but of letters. They claimed that more people chose glass M over glass Q not because they preferred the cola in glass M but because they liked the letter M better than they liked Q. This hypothesis was supported when most people tested still claimed to prefer the drink in the M glass when *both* glasses contained Coke.

In this example, the letters were apparently a confounding variable. Because they varied systematically with the colas in the original test, the drinkers' preference for the colas could not be distinguished from their preference for the letters.

Random Variables

We have decided to allow some circumstances to vary, and we have seen the importance of avoiding confounding variables. In what way can we allow the circumstances to vary and still be sure that they will not confound our experiment? One alternative is to permit some of the circumstances to vary randomly. These variables are termed **random variables.**

A random variable is allowed to change levels in an uncontrolled way, but as an experimenter you must be sure that a random process is determining the levels. As long as the random process is allowed to operate many times, it is unlikely that the levels selected will be biased, turning a random variable into a confounding variable. For example, suppose you randomly choose 100 6-year-old children to assign the task of watching violent television shows versus 100 randomly chosen to watch nonviolent television shows. You wish to determine the effects of television violence on aggression. Is it possible that most of the first group attend violent schools or eat lots of sugar, while few of the second group do? Yes, but if the selection was done in a truly random fashion, it is statistically unlikely for such large samples to be biased.

There is no particular trick to random selection. Any device that allows each item in a population an equal chance for selection can be used. If two items are in your population, you can flip a coin to select from the population.* If there are six, you can throw a die. If there are 33, you can use 33 equal-sized slips of paper. Most mathematical handbooks and many statistics texts have random-number tables based on a process equivalent to drawing from 10,000 slips of paper. Using any column or columns in a table of random numbers, you can assign each of your items a number and select the item when that number occurs. If you happen to be a computer bug, you can use the computer to generate random numbers or events.†

If you have chosen to make a circumstance into a random variable, you must be sure that it varies in a truly random way, because not all events that appear random really are. For instance, if you try to randomize conditions in an experiment by assigning events yourself, you have not randomized! Humans are notoriously bad at producing random events. If you assume that subjects will show up for an experiment throughout the day or throughout the semester in a random order, you are wrong! People who are morning subjects or afternoon subjects or early-semester or late-semester subjects have different characteristics. Mistakes in randomization are commonly made by new experimenters. Don't you make them!

The major advantage of using random variables is the generalizability of the results. As we discussed earlier, every time we choose to make a circumstance into a control variable, we can generalize our results only to situations at that level. However, if we make a circumstance into a random variable and randomly select levels from a population, we can generalize the results to that entire population. Thus, randomization can be a powerful experimental tool.

Randomization Within Constraints

In some cases you may not wish to make a circumstance into either a random or control variable. Actually, randomization and control define opposite ends of a continuum. Falling between these two extremes are various degrees of **randomization within constraints.** In this case, you control part of the event assignments and randomize the other part. Suppose in our reaction-time experiment we knew that practice could be an important vari-

---

*Actually, most coins are slightly biased in favor of heads, but, unless you are running an experiment with over 10,000 subjects, don't worry about it.

†Computers are also less than perfect at generating random events, but they're much better than coins. For the purpose of assigning events in an experiment, it doesn't make much difference which method you use.

able. If we present all the low-intensity trials first, followed by all the high-intensity trials, we could be accused of confounding the experiment; any difference between response times to low- versus high-intensity light might, in fact, be due to short versus long practice. To avoid this problem, we could decide to control the practice variable and give only one trial to each subject. Or we could assign the low- and high-intensity trials randomly over, say, 12 trials by flipping a coin and presenting a high-intensity light whenever a head occurs and a low-intensity light whenever a tail occurs. This alternative might not be the most attractive, however, because it could result in an inadequate representation of high and low intensities. (The flipping of the coin might result in only three high-intensity trials, for example, and nine low-intensity trials.) To avoid this possibility, we decide to have an equal number of high- and low-intensity trials. Thus, as a solution we establish a constraint on the assignment of trials (an equal number of each type of trial), and we make a random assignment within this constraint. We might write the word *high* on six slips of paper and the word *low* on six and draw them out of a hat to determine the order of presentation. This procedure would fulfill the requirement that the conditions be randomly ordered across trials within the constraint that the two intensities be equally represented.

Other constraints, of course, are possible. We might wish to avoid the possibility that too many trials at a particular intensity occur early in the sequence. We could then **randomize within blocks,** with the block serving as our constraint. Using this alternative, we could choose three blocks of four trials each, assuring that two high-intensity trials and two low-intensity trials are randomly selected within each block. To describe this procedure, we would say that conditions were randomly assigned to three blocks of four trials each, with the constraint that each intensity be represented an equal number of times within each block.

Many such constraints can be legitimately used as long as they are specified. However, the more constraints you specify, the less random is your selection process, and the less generalizable are your results.

Summary of Experimental Method

Figure 1-2 summarizes the general experimental model we have outlined so far. Because all circumstances in an experiment must be either controlled or randomized to avoid confounding the experiment, the circumstances on the left have been partitioned into an independent variable, control variables, random variables, and variables randomized within constraints. While partitioning the variables, we should keep in mind that a decision to control increases the precision of the results (because the circumstances are less variable) but decreases their generality. On the other end of the continuum, a decision to randomize decreases the precision but increases the generality.

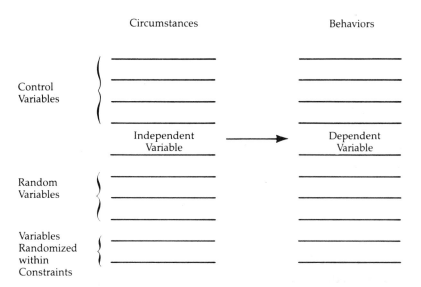

Figure 1-2. A diagram representing an experiment. One of the circumstances has been chosen as the independent variable. The others have been partitioned into control variables, random variables, or variables randomized within constraints. One of the behaviors has also been chosen as a dependent variable.

Correlational Observation

In establishing relationships that add to our knowledge of human behavior, it is not always possible to conduct an experiment. In such cases, **correlational observation** is often appropriate. In correlational observation we try to determine whether two variables are related without attempting to experimentally manipulate either one. Suppose, for example, we were interested in finding the relationship between parental discipline and rate of juvenile delinquency. To fit this problem into the experimental model, we would have to make parental discipline the independent variable and force the parents of a cross section of newborn infants to discipline their children at a particular level of strictness or leniency. When the children reach age 18, we might count the number of appearances before juvenile court for each child. Obviously, few parents would agree to such an experiment, nor would our society smile on our sincere effort to do good research. Rather than give up on what might be an important question, however, we could consider using a correlational observation.

In making such an observation, we could choose a number of children randomly and send their parents questionnaires asking such questions as "How often do you spank your child?" "Does your child have a specific time to be in bed?" and so on. Based on the answers to these questions, we could assign each set of parents a number on a scale from strict to lenient.

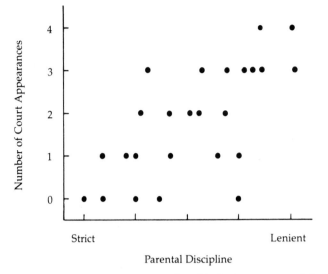

Figure 1-3. Fictitious data showing the relationship between parental discipline and the number of court appearances for children.

Then we could survey court records to determine the number of offenses for each child and determine if a relationship might exist.

Data* from correlational observations are typically pictured in a **scatterplot,** in which each variable is represented on an axis and each point represents a single measurement. For example, hypothetical data from our parental-discipline study are plotted in Figure 1-3. In this case, each point represents the parental-discipline score and the number of court appearances for each child. For example, the upper right point in the figure represents a child having four court appearances and a lenient parental-discipline score, the lower left point a child with no court appearances and a strict parental-discipline score. This scatterplot shows that there is a moderate relationship between parental discipline and court appearances in our fictitious example. Children whose parents are strict tended to have fewer court appearances. We agreed at the beginning of this chapter that the business of scientists is establishing relationships between events, why then is this result not as good as the result of an experiment? When we conduct a good experiment, we can conclude that the independent variable caused a change in the dependent variable. From a correlational observation, however, the best we can do is conclude that one variable *is related to* a second variable.

You may be wondering why we can't say that leniency *causes* juvenile delinquency in the same way that we can say that changes in an indepen-

*Every good experimenter must remember that **data** is a plural word; a datum is, but data are. If you chant to yourself "these data are" three times each morning when you wake up, you'll probably still forget!

dent variable cause changes in the dependent variable in an experimental situation. Perhaps the following example will illustrate why it is difficult to make causal statements based on correlational observation. The U.S. Army conducted a study of motorcycle accidents, attempting to correlate the number of such accidents with other variables such as socioeconomic level and age. The best predictor was found to be the number of tattoos the rider had! It would be a ridiculous error to conclude that tattoos cause motorcycle accidents or, for that matter, that motorcycle accidents cause tattoos. Obviously, a third factor is related to both—perhaps preference for risk. A person who is willing to take risks likes to be tattooed and also takes more chances on a motorcycle.

If we were to try to fit a correlational observation into our experimental model (Figure 1-2), we might say that the investigator has allowed all the circumstances to become random or confounding variables. The experimenter has no control over any of the circumstances—including the circumstance of major interest. Rather than choose one of the circumstances as an independent variable and then manipulate that variable, the investigator permits all variables to vary randomly and then samples from at least one variable. We cannot call it an independent variable, because the levels were not independently chosen by the investigator. For this reason, the chances are high that some other circumstance is changing along with the variable of major interest and that this circumstance may be causing the observed change in the behavior.

Another example of this problem is the Surgeon General's position on cigarette smoking and lung cancer. Although it had been known for some time that there is a positive correlation between the number of cigarettes smoked and the incidence of lung cancer, the Surgeon General was reluctant to say that smoking caused lung cancer. While some of this reluctance may have been politically motivated, much of it was justifiable scientific caution, for there could have been a third variable that caused the cancer but was related to smoking. For example, people who are nervous might produce a chemical that keeps the body in an irritated state, producing irritated cells that are prone to malignancy. It might also be true that nervous people smoke more cigarettes. Nervousness, then, could have caused the change in both variables.

Thus, the Surgeon General's office would have to perform an experiment to say definitively from one study that smoking causes lung cancer. Such an experiment might require 1000 people to smoke 40 cigarettes a day, another 1000 people to smoke 30 a day, and so on. In this design, experimenters could determine the probability that an individual in each group would have gotten lung cancer during his or her lifetime. Assuming that no confounding variables were present, any real difference in the incidence of cancer between the groups could be said to be caused by the cigarettes. Because the use of cigarettes would be independent of the subject's preference, the number of cigarettes smoked would be an independent variable. However, our society requires that a person's preference be honored, so ethically such an experiment could not be and was not conducted. How, then, did cigarette packs come to have the following warning printed on them: "SURGEON GENERAL'S WARNING: Quitting Smoking Now Greatly Reduces Serious Risks to Your Health"?*

In this case, correlations were determined for many of the other variables that could have been related to cancer and smoking. As more and more of these variables were eliminated, it became increasingly likely that cigarette smoking was the cause. The Surgeon General apparently felt that all the logically possible mediating variables had finally been eliminated. That fact, in combination with animal experiments that did show a causal relationship, convinced him that such a statement could be made.

The point, then, is that sometimes we must collect correlational data to establish important psychological relationships. However, we must consider these data carefully to avoid the common error of interpreting the results of a correlational observation as a causal relationship.

In applied field settings it is often possible to satisfy most, but not all, of the randomization and control requirements of an experiment. For example, two different teaching techniques might be used with two third-grade classes. Although most variables can be made into control or random variables, perhaps the assignment of children to the classes cannot be. For practical reasons, already existing classes, which were made up on some basis other than random selection, probably will have to be used. Obviously, a number of potentially confounding variables might be correlated with class assignment. In this case, we have neither a pure experimental design

---

*There are actually several statements that warn of the dire consequences of smoking, but they all imply that it is smoking that *causes* health problems.

nor a correlational observation. The design falls somewhere in between and is called a **quasi-experimental design.** These designs will be discussed at length in Chapter 8.

Naturalistic Observation

Some psychological questions cannot be studied even with a correlational study. Some psychologists would argue that the act of filling out a questionnaire or reporting for an experiment could distort the behavior of a subject. Suppose we were interested in whether consumption of alcohol was related to social aggressiveness. We could set up an experiment in which groups of subjects drank measured amounts of alcohol. They would then interact while the experimenter sat in the room and noted the amount of aggressive activity. How aggressive do you think the drinkers would be in this situation? They would probably resemble a church congregation more than a bar crowd.

To get an effective answer to our question, we would probably have to go to a bar and observe its customers. This technique in psychological research is called **naturalistic observation** because experimenters observe behaviors under the conditions in which they normally occur. Naturalistic observations are required when we wish to investigate any behavior that we feel might be distorted by the artificiality of an experimental situation. Children, for instance, are typically inhibited by the presence of adults, particularly strangers. We would expect the behavior of children playing at home with their own toys to be far different from their behavior in a psychology lab with unfamiliar toys and a strange-looking psychologist present.

For a long time, comparative psychologists* wondered whether any animal other than humans used tools, and naturalistic observation provided them with the beginnings of an answer. Initially, data collected by observing

*A comparative psychologist is not someone who makes television commercials in which Brand X loses out to Brand Y. A comparative psychologist compares the behavior of animals, including humans, across species. Comparative psychologists contend that the rest of us are far too egocentric in our research; humans form only a small part of the animal kingdom.

chimpanzees in zoos supported the general belief that other animals did not use tools. After a while, however, "chimpanzeeologists" began to wonder if maybe zoo chimpanzees were not using tools because no tools were available in the zoo. They gave them tools like pliers and screwdrivers, but the chimps still didn't use them. Finally, a particularly bright investigator named Jane Goodall moved into the forest with the chimps. She lived with them and constantly observed their behavior for several years. One day she noticed that a particular chimp would take a branch, peel off the leaves to make it smooth, trim it to length, and dip it into a termite hill and lick off the termites that were clinging to the stick. Although it is not as sophisticated as a human's tools, some investigators consider the stick an appropriate chimpanzee tool. Without naturalistic observation, chimpanzeeologists would still be sitting around watching zoo animals not using tools.

Some sciences other than psychology use naturalistic observation as their primary tool because they cannot achieve control over the variables they are investigating. Astronomers, for example, must pretty well investigate the universe as it occurs naturally. The same is usually true for archeologists, paleontologists, ethnologists, and anthropologists. This limitation has not prevented these scientists from discovering important scientific phenomena such as evolution. Because of problems with control, naturalistic observation in psychology is often used to suggest hypotheses that can later be more carefully investigated through experimentation in the laboratory. Used in this way, naturalistic observation can be a valuable research tool.

The major problem with naturalistic observation as a research technique should be obvious to you after our discussion of confounding variables. Because investigators have no control over any of the variables they are observing, one variable may be changing systematically along with the primary one being observed. In our bar example, for instance, an investigator might observe that the more alcohol the customers drink, the more aggressive their social interactions become. However, the observer may not notice that as the evening wears on and more drinks are consumed, the number of bar patrons also increases. Maybe aggressiveness is related to crowding. Or perhaps the bartender is getting tired and brings the drinks at a slower rate. Maybe aggressiveness is related to frustration.

Thus, while naturalistic observation has an advantage in realism, it also has disadvantages in its lack of control. As with correlational observations, experimenters must be aware of potential confounding variables and must avoid making causal statements.

Case History

The final research technique available to a psychologist is the **case history.** A case history is a detailed account of the relevant events in one person's life. Usually this account is purely verbal, with no quantification. If you were a therapist who had a pair of Siamese twins with dual personalities as patients, you might be interested in exploring why Siamese twins get dual personalities. You would immediately realize that trying to conduct an experiment to answer the question would be futile. Even if you could find enough Siamese twins to do an experiment, it is considered unethical to make Siamese twins mentally ill; it is also unethical to make non-Siamese twins mentally ill!

You might consider a correlational observation next. Perhaps you could correlate the number of personalities in Siamese twins with degree of childhood stress. Again, you would need to find a number of Siamese twins who have dual personalities. Because this task is virtually impossible and a correlational observation based on one data point is meaningless,* you would have to abandon this approach also.

The only option left open would seem to be a case history outlining the factors in the lives of the Siamese twins that have contributed to their development. First, you would spend many hours interviewing the twins to establish a history of their life from birth to present. In addition, you would talk with their relatives and friends and examine any school, medical, and psychological records that were available. Because all this information would require far too much space to report, you would select what you felt were the most important aspects.

The case-history technique has built into it all the dangers that have been mentioned for the other methods, including unknown confounding variables and inability to establish causality. This method also has additional pitfalls. For one thing, the investigator is generally trying to reconstruct past events from the subjective reports of those who were associated with those events, and research has shown that people are terrible at recalling the past. One investigator found that mothers were inaccurate about recalling the details of their pregnancy and the birth of their child six months to

---

*It is pretty difficult to establish a relationship between two variables with a single point. It is not difficult to establish a relationship with two points, however, because only one straight line can be drawn between them. Reporting a relationship based on two points is a lot like bragging—it's easy to do but no one pays any attention.

a year after the experience. You can imagine the problems involved when the memories are 20 years old!

A second possible pitfall of the case-history method is the investigator's bias in selecting events to be reported. In a psychology course, I was once required to support a particular personality theory using events from the life of the major character in the book *Crime and Punishment*. It was easy to select events that offered convincing support for my theory. However, I discovered that the other students in the class had used the same book to support three other personality theories, also in a convincing way. They had either chosen different events or given a different interpretation to the same events I had chosen. Even with the limited set of events described in a single book, bias was extremely important in determining the relationships we established. Is it any wonder that investigators can find support for their own pet theories from the nearly unlimited set of events in a person's life?

A number of books have been written that analyze the lives and personalities of famous historical figures, such as Richard Nixon, John Kennedy, and Sigmund Freud. Although they may make interesting speculative reading, these so-called psychohistories are subject to all the dangers inherent in a case history. In addition, most of the events the authors use as support for their theories are based on secondhand reporting in the public media. Thus, they are one more step away from the objective truth. (For example, one author concluded that Nixon was psychotic, while another concluded that he was neurotic.)

A case-history approach has also been used in applied experimental settings for investigating infrequently occurring events. For example, it is basically impossible for a psychologist interested in the causes of aircraft accidents to set up appropriate experiments. What these investigators often do is reconstruct the events preceding an accident in as much detail as possible. By collecting enough of these critical incidents describing accidents and near-accidents, they hope to establish a pattern that will allow them to hypothesize the causes. These hypotheses may then be more thoroughly investigated under controlled experimental conditions.

Even in clinical settings, a case-history approach can be combined with experimentation and quasi-experimentation. For example, a therapist may have only one client with a particular diagnosis yet may wish to determine the effectiveness of a particular therapy for this disorder. In this case it may be possible to establish the consistency of a given abnormal behavior, apply the therapy, and again observe the behavior. Perhaps the therapy could even be temporarily discontinued to find if the behavior reverted to its former level. This therapist would be combining a case-history approach with a baseline design, discussed in Chapter 6. The combination of approaches would add considerable strength to the research conclusions.

Thus, the case-history approach when used by itself has many potential drawbacks. It can be of value when the behaviors or subjects under investigation are so unusual that finding similar cases is impractical. It can also provide evidence that is useful in forming hypotheses. These hypotheses can later be investigated with research methods that permit more control, such as experimentation. In any event, the interpretation of the data reported in a case history should be regarded as speculative until confirmed by other methods.

Summary

As scientists of human behavior, psychologists have a number of research techniques available to them, all of which aim to establish relationships between events and to fit these relationships into an orderly body of knowledge. The **experimental method**, which is the primary focus of this book, requires that a particular circumstance called an **independent variable** be related to some aspect of behavior called a **dependent variable.** The other circumstances in a given experiment can be treated as **control variables, random variables,** or **variables randomized within constraints.** Throughout an experiment, investigators must guard against **confounding variables** that change systematically with the independent variable and distort the relationship between the independent and the dependent variables. Sometimes when an experimental approach cannot be used, it is necessary to use **correlational observations** in which variables are observed and their relationship recorded. The results of such a study cannot be used to establish causal relationships, because none of the variables are under the control of the investigator. When the artificiality of the experimental approach would distort the results of an investigation, psychologists may use **naturalistic observation** as a method—that is, they observe behavior in a realistic setting. Finally, a **case-history** method may be necessary if an experiment is not appropriate and the potential number of observations is limited.

References

Staff. (1976, July 26). Coke-Pepsi slugfest. *Time*, pp. 64–65.

2

How to Get an Experimental Idea

A fair idea put to use is better than a good idea kept on the polishing wheel.*

As he was testing hypothesis number one by experimental method a flood of other hypotheses would come to mind, and as he was testing these, some more came to mind, and as he was testing these, still more came to mind until it became painfully evident that as he continued testing hypotheses and eliminating them or confirming them their number did not decrease. It actually *increased* as he went along.†

You can observe a lot by just watching.
Yogi Berra

I was once so bold and foolish as to assign introductory psychology students the task of proposing seven experiments as a course requirement. At first I was puzzled by their reactions to this assignment. Above the din of gnashing teeth, the moaning, and the groaning could be heard the plaintive wail of my stupefied students, "How do we get an idea?" Not only did I find it difficult to understand why getting an idea would pose such a problem, I also found it impossible to answer the question. I have now pondered this pervasive problem and formed an opinion about why it occurs and what can be done to solve it.

I don't believe the problem is that students have no ideas. As small children, we are curious about everything, including human behavior: "Mommy, why is that man so fat?" "How does Jenny eat with her left hand?" "Why can't I spell as good as Betty?" "Why do Tommy's parents spank him so much?" I refuse to believe that this curiosity simply fades away. In fact, the same students who "could not get an idea" seem to have plenty of thoughts about human behavior at parties or bull sessions: "What's the best way to study for my bio exam?" "Should I marry him or just move in with him?" "Am I more creative in the morning?"

For this reason I will refuse to believe you if you tell me you don't have any ideas for an experiment. It's not true that you don't have any ideas, but it may be true that you are afraid something is wrong with the ideas you do have! This fear can paralyze your natural creativity, and, after a while, all your ideas seem inadequate to you.

---

*Osborn, A. F. (1970). *The Journal of Creative Behavior, 4*, cover.
†Pirsig, R. M. (1975). *Zen and the art of motorcycle maintenance*. New York: Bantam, p. 107.

Fearing Experimental Ideas

Fears about experimental ideas are usually irrational, stemming from a mis-understanding of psychology experiments. Psychologists call irrational fears **phobias.** Since I am a psychologist, I cannot resist the temptation to name the phobias behind our inability to get experimental ideas. The following phobias seem to be the most common.*

Geniephobia (Fear of Geniuses)

Geniephobia stems from the common belief that anyone doing research must be a genius and that your modest brainpower couldn't possibly mea-sure up. Researchers often do little to counteract this belief, and a few have been known to cultivate it. For years, every time I read a journal article I pictured the author as a wise-looking old man with flowing white locks. It was a shock to find that many experimenters are young, ordinary-looking people who make silly mistakes and say stupid things just like the rest of us.

My own geniephobia is still being cured. The more experimental psy-chologists I meet, the less I think only geniuses can do this kind of work.[†] So, relax. Your ideas are probably as good as theirs were when they were getting started.

Imitatophobia (Fear of Imitating)

Those people with imitatophobia are afraid to propose any idea unless it is absolutely original. An imitatophobic who combines this fear with a belief that everything worthwhile has already been thought of often reaches a state of total paralysis. Truly original experiments are few indeed in psy-chology. Most experiments use variations of somebody else's method to test somebody else's theory. In the next chapter you will learn how to find out what other experiments have been done in your area of interest, and you will find out exactly how unoriginal you are. Don't be afraid to move science along in small steps, however. That's what the rest of us do.

Paraphernaliophobia (Fear of Apparatus) and Manuphobia (Fear of Doing It by Hand)

If the sum total of your mechanical knowledge of the automobile is that the right pedal makes it go and the left pedal makes it stop, you are a prime candidate for paraphernaliophobia. This malady will scare you away from any experimental idea requiring apparatus more sophisticated than a deck of cards.

---

*Any resemblance of these names to accepted psychological terminology is purely coincidental.
[†]I do not mean to imply that experimental psychologists are dumber than other scientists. Biologists and physicists can be dumb, too.

A PREPHOBIC HAVING
LOTS OF IDEAS

On the other hand, if you will not consider doing any experiment unless it requires sophisticated scientific equipment, you are a victim of the opposite affliction, manuphobia. Everyone knows that the more complex the equipment, the better the research.

Both positions are unfounded, however. Some of the best research uses little or no apparatus. Piaget developed a major area of child psychology with no more apparatus than toy blocks, water glasses, and modeling clay. Other areas of psychology, such as verbal learning, concept formation, attitude assessment, and personality, require no more than pencil and paper. Apparatus can help you do research, but it isn't the research itself. And when apparatus is necessary, someone will be available who can teach you how to use it.

Parsimoniophobia (Fear of Simplicity)

Parsimoniophobics think they must come up with grandiose experiments that will change the course of science in one fell swoop. Their motto is: If it's simple, it can't be science. While there are some advantages to complex experiments, generally you should aim for the simplest experiment that can answer your experimental question. People with parsimoniophobia seldom complete their majestic experiments; when they do, they usually cannot interpret the results. To start with, then, think simple. You can always pursue more complex questions later. (In Chapters 6 and 7 we will talk about what we mean by simple and complex experiments.)

Calculatophobia (Fear of Statistics)

Some people dread having to do any calculations tougher than counting their fingers. If you never can remember how to figure out your car's gas mileage or how to keep your checkbook straight, you are a potential calculatophobic. If you will consider only those experiments that require the

A CALCULATOPHOBIC

simplest statistical tests, remember that such tests are tools that can help you interpret your results; they should not cause you to throw out good experimental ideas. You can always find someone who enjoys playing with numbers to help you analyze your data. I am not saying that a knowledge of statistics is unimportant, but it is, after all, just a tool used in science, not science itself.

Imperfectaphobia (Fear of Being Imperfect)

An imperfectaphobic will not tell you about an experimental idea until every tiny detail is perfectly worked out, and his or her proposal looks like the final report. This attitude often stems from having read too many pristinely presented journal articles. As we will discuss in Chapter 13, journal articles are end products; they seldom reflect the sloppy thinking and general air of confusion that precedes most experiments. Completed experiments are often quite different from the experimenters' original ideas. The original idea for an experiment simply forms the kernel; the experimental procedure will evolve as you set up and conduct the experiment. If you take the plunge and begin talking about your experiment in rough form, others may be able to help you mold it into a perfect experiment. Well, almost perfect.

Pseudononphonoscientiaphobia (Fear of Not Sounding Scientific)

People with this hideous affliction can only recognize a great idea if it is expressed in **scientific jargonese.*** Scientific jargonese is a pseudolanguage that some scientists make up to sound good when they talk with other scientists who do similar research. It helps obscure the research from the

---

*I am using the word *jargonese* to represent the fourth dictionary definition of jargon (speech or writing characterized by pretensions, terminology, and involved syntax) as opposed to the first definition (the language peculiar to a particular trade, profession, or group). The line between jargon and jargonese is thin indeed.

general public—and sometimes from other scientists as well. For example, in jargonese an experiment designed to determine whether people remember words better when the words are in groups is described as an investigation into "the effect of taxonomic and categorical clustering on the retention of verbal material." Or a notion that people from ethnic groups live in the same neighborhood because of pressure from their friends is described as an experiment examining "the effect of demographic distribution by ethnic affiliation as a function of peer-group coercion." Jargonese can also be translated into everyday language. If you are interested in "the effect of affiliative preference on the salience of dimensions in person perception," you are actually trying to find out whether people who join certain organizations differ in the way they see other people. Try translating one yourself: "the effects of maternal employment on sibling aggressive tendencies."*

As you can guess from the way this book is written, I believe that most pseudoscientific jargonese is nonsense. Good scientists need not hide behind their language. A good idea is a good idea regardless of the words used to express it.

Ergophobia (Fear of Work)

Sorry, there is no known cure for this affliction.

Now that we are aware of what fears might block our creativity, let's try to get some experimental ideas. What is the best way to start?

Observation

Someone once said that it's easy to write: just sit at the typewriter and stare at the keyboard until drops of blood appear on your forehead. This also describes the best way to avoid coming up with experimental ideas. Because we are interested in human behavior rather than typewriter behavior, the best thing to do is observe humans, not typewriters!

Getting experimental ideas is simply a matter of noticing what goes on around you. Once you become a good observer, your natural curiosity will provide you with experimentally testable questions. One week of constant observation should provide you with enough experiments to last three careers.

Indeed, some of the classic research in experimental psychology started with a simple observation. If Ekhard Hess' wife had not noticed that his pupils got bigger when he was looking at bird pictures, pupillometrics might never have gotten underway. If Ivan Pavlov had not noticed that his dogs were salivating to stimuli other than meat powder, Igor Nosnoranovitch might have been the father of classical conditioning instead. If Jean

---

*If you came close to "Do working mothers' kids fight more?" then you are catching on. Be sure to buy my next book: *Scientific jargonese for fun and profit*.

Piaget had not noticed that his daughter Jacqueline stopped making gurgling noises when she could no longer see her bottle, he might have been a famous Swiss watchmaker. Most revolutionary experimental ideas have been generated by simple observation.

Public Observation

After reading the next couple of paragraphs, take a paper and pencil, leave the room you are in, and walk outside where there are people to observe. As a training exercise in observation, make notes of possible experimental questions that occur to you as you stroll around.

First I'll go on a stroll to show you what I mean: I wander outside, and I see that the sun is shining.

1. Do people get more or less work done when the weather is nice?

I walk past two workmen laying concrete for a bike rack. One is working; the other is standing and watching.

2. Do workers stand around more when they are unionized?

A couple of joggers run by.

3. Do people who exercise regularly sleep better at night?

A young woman is sitting over there under a tree with a young bearded fellow. They are looking rather amorous, and I feel like a peeping Tom. Better move on.

4. Do women find men with beards more attractive than men without beards?

I see a large group of students filing into a classroom.

5. Do students in large lecture classes make better grades than those in small classes?

I arrive at a crosswalk. Will that car stop? Yes, it did. Across I go.

6. Are drivers more likely to give the right of way to pedestrians of the opposite sex?

I stop to watch a sports car zooming down the street.

7. Do people drive sports cars faster than regular cars?

I head back past the library.

8. Do students who study in the library retain information better than those who study in the dorm?

I pass the bike rack at the front of my office building and see lots of bikes.

9. Are ten-speed bikes easier to ride than three-speed bikes?

ME WAITING

I lope upstairs to my office. I am back.

I just got nine potential ideas for experiments. That's almost one per minute! Now you try it while I wait.

Welcome back. Did you get plenty of ideas? Think about the ideas you could get if you were that observant all the time. Now the problem is "which idea should I turn into an experiment?" because not all important questions can be answered by experiment. All experimental questions must pass the ROT test: they must be **Repeatable, Observable,** and **Testable.** For example, science cannot answer moral questions, such as: "Is abortion wrong?" "Is it proper for women to wear short skirts?" "Is dope evil?" While we can certainly use the scientific method to determine people's opinions about these questions, we cannot devise any test that could answer the questions themselves. We must therefore eliminate all such questions from any list of experimental ideas. Other questions fail because they are not observable: "Do dogs think like humans?" "Is my experience of the color red the same as yours?" Finally, some questions fail experimentally because they cannot be reliably repeated. Some supporters of ESP (extrasensory perception), for example, claim that ESP occurs only under certain conditions and that it is impossible to predict when the conditions are right. In other words, ESP works only some of the time. As long as this basic tenet governs ESP effects, it is impossible to test for the existence of ESP.

Do all the questions in your list of ideas meet the ROT requirements? Take a moment to go through your list and eliminate any that fail to do so.

After reading Chapter 1, you should also recognize that some questions must be answered by correlational observation rather than by experimentation. For example, if, as in question 7, we want to know whether people who choose to drive sports cars drive at a faster speed than those who drive other types of cars, we must do a correlational observation to answer the question. On the other hand, if we wish to know whether any driver tends to drive faster when driving a sports car, we could design an experiment to answer the question. Take another look at your list of ideas, and label each idea experimental or correlational.

Our little walk has been interesting, but people in public provide us with a limited set of behaviors. Whom else can we observe?

NOT ALL QUESTIONS
MAKE GOOD EXPERIMENTS.

Observing Yourself

As you may know, introspection was one of the earliest techniques in experimental psychology. Introspectionists, however, concentrated on looking at their own mental processes rather than their own behavior. Because a controversy developed about whether a person can know his or her own mental processes, experimental psychologists stopped watching themselves altogether. Rather than follow the dictum "Know thyself," they resolved to "Know not thyself."* It is still generally frowned on to do an experiment with yourself as the only subject; nevertheless, you can get some good experimental ideas this way. Not only will you be able to collect many samples of the behavior you are interested in, but you might even have some idea why you did what you did. The former can give you an idea for an experiment, the latter an idea for a theory.

With a little effort, you can begin to notice your own behavior. It may seem ridiculous to suggest that you do not notice yourself, but it is probably true. When dressing, which arm do you put into your shirt or blouse first? When you brush your teeth, do you brush the left side first or the right? Do you put the key to your house or room into the lock rightside up or upside down? When you cross your legs, do you put your left leg or your right leg on top more often? These are all things you do every day. Do you notice them? Observing yourself can be entertaining[†] as well as a good source of ideas. Write down the ideas as they occur to you.

Observing Your Friends

Your friends are also good sources of experimental ideas. It is important, however, to observe their behavior in as unobtrusive a manner as possible. Staring is considered impolite at best and grounds for a fight at worst. People sometimes avoid paying attention to their own behavior because they are not particularly fond of the way they behave. Consequently, to

---

*Some experimental psychologists still don't know who they are.
[†]If you develop this skill, you will have to learn to control yourself in public. You may be
considered strange if you break into gales of laughter over your own behavior.

KNOW THYSELF.

avoid losing friends, keep your observations to yourself. Pointing out your insights, no matter how brilliant, will not help you win friends and influence people.

Observing Children

Observing children is a necessity if you are interested in doing experiments in the area of developmental psychology, but children can also give you good ideas for other areas of research. If you are not blessed with* children, you probably have friends and relatives who would be more than happy to let you watch theirs for a while. Unlike adults, who have learned that their behavior should appear rational, logical, and consistent to an outside observer, children generally behave in ways that are uncomplicated by complex patterns or social inhibitions. Because most kids couldn't care less about adult standards, you will be able to observe relatively uncontaminated behavior patterns in children.

Observing Pets

Animals are interesting to study in their own right, but much of their behavior can also be generalized to humans. Furthermore, you will find that pets are even less inhibited than children; because they are less capable of highly complex behavior patterns, their behavior is often easier to interpret. In addition, you can manipulate your pet's environment without worrying as much about the moral implications of possible permanent damage (see Chapter 13 for a discussion of the ethics of animal treatment).

*Or plagued by (depending on your point of view).

Vicarious Observation

Although you may find it less exciting than direct observation, you can also get experimental ideas by reading other people's research. You might feel that this technique of **vicarious observation** feeds off other people's creativity, but nonetheless this approach has certain practical advantages. For one thing, because the broad experimental question you are researching already has a stamp of approval from the author and journal reviewers, you know that the questions being asked are considered important. Second, somebody else has already fit the experimental result into the existing body of knowledge, thereby structuring the area of research for you and saving you time and effort. Finally, earlier researchers have devised a method of attack that apparently works and that you may be able to modify and use in your research.

In beginning your search for an idea, you should first identify an area of research that interests you. You will then know what types of journals you should read. Your topic should be as specific as possible: competition in small groups, play therapy in schools, perception of visual illusions, development of arithmetic abilities, and so on. For the more general topics you specify, you can simply scan journals having related articles. For more specific topics, this procedure is rather inefficient, and you will need to do a literature search as described in Chapter 3. In either case, as you read the journal articles, make a note of the experimental questions left unanswered by the research. The author will sometimes help you discover what these questions are by suggesting where future research should go. You might select one of these experimental questions for your experiment.

Expanding on Your Own Research

Once you have done several experiments, you will find that your own research may provide many experimental ideas. Every experiment you do will leave a number of questions unanswered. For example, after using several levels of an independent variable in an experiment, you may want to see what happens when you choose other levels. Or you may have controlled a certain variable at a particular level in one experiment and may wonder what would happen if you set it at a different level. Or you may come up with unexpected results and want to find out why the outcome was not as predicted. Each experiment usually brings up more unsolved questions than it answers.

This picture of science as a continual growth of new questions is different from that held by many people who think of science as a fixed body of knowledge we need only uncover. This latter concept views scientific research as leaving fewer and fewer questions unanswered as it proceeds. In reality, however, each experiment actually increases the number of questions to be answered. Instead of working ourselves out of business, we are working ourselves into more business than we can possibly handle.

This open-ended view of science can be very discouraging and very exciting. It can be discouraging because it is sometimes difficult to chart our progress through an ever-expanding universe in which we sometimes seem to take five steps backward for every step forward. On the other hand, it is exciting because we end up asking better and better questions. Perhaps the goal of science is not to find answers to all possible experimental questions but to answer ever more promising and important questions. In following up on your own research, you will find that your main problem is not "How can I get an experimental idea?" but "Which idea is the most important one to work on?"

Focus on a Practical Problem

If you have a practical problem crying for a solution, you may also have the kernel of an experimental idea. So far in this chapter we have been pretending that all research is **basic research***—that is, research done for the sole purpose of increasing the scientific body of knowledge. It is not necessary to justify such research as a solution to any practical problem, although basic research can help solve practical problems. Today's behavior-modification techniques, which provide some of the most powerful procedures for correcting human behavior problems, are based on basic research done in the rat laboratories of yesteryear. Adams (1972) found that many of our military systems were designed using information from basic research done more than 20 years earlier. Thus, basic research does at times prove valuable for solving practical problems. In general, however, such research is done in the name of the advancement of science.

Research designed to solve a specific practical problem is called **applied research.** Perhaps you need to know how humans read handwritten numbers so that you can design a machine to automatically read ZIP codes. Or you may wish to know whether daily quizzes will improve a student's

---

*Basic research is sometimes also called **pure research,** perhaps because one is not supposed to have mixed motives for doing it. Unfortunately, some people who do this kind of research seem to prefer other dictionary definitions of pure—for example, untainted with evil or guilt. I have never heard pure scientists defend the position that they are physically chaste, even though I suspect that this is the subconscious reason behind wearing white lab coats.

classroom performance on major examinations. Or you may want to know whether transactional analysis is a more effective therapy than psycho-analysis. Many such practical problems need immediate answers that basic researchers might never find. Needing an answer to a practical problem is a perfectly legitimate reason for doing research, and it can be satisfying if your findings have an immediate impact on the world.

Observation is again the key to getting ideas for applied research. Find-ing a practical problem is simply a matter of carefully observing human behavior and permitting your curiosity free rein. As with the other proce-dures that we have discussed for getting experimental ideas, you will find that more practical problems need to be solved than you can possibly do experiments to solve. As before, the question becomes "What should I do first?" not "What can I do?" We will deal further with this question in Chapter 11.

Summary

Although we all have natural curiosity about human behavior, many of us develop irrational fears that block our ideas. Some of us fear that all other researchers are geniuses and that our ideas will not be original. Some people are afraid to propose an experiment requiring complex apparatus, while others are afraid of experiments with simple apparatus. Others fear that their idea is too simple, that their experiment will require complicated sta-tistics, or that their idea is not perfect when it is proposed. Finally, many people do not believe they have good ideas until they translate them into scientific jargonese.

The major key to getting experimental ideas is to learn to **observe** the world about you. You also need to know which ideas are scientifically appropriate. Ideas must be **repeatable, observable,** and **testable** to be exper-imental ideas. To get ideas you can observe yourself, friends, children, and even pets. Although some of the best ideas come from direct observation, you can also get ideas by reading other people's research (vicarious observation) and from following up your own research. Finally, some of the best ideas come from having a practical problem that needs to be solved. Research designed to solve a practical problem is called **applied research,** while research aimed primarily at advancing scientific knowledge is called **basic** or **pure research.**

References

Adams, J. A. (1972). Research and the future of engineering psychology. *American Psychologist, 27,* 615–622.

3

How to Find Out What's Been Done

Polonius: What do you read, my lord?
Hamlet: Words, words, words.*

But why do we have to endure the academics who insist on making verbal mountains out of intellectual molehills?†

Perhaps while you were reading Chapter 2, a terrific experimental idea came to you in a blinding flash of inspiration. On the other hand, an idea may have appeared with a dull thud. In any case, some interesting experimental idea has begun to form, and you may be getting eager to start your experiment. You should consider one thing first, however: your terrific idea may already have been somebody else's terrific idea.

Why Search the Literature?

Although psychology is a relatively young science, more than 4000 research articles are published in a typical year. Although another investigator probably has not done exactly what you are planning to do, it is likely that out of all the articles accumulated over the short history of psychology, somebody has done something quite similar. It would be counterproductive for you to repeat an experiment unless you, for some reason, did not think the results were reliable.

You might also find it helpful to discover how other investigators have attacked similar problems. Perhaps they have used experimental techniques with which you are unfamiliar. You might also find that other investigators have already discovered a number of pitfalls you would rather not waste your time rediscovering.

Science is an organized body of knowledge, not a random collection of facts built by scientists doing small isolated experiments. Thus, the most important reason for knowing what experiments others have done is that you will be required to fit your findings into this existing scientific body of knowledge. When you have completed your experiment, you will be required to say not only "This is how it came out" but also "This is where it fits in." To know where your work fits in, you obviously have to know what the

*Hamlet, Act II, scene ii, line 195.
†Senator S. I. Hayakawa (1978, June–July). *Change,* p. 6.

body of knowledge was like prior to your experiment. This chapter discusses how to find out what is in that body of knowledge through a **literature search.***

While you are doing a literature search in the library, be sure to keep a record of what you find. Each time you find an article or book that might be useful, make a note of the important points and write down the complete reference. Include the names of the authors,[†] title of the work, name of the journal or book, date, volume number, page numbers, and for a book, the publisher. You will need all of this information later if you decide to refer to the article in your experimental report. Some people find it helpful to use an index card for each reference. The more orderly you are the first time through, the less time you will waste later looking for references that you put on the back of a long-lost gum wrapper.

Although a literature search is not particularly difficult to do, it can be time-consuming[††] and not particularly inspirational, since it involves lots of paper shuffling. Knowing the literature, however, is an absolute necessity. Nothing is more embarrassing when presenting the results of your life's work than to hear someone remark, "You are, of course, familiar with Klip and Klap, 1990, who did this same experiment last year?"

---

*Psychologists traditionally have called this process a literature search despite the sneers of Shakespeare and Dickens buffs who probably would not call journal articles "literature."

[†]People who are new to psychology sometimes find it strange that experimental psychologists talk about experiments by author rather than by subject. If you hear your instructors say such things as "The Carothers, Finch, and Finch, 1972, findings agree with Peterson, Bergman, and Brill, 1971," they are talking not about law firms but about experimenters.

[††]One of the most time-consuming and exasperating things that can happen is to uncover references that have been ripped off or ripped out. It's enough to make the most ardent pacifist have fantasies of catching the scalawags and hanging them by their thieving thumbs in the town square.

The Timeliness of Sources

Assuming you have found your way to the library as the most logical place to conduct your search, where do you start once you are there? Here is one good way to learn about the sources available and how up-to-date each source is: follow the history of a typical experiment as it is communicated to the scientific community. Figure 3-1 summarizes this process on a time line in which zero represents the time a project is started.* After collecting data, the investigator may present preliminary results to a small gathering of friends at a local institution. Assuming the researcher isn't laughed out of the room, he or she may decide to attend a professional meeting such as an annual convention and read a paper summarizing his or her research.†   Again, assuming that this somewhat more hostile audience offers a little support, the investigator might decide to write a manuscript based on the research and submit it to a journal. If the article is accepted, it will appear in the journal about nine months to a year later. Following journal publication, *Psychological Abstracts* will publish an abstract of the article. If the article is important, it might appear later in the *Annual Review,* be cited in other articles, and perhaps be mentioned in a publication such as *Psychological Bulletin.* Finally, after several years, a textbook author might mention the research as part of the accepted body of knowledge.

Figure 3-1 points out the **time lag** involved in the scientific communication process. If you use the library, your first access to an experimental result is its appearance as a journal article. As you can see, you have lost considerable time at this point because the research was probably started at least three years before its publication in a journal. If you begin your experiment at this point and go through the same process, the other author will have to wait three more years before your results will be reported in a journal article. (Even the U.S. mail has better turnaround time than this!) Because of the need to avoid such delays, fewer than one in seven research efforts originate from formal sources such as journal articles (Garvey & Griffith, 1971). Most ideas originate from more informal communication among scientists in a given field. However, as a new investigator without the contacts necessary for such informal communication, you might have to be content with the formal sources for the time being. If you continue to work in a particular area of research, you will find out who else works in your area and will get to know your fellow researchers personally. You will then be ahead of the journals and the "new" new investigators.

---

*This figure is based on research that is now a bit old. It is likely that, with technological advances in publishing, the time line has been compressed in recent years. However, I know of no more recent research that speaks to this issue. I believe that the order of events is essentially unchanged today and that the figure still provides a useful way to organize our thinking about the publication process.
†This is where your professors go when they miss class. And you thought they were on vacation having fun.

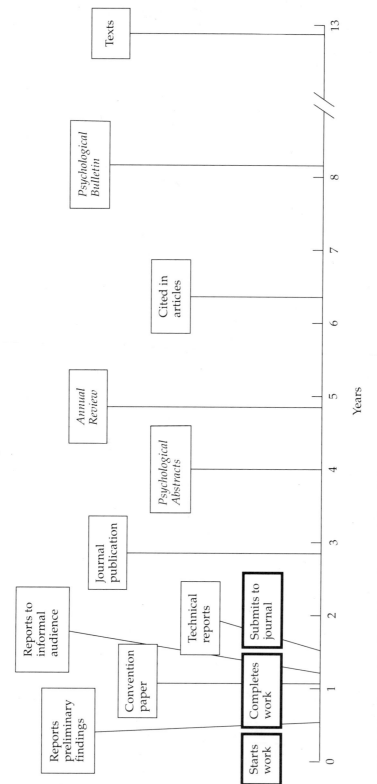

Figure 3-1. The publication history of research from its inception until its appearance in the psychological literature. Adapted from "Scientific Communication: Its Role in the Conduct of Research and Creation of Knowledge," by W. D. Garvey and B. C. Griffith, *American Psychologist* 1971, 26, 353. Copyright 1971 by the American Psychological Association. Reprinted by permission.

In the following section we will consider the formal sources in more detail, discuss the advantages and disadvantages of each, and determine how to locate relevant sources. Let's start with books and work our way to more recent sources.

Formal Sources

Books

Because books only include research that was begun years earlier, you might think that books would be the worst possible source. However, this enormous time lag makes them the best as well as the worst source. An important process occurs between the time research is completed and the time it is reported in one of the sources: the research is screened on the basis of importance and quality so that by the time it appears in a book it has been integrated with other research to form a coherent body of knowledge. Thus, the value of book research lies in the fact that the author thinks it is well done and important and that it fits into the growing body of knowledge. The author has already done much of your work for you; it's just a bit obsolete.

A good place to start your literature search is to find a recently published book that deals with the general research topic you are interested in. If the author has done a good job, you can have some confidence that you have a good summation of the most important research from the start of psychology up to about 13 years prior to the publication date of the text. Your job is now considerably easier: to find out what has happened during the last 13 or so years.

One problem with this approach is that the author has had to be selective and has not been able to include all the research done on a particular topic since the beginning of psychology. Each book author is biased toward some theoretical or methodological approach and selects research based on this bias. Thus, to be sure you can trust the author's scholarship and bias, try to develop a consensus of several resource books; at the least, try to discover the author's particular bias.

There are several ways to find appropriate books. The library card catalog is a primary source. In many libraries now the catalog is really no longer a set of cards, but a computer file. Such files are easy to use and some allow more complete subject searches than cards do. If you have never used a card-catalog index or the computer equivalent, by all means ask one of the librarians how to use it. They are most anxious to be helpful. Many libraries also participate in interlibrary loans. It may take time to get books this way, so visit the library early in your research. Do not wait until your research is done and you are writing the report before you decide to do your literature review.

Prior to your library visit, you might also look in an introductory psychology book under the topic you are interested in. Most basic texts will reference some suggested readings that get you started. You might also talk to an instructor in your psychology department who does research in the area. He or she will probably be happy to give you some book references. Finally, the American Psychological Association's *Library Use: A Handbook for Psychology* (Reed & Baxter, 1983) should be helpful to you in learning library skills specific to psychology.

Review Articles and Books

Several other sources make an attempt to summarize and integrate research within particular areas of psychology. These sources are more up-to-date than textbooks, and consequently there has been less time for the research to be put into perspective. One such source is a journal published by the American Psychological Association called *Psychological Bulletin*. The inside cover of this publication states, "The *Psychological Bulletin* publishes evaluative and integrative reviews and interpretations of substantive and methodological issues in scientific psychology." Here are some titles from recent issues of the *Bulletin:*

Arousal and the Inverted-U Hypothesis: A Critique of Neiss's "Reconceptualizing Arousal"

Attributions in Marriage: Review and Critique

Gender Differences in Mathematics Performance: A Meta-Analysis

Effects of Alcohol on Human Aggression: An Integrative Research Review

Hindsight: Biased Judgments of Past Events After the Outcomes Are Known

Ideas About Causation in Philosophy and Psychology

Psychotherapy for the Treatment of Depression: A Comprehensive Review of Controlled Outcome Research

Children of Depressed Parents: An Integrative Review

Science and Morality: The Role of Values in Science and the Scientific Study of Moral Phenomena

As you can see, the topics covered in these articles are generally narrower than textbook topics. A *Bulletin* article may also take a previous summary article as its starting point rather than the beginning of psychology and fall short of a complete survey. Nevertheless, a recent review article can save you a great deal of search time. And, generally, they are more timely than books.

For those experiments that are similar to the one you are planning, a review article will not go into enough detail for you. In this case, the original sources cited at the back of the article will allow you to quickly find which references are important and to determine how your experiment will fit in with past research.

Another source of research reviews is the *Annual Review of Psychology,* published by Annual Reviews, Inc. This series of books is published one volume per year, with the topics varying from year to year depending on the decision of an editorial board. Each chapter is written by an author who is a recognized expert in the field he or she is writing about and whose job is to bring the field up-to-date by summarizing and integrating the research done since the topic was previously included in the series. The topics are generally broader than *Psychological Bulletin* topics:

Personality
Developmental Psychology
Spatial Vision

However, some topics are a bit narrower:*

Intervention Techniques: Small Groups
Social and Cultural Influences on Psychopathology

In recent years, many edited books have appeared. Some of them summarize the most recent work in a particular area of psychology. Each chapter is usually written by a researcher who gives an up-to-date review of an even more narrowly defined research area. These chapters resemble review articles, and if you can find a chapter that is relevant to your research, you will save search time. For this type of book in particular, the publication lag is much shorter than for more standard textbooks. Many of them, in fact, are now produced by "desktop publishing" in which the lengthy process of typesetting, editing, and producing a final copy is considerably shortened. In this case some of the research reported may be only a year or two old.

Because the number of edited books has increased so rapidly, it is not as easy as it once was to browse through the few books relevant to a particular area of research. Indeed, the promoters of a new reference source called *PsycBOOKS* claim that more than one-third of scholarly writing in psychology now appears in the form of chapters and books. For this reason, *PsycBOOKS*, which may be available in your library, provides bibliographic citations, lists of chapters and their authors, and short statements about content. A search of these references can be conducted using key terms descriptive of the research subject or using author names in a way similar to that used in searching for articles in the journal *Psychological Abstracts*. (I will discuss how to do such a search shortly.)

Journal Articles

Psychological journals form the backbone of our science. They are called **primary sources** because they present the basic results as interpreted by the experimenter or experimenters who did the research rather than by third parties such as those who compile reviews. To do a really thorough literature search, you must use journal articles. As you recall, they are the most up-to-date of the formal sources, following the actual research by only a few years. Thus, although article authors try to integrate their work with

---

*Did you notice the interesting relationship? The broader the topic, the shorter the title.

the existing body of knowledge, their effort can be only partly successful because they cannot know about other research being done at the same time. Therefore, you will have to do some integration yourself to make the research form an orderly body of knowledge.

We cannot possibly list all the journals related to psychology here. Many professional organizations publish journals for their members, with a number of publishing companies sponsoring individual journals as well. However, to give you an idea of the kinds of journals available, here is a listing of some journal titles:

> *American Journal of Psychology*
> *Animal Learning & Behavior*
> *Audiology*
> *Behavioral and Brain Sciences*
> *Behavioral Neuroscience*
> *Cognition*
> *Cognitive Psychology*
> *Developmental Psychology*
> *Journal of Abnormal Psychology*
> *Journal of Applied Psychology*
> *Journal of Comparative Psychology*
> *Journal of Experimental Psychology: Animal Behavior Processes*
> *Journal of Experimental Psychology: General*
> *Journal of Experimental Psychology: Human Perception and Performance*
> *Journal of Experimental Psychology: Learning, Memory, and Cognition*
> *Journal of Personality and Social Psychology*
> *Learning and Motivation*
> *Memory & Cognition*
> *Motivation and Emotion*
> *Perception & Psychophysics*
> *Perceptual and Motor Skills*
> *Psychological Record*
> *Psychological Reports*
> *Psychological Review*
> *Quarterly Journal of Experimental Psychology: Comparative and Physiological Psychology*
> *Quarterly Journal of Experimental Psychology: Human Experimental Psychology*
> *Verbal Learning and Verbal Behavior*

Psychological Abstracts

As you can see, it would be nearly impossible to look through every article published in every journal since psychology began. Fortunately, there are publications that have done this survey for you. *Psychological Abstracts*, for example, will be your main tool in doing a literature review. Published monthly by the American Psychological Association, *Psychological Abstracts* publishes an abstract or short summary of every article published in the field of psychology in all countries of the world. It also abstracts books, review articles, and government documents. The *Abstracts* scans more than 1000 journals and reports regularly and further simplifies your task by classifying and indexing each abstract by topic and author.

Using the *Abstracts* can seem a bit frightening at first. Some students who know about *Psychological Abstracts* still do not use it because they are not familiar with a few simple procedures that make it easy to use. When you locate the *Abstracts* in your library, you will find a complete wall of rather imposing books staring at you. Glancing in one of the books, you will find paragraph upon paragraph of terse-sounding summaries and lists of authors and terms. Once you understand how to use the *Abstracts*, however, you will find that it is only slightly more difficult than using a dictionary.

Let's begin by discussing what happens to an article when it is processed by *Psychological Abstracts*. Several months after an article is published in a journal, an abstractor will put together one of the listings you see in the journal. The listing will be given a number. The authors will be listed, followed by parentheses containing the first author's institution. Next comes the title of the article, the name of the journal in which the article appeared, the date of appearance, the journal's volume number, and the page numbers for that article. If the author wrote a summary of the article, this abstract will follow. If not, the abstractor will write one and include it. Here is a typical but fictitious listing:

> 4603. **Follicle, Harry R.** (Southern Idaho State U.) **Beard growth during sexual fantasy.** *Journal of Whisker Behavior,* 1990 (Jun), Vol 3 (4), 444–447.—Exposed one group of Papago men to appropriate stimuli for sexual fantasizing while isolating a second group. The weight of the hair shaved from the face of each subject was measured daily to see whether sexual fantasizing is related to beard growth. It was concluded that Papago men do not have sexual fantasies because none of the subjects produced measurable facial-hair growth (10 ref).—*Journal abstract.*

To help you find the listing, the abstractor adds the name of each author and the listing number to an author index at the end of each monthly issue. In addition, the abstractor determines several key words that describe the article and includes these in the subject index. Suppose the article is about the effects of *cannabis resin* (a marijuana-type drug) on the social behavior of mice. The key words "cannabis" and "animal social behavior" would be added to the subject index along with the number for the listing. Finally, the abstractor would determine the major classification and subsection classification for the listing. In the previous example, for instance, the major classification would be "Psychopharmacology" and its subsection would be "Physiological Intervention and Drug Effects." The abstract would then be grouped with other articles on the same topic in the monthly issue.

Psychological Abstracts publishes an annual index for every year of abstracts. Some libraries may also have cumulative indexes that cover a period of two

LITERATURE SEARCH

or three years. Let's pick a topic and see how you would use an annual subject index to search a year's period of time. Suppose you want to know whether being the oldest child in a family affects a person's success in school. If you looked under the subject of "Birth Order" in the *1989 Subject Index*, you would find 35 listings, such as:

> birth order & level of education & race & fear, males vs females, 1432.

Because this article seems relevant to your subject, you would make a note of the listing number. Others that you might want to examine more closely would be:

> birth order, patterns of psychological problems, children, longitudinal study, 11897.

> birth order, intellectual ability & personality & academic interests, 13–16 yr old students, India, 24088.

Most of the listings would not be worth your time, such as:

> birth order & criminal behavior & substance abuse, substance abusing adults, South Africa, 22829.

Once you have jotted down the numbers of all likely-looking articles, you can use these numbers to look up the original abstracts from individual *Psychological Abstracts* published during that year, deciding as you go whether each reference is worth looking at more closely. If you are still interested after reading the abstract, write down the reference, find the original article in the library, and read it. At each point of your search, you need look at only enough information to determine whether to pursue each reference.

In this manner you can search through large amounts of material efficiently.

If you have never used *Psychological Abstracts,* you might find it helpful to select several specific topics, head for the library, and try your hand at finding relevant articles. If you cannot think of any topics,* try these:

The attitude of various races toward segregation
Differences in emotional adjustment of smokers and nonsmokers
Leadership capabilities of female managers
Brain-hemisphere effects on motor skills
The effect of alcohol on traffic accidents

Once you have used the subject indexes to find all the research related to a particular topic, you might wish to double-check by using the author indexes. Look up the names of the authors of the articles you have tracked down to make sure you have identified all their relevant work. Find the listing numbers of any additional articles and again select relevant articles based on their abstracts.

The *Psychological Abstracts* will give you access to all the formal sources except those articles less than about six months old. To be thorough, look at the article titles from the final half-year of the journals in which you have previously found relevant research.

"Treeing" Backward Through the References

There is another way to do a literature search that is not nearly so thorough as using *Psychological Abstracts.* However, it is a good way to determine whether you have missed any key research in your previous search. I will refer to this technique as **treeing backward through the references.** The first thing to do is find the most recent article that deals with the topic of interest; this article will form the "trunk" of your research tree. Find the references at the end of the article. Many of these references should also be relevant to your topic (with any luck most of them are already on your list). Each of these articles will also have a reference list from which you can select in the same way. Follow each reference list backward through the literature until you have found all the important articles that form a new set of branches on your tree. This method can be helpful, but do not rely on it as your sole technique, since you cannot always assume that every author has done a scholarly job of finding the important references.

"Treeing" Forward Through the References

To be thorough in your literature search, you can tree forward through the references as well as backward. For example, if you find a key article that is several years old and want to find more recent articles that have refer-

---

*If you cannot think of any topics, you must have missed Chapter 2. Go back and read it!

TREEING THROUGH THE REFERENCES

enced that article, you can use the *Science Citation Index* or, depending on the topic, the *Social Sciences Citation Index*. The SSCI is published quarterly and cumulated annually by the Institute of Scientific Information. It covers nearly 1400 journals from virtually every social science discipline. The SCI also covers topics that may be of interest to psychologists.

After you get the hang of the abbreviation system, you will find the *Citation Indexes* fairly easy to use. Suppose that key article you found is five years old. You would first find the shelf that contains the *Citation Index* for the year following publication of the article and get the volume that lists the part of the alphabet containing your author's name. Look through the alphabetical listing of names until you find your author's name and initials. Notice that articles by several people with the same name may be listed under this heading.* Look for a listing of your key article. If it isn't there, you can assume that nobody cited it during this year. If your article is listed, you will find a list of authors' names and journals. These references are for articles that cited your key article. Write them down. Repeat this process for each year up to the most recent, and you will have found every article that included the key article as a reference.

A typical column from the *Science Citation Index* is shown in Figure 3-2. Suppose the early key article you were interested in was D. Aaronson's 1967

---

*For example, whenever I look up my listing, I can find out what my father, who is a physicist, has been doing. He is also D. W. Martin.

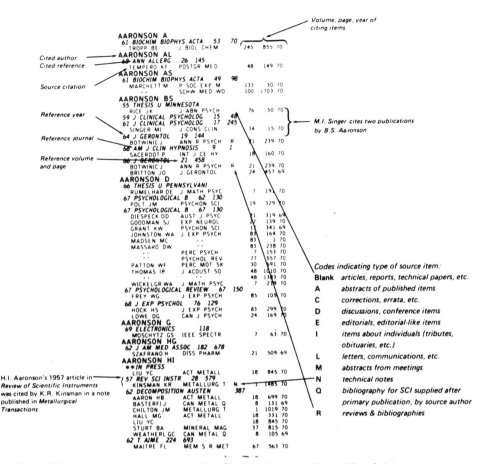

Figure 3-2. A typical column from the *Citation Index* portion of the *Science Citation Index*.
SOURCE: M. Weinstock, 1971.

article that appeared in Volume 67 of *Psychological Bulletin*. You can see that it is listed as the third entry under Aaronson's name. It was cited in the 12 listings that appear under it. For example, Wicklegren referenced it in 1970 in Volume 7, page 219, of the *Journal of Mathematical Psychology*. Citations for other key articles can be found in a similar manner.

You can also recycle yourself by finding each article that cited the original article, then treeing backward using the references for each of these new articles. You may wish to take some of these newly acquired references, use them as key references, and go forward again. You can continue this process until you feel you have covered all the important references.

HOW TO RECYCLE YOURSELF

Current Research

The Smithsonian Science Information Exchange provides a way of finding out what is going on in current research. Their current file contains records for more than 14,000 projects in all areas of the behavioral sciences. All these projects are being supported by a funding agency such as the National Science Foundation. Each listing contains a 200-word description of the work being performed. You can order a package containing the listings for general topic areas such as "Insomnia" or "Behavior therapy with alcoholics." There is a fee for this service that depends on the number of listings. The disadvantages of this system are the cost and the fact that only funded research is listed. However, it is one of the few means of finding out about ongoing research.

Computerized Searches

Databases of the psychological literature can now be examined using computerized searches. Several such databases have been established that contain all of the articles or abstracts published during a given time span. For example, the American Psychological Association (APA) has produced a database, called *PsycINFO,* containing all of the abstracts from *Psychological Abstracts* published since 1967. This information can be searched using authors' names or key terms or identifiers in a way similar to manually searching *Psychological Abstracts.* There are three ways that such a computerized search can be done. The most time-consuming way is to fill out appropriate forms indicating how you wish the search to be accomplished and then have the search carried out by an organization in the APA set up to provide this service (at a considerable cost). A second way is to use a library equipped with terminals that can tap various databases. Many university libraries now provide such services, sometimes for free and sometimes for a nominal charge. In this case, the search can be done "on line" so that it is possible to immediately see the results of the search and to pick and choose which information to save and print and which to discard. If this service is available in your campus library, a librarian will be happy to work with you in your literature search. Finally, some databases are now available on compact discs with read-only memory (CD-ROM). For example, *PsycLIT* provides summaries of over 1300 journals cumulated since 1974, on only two discs! It also provides a search system that can be used on the more popular personal computers. This system is very convenient and an unlimited number of searches can be done. However, the annual fee is relatively large so the availability of such systems may be limited to large universities. If you want to learn the details of how to do computerized searches, the APA publishes a step-by-step instructional guide for students called *Search PsycINFO* that you might wish to order.

A computerized search takes little of your time, and it is fast. You get printed references and abstracts appropriate for filing with no mistakes; you get just what you asked for.

There are also several disadvantages of a computerized search. You do get just what you asked for, but sometimes it is difficult to know quite what to ask for. When you are doing the search by hand, you sometimes find out what you are searching for while you are searching. The computerized searches that are not done "on line" require that you specify exactly what you are looking for prior to the search. A second disadvantage is that once you get the results of the computerized search, you still have not completed the search process. You still have to sort the listings and examine the original articles. The final disadvantage—cost—is getting to be less of a problem. Charges for the service vary. In some cases a library may subscribe and there may be no charge. In other cases there may be a flat charge or one based upon the number of abstracts you have printed.

While we are on the subject of money, here is a final word on how poor people like us can get free journal articles. When authors get articles published, they usually order 100 or so reprints of the article from the journal. As long as these reprints last, the author will send one to you if you ask nicely. The usual way is to send a postcard saying "I would very much appreciate receiving a reprint of your article entitled ＿＿＿＿＿＿＿ that appeared in ＿＿＿＿＿＿＿ ." Be sure to include your address. The author will send you a copy as a professional courtesy. Don't be embarrassed to send out these **reprint requests.** Many younger investigators who are trying to become familiar with research in a particular area but do not have the resources to buy their own journals send out reprint requests.

Technical Reports

Technical reports are often ignored as a source of psychological literature, but they can be helpful in certain areas of research. When the federal government supports research, particularly Defense Department research, the investigator is usually required to report it in the form of a technical report. This report is similar to a journal article but usually goes into more detail about the procedure and the apparatus, and sometimes it even lists the data. Technical reports are automatically distributed by the supporting governmental agency to other investigators who are doing similar research supported by that agency.

About one author in ten produces these technical reports, and only about one-third of these reports are later published in a journal (Garvey & Griffith, 1971). Most libraries do not routinely order technical reports, because they would quickly fill up the shelves and are difficult for a library to organize and classify systematically. Investigators who are working on defense grants or contracts get a monthly publication listing abstracts of all technical reports. *Psychological Abstracts* also lists many of these reports. Unfortunately, technical reports are often difficult to obtain. To purchase them, you must send to the Defense Documentation Center in Alexandria, Virginia, and you must know the document number and the price of the report you want.

Searching through technical reports is a waste of time for some areas of research. However, if you are working in an area supported by a major government agency, the technical report is a valuable source of information. Some examples of government-supported research are automobile driver safety, personnel training and selection, operator control of complex machines, and human decision making.

Informal Sources
Professional Meetings

As we mentioned earlier, to be completely up-to-date on the research in a particular field, you must become familiar with informal sources of communication. About 15 to 18 months prior to journal publication many investigators present their research at a professional meeting by reading a paper. In fact, about one-fifth of the articles published in major psychology journals are based on material previously presented at an American Psychological Association (APA) convention (Garvey & Griffith, 1971). The APA annually sponsors a national meeting and six regional conventions. In addition, many other non-APA professional groups, such as the Psychonomic Society, the Psychometric Society, the American Psychological Society, and so on, sponsor meetings.

Of course, you can't attend every single meeting or convention in your field. Thus, some of the meetings publish papers in a bound volume called a **proceedings**, which is available in most libraries. In addition, just prior to the meetings, members of these organizations receive convention programs. You might be able to find faculty in your psychology department who are members of these organizations and get programs prior to the meetings. Once you know that one of these papers is of interest to you, simply send the author a reprint request. You will understand the paper better if you read it than if you listen to it anyway.

The real reason for attending conventions, aside from engaging in superfluous hedonistic activities,* is to talk to other researchers presently doing work in your area of interest. Depending on how defensive they are, you might even find out what they are planning to do in the near future. In this way, you can fill in the information gap between "starts work" and "convention paper" in Figure 3-1.

By the way, if you learn something in one of these discussions that you might wish to quote in an article, be sure to write it down, note the date, and get the person's permission to use it. You can then cite the source in an article as a **personal communication**.

After you have established these informal contacts, you can work out an agreement by which other investigators routinely send you **preprints** of articles and papers as soon as they are finished. You in turn agree to send them preprints of your work. Sometimes a number of researchers working in a specific area will join to form a preprint group.† Usually, however, informal contacts are more valuable when they are on a one-to-one basis.

While the written record of our science is maintained by the formal sources, the informal sources also perform a vital service for science. They offer a forum for saying stupid but creative things. Your informal colleagues will chuckle quietly and tell you where you are wrong. Your formal colleagues are forced to guffaw loudly and boisterously tell the world where you have gone wrong. With only the formal sources, few of us would have the courage to try to move science by leaps and bounds, and we would stick with small conservative steps. The encouragement and friendly discouragement offered by informal contacts are important in shaping our thoughts into a form suitable for the formal literature.

---

*Havin' fun!

†I was once a member of a collection of psychologists interested in human decision making that was quaintly called "the group." Unfortunately, as "the group" grew, some groupers turned into groupies and rules had to be made. The group also became larger and more ritualized. Suddenly we were an institution! At that point informal lines of communication became formal, the purpose was lost, and the group faded away.

I have tried to make this discussion of searching the literature as complete as possible. I hope that in doing so I haven't made the process sound more complex than it really is. Many new investigators believe that a literature search requires some sort of mystical power and many years of experience. However, if you follow the simple steps outlined in this chapter, you will find that doing a thorough literature search can be a straightforward, satisfying experience.

Summary

A **literature search** is necessary to find out if your experimental idea has already been investigated, to determine whether similar experiments have been done, and to see how your experiment will fit into the current body of knowledge. To do this search efficiently, you should understand the lines of communication within the scientific community and the **time lag** associated with various sources of information. It is usually most efficient to begin your search in **books** that are relevant to your area of interest. Books describe research from the beginning of psychology up to about 13 years prior to current research. You can then use **review articles** to bring you within five to eight years of current research. **Journal articles** will form the backbone of your literature search. You can track down relevant articles through the subject indexes and author indexes from *Psychological Abstracts*. You can double-check your search by **treeing backward through the references** of recent journal articles. The *Social Science Citation Index* also allows you to **tree forward through the references** by determining which articles have cited a particular earlier article. **Technical reports** can be an important source of information, particularly in applied fields. **Computerized searches** of formal sources can now be done using commercial search services, library terminals, or personal computers equipped to read compact discs. Informal sources such as **papers read at professional meetings, personal communications,** and **preprints** are a valuable way to learn about current and future research.

References

Garvey, W. D., & Griffith, B. C. (1971). Scientific communication: Its role in the conduct of research and creation of knowledge. *American Psychologist, 26,* 349–362.

Reed, J. G., & Baxter, P. M. (1983). *Library use: A handbook for psychology.* Washington, D.C.: American Psychological Association.

4

How to Decide Which Variables to Manipulate and Measure

> We believe that a concept has no meaning beyond that obtained from the operations on which it is based.*

We discussed a general model of an experiment in Chapter 1 and how to get experimental ideas in Chapter 2. In Chapter 3 you probably learned more about doing a literature search than you wished to know. Now it's time we got to work doing what experimental psychologists are supposed to do—experiments.

In this chapter, we will consider two decisions that have to be made when planning any psychology experiment, from the simplest to the most complex. We need to choose the independent and dependent variables.

Choosing an Independent Variable

Recall from Chapter 1 that the independent variable is the one that the experimenter manipulates. Since the whole purpose of any experiment is to find the effect of the independent variable on the subject's behavior, choosing this variable is about the most important decision you have to make. At first blush it may seem that the decision should be rather straightforward. And for some experiments it is. For example, if you want to know whether people press a button in response to a light more quickly when a tone is given as a warning signal, the independent variable is rather obvious— the presence or absence of the tone. If, however, you want to find out if children are more aggressive after exposure to violent versus nonviolent television programs, the independent variable (violence) may be tougher to define. What constitutes violence on television? Is *Monday Night Football* violent? Are *Roadrunner* cartoons violent? Is *Wild Kingdom* violent? Not everyone would agree on a particular definition of violent television programs.

The problem here is that there is a difference in precision between what the general public will accept in defining a term and what experimental psychologists will accept. Experimental psychologists require **operational definitions** of the independent and dependent variables. This means that they must specify the operations they would go through to determine if a

---

*Garner, W. R., Hake, H. W., & Eriksen, C. W. (1956). Operationalism and the concept of perception. *Psychological Review, 63,* 158.

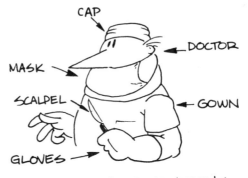

OPERATIONAL DEFINITIONS

television program were violent and outline the specific steps they would take to classify television programs.

For example, if you were conducting our television experiment, you could operationalize the concept of a violent television program by showing each program to a randomly chosen group of 100 people and requiring that 75% of them indicate a program is violent before you operationally define it as violent. Another alternative is to devise a checklist with such items as: "Is there physical contact of an aggressive nature?" "Has an illegal act taken place?" "Did one person act so as to make another feel inferior?" Perhaps you would require that each program have at least two out of ten such items checked "yes" for it to be considered violent. Again, such a procedure would specify exactly what operations any other experimenter must carry out to meet your operational definition of violent television programs.

Psychology researchers have more difficulty agreeing on operational definitions than do physical scientists.* Galileo did not have to ponder over a definition for mass before determining whether objects that have different masses fall at the same speed in a vacuum. Yet a great many important psychological questions require complex operational definitions: Do people whose mothers were affectionate make more successful marriage partners? Do students learn more from popular professors? Does a worker's morale affect work output? Does anxiety cause depression? Before doing an experiment to answer any of these questions, you need operational definitions for the terms *affectionate, popular, morale,* and *anxiety.* Try making up operational definitions for these terms; you will quickly see the psychology researcher's challenge.

Choosing the Range of Your Independent Variable

Once you have defined your independent variable, you still have to choose the range of the variable. The **range** is the difference between the highest and lowest level of the variable you choose. For example, suppose we decided

---

*A physicist first used the term *operational definition.* However, in the physical sciences, operational definitions are usually so widely accepted that physical scientists spend considerably less time agonizing over them than behavioral scientists do.

to define violent television programs using our group of 100 people to classify each program as violent or nonviolent. We could choose to use two levels of violence in our experiment—those programs classified as violent by 100% of the people and those that nobody thought were violent. These two levels of the independent variable give us the largest possible range.

On the other hand, we might have chosen the programs rated violent by over 50% of the people as violent and those rated violent by less than 50% as nonviolent. These levels obviously create a much smaller range.

How do we determine what the range should be? Unfortunately, I can't give you any hard and fast rules for making this decision, for it is as much an art as a science. However, following are some guidelines that you might find useful.

Be realistic   First, you should try to choose a range that is **realistic** in that it is similar to the levels found in the situation you will be generalizing to. You should avoid "sledgehammer" effects caused by setting the levels of the independent variable at such extremes that you are certain to find a difference in behavior. Some of the early medical research on marijuana was plagued by sledgehammer effects. In some cases, experimenters gave mice the human equivalent of a truckload of marijuana per day! The experimenters got impressive but impractical results.

Select a range that shows effect   Within realistic limits, you should have a range that is large enough to show an effect of the independent variable on the dependent variable if such an effect exists. For example, if you were interested in the effect of room temperature on manual dexterity in a sorting task and you chose temperatures of 23° C and 25° C,* you might conclude falsely that room temperature has no effect on manual dexterity.

*For those of you who refuse to be converted to converting Celsius, 73° F and 77° F.

Real-world* experimental situations require special attention to choosing a large enough range because the experimenter does not always have complete control over the levels of the independent variable. You can choose an approximate level, but the actual level may vary from trial to trial. For instance, in a lecture-pace experiment, I once attempted to vary my lecture pace by speaking at a slow, medium, or fast rate. The levels I attempted to achieve were 100, 125, and 150 syllables per minute. Because I am not a machine that can be set at a particular speaking rate, I was bound to produce some variability around the desired levels. To determine my actual rate, we recorded the lectures and counted the number of syllables per second. Fortunately, the fastest lecture at the slow pace was still slower than the slowest lecture at the medium pace, so there was no overlap of levels. If I had chosen a smaller range, however, I would have had less chance of producing these reliable differences among the levels of the independent variable. Thus, in some nonlaboratory experiments, you must remember to make the range large enough that differences in the levels of the independent variable are not covered up by the uncontrolled variability of that variable.

Do a pilot experiment   Determining the best range for an experiment is to some extent guesswork. In some cases, you may find experiments using the same independent variable you are planning to use that can give you an idea about an appropriate range. However, if your experiment is original and nobody else has used an independent variable similar to yours, you may choose to do a **pilot experiment.**† A pilot experiment is a small-scale version of the experiment you are planning, done so you can iron out any problems before you proceed. Because you need not report the results of this experiment, you may break some of the rules of experimentation. For example, you might cajole your friends into serving as subjects, and you might even serve as your own subject. You can also change the levels of your independent variable halfway through a trial, stop the experiment, or do only part of the experiment, depending on what you learn as you proceed.

When doing a pilot experiment, you will sometimes find that what looked good on paper just does not work. For example, I once discovered during a pilot experiment that a supposedly simple experiment I had designed required at least three experimenters to operate the equipment. The pilot experiment may also help you determine whether the levels of your independent variable are what you expected. Levels that seem realistic during

---

*I use the term **real world** to refer to nonlaboratory experiments designed to find answers to applied problems, not to imply that most people in universities are unreal. People who live in ivory towers shouldn't throw snipes.

† I suppose the term *pilot* in this case is used in the sense of "guiding through unknown places," as when a ship's pilot comes on board to steer a vessel through unknown waters. The pilot experiment becomes the guide for future experiments, guiding the experimenter through uncharted waters.

SUBJECT FOR A
PILOT EXPERIMENT

the planning stage of an experiment may seem unrealistic to the laboratory subject. By having a trial run, you can change an obviously inappropriate range of the independent variable before investing a great amount of time and effort in the experiment.

Although searching the literature and doing pilot experiments can give you some idea of an appropriate range for your independent variable, in the end you still have to make your best guess. If you turn out to be right, you can claim good judgment. If you are wrong, you claim bad luck.

Choosing a Dependent Variable

As we know from Chapter 1, the dependent variable is some measure of the subjects' behavior. We saw that there are an infinite number of things we could choose to measure. In selecting our dependent variable, we must decide what we will measure.

Operational Definitions Again

Let's return to the question "Will violent television shows cause a change in a child's aggressiveness?" In this experiment, we clearly want to measure aggressiveness, but again we need an operational definition of aggressiveness so that we can determine whether a child's behavior changes after viewing violent television shows.

One way to develop an operational definition in this example would be to have a panel of judges watch a movie of each child in a free-play situation and then rate the child's aggressiveness on a seven-point scale. Or we could tell each child several stories about other children in frustrating situations and ask the child what he or she would do in each situation. We could then use the number of "direct-attack" responses as a measure of aggressiveness. Another alternative is to observe children as they play with a selection of toys we had previously classified as aggressive (such as guns, tanks, and knives) or nonaggressive (such as trucks, tools, and dolls). We could then measure the percentage of time that the child played with each type of toy. You can undoubtedly think of many other behaviors that would be an indication of a child's aggressiveness.

Sometimes, even when a dependent variable seems quite straightforward, there can be problems with operationally defining it. For example, two investigators wished to determine whether some predictions from a theory of evolutionary psychology would be supported by homicide figures (Daly & Wilson, 1988). The theory predicts that people are much less likely to kill blood relatives living with them than to kill genetically unrelated people living with them.* Now, it would seem to be a pretty simple matter to count homicides within a particular sample. But what exactly is a homicide? In several countries homicide figures include all "murders, attempted murders, and manslaughters." Should attempted murders and manslaughters be counted for this study? For most manslaughters, such as a reckless auto accident, there is no intent to kill. Is intent important? If intent is important, perhaps attempted murders should be treated as murders. Should only the cases in which a conviction was obtained be counted? At first that might seem appropriate; we would not want to include a case if the person were innocent. But counting convictions may be even more misleading. In a sample of homicides committed in Detroit in one year, 20 men were convicted for killing their wives, and 9 women were convicted for killing their husbands. One might conclude that men killed their wives more often. Actually, though, women killed their spouses more often. But homicidal wives had their cases dismissed without trial 75% of the time, whereas homicidal husbands were spared a trial only 20% of the time. As the researchers point out, counting only convictions may say more about the behavior of prosecutors than about the behavior of offenders! Unfortunately, as this example illustrates, operationally defining dependent variables is no easier than doing so for independent variables.

With dependent variables, not only do we have to be concerned with determining an operational definition, but we have to know whether the measurement is **reliable** and **valid.**

Reliability and Validity

A measuring instrument is perfectly reliable if we get exactly the same result when we repeat the measurement a number of times. The more variable the results, the less reliable is the measuring instrument. A rubber ruler, for example, would not be very reliable. It might measure a tabletop at 18 inches one time and 31 inches the next time. To find out how reliable the ruler is, we would have to measure a number of objects at least two times and see how the results correlate (Chapter 1). If the result of the first mea-

---

*For your information, they found that unrelated cohabitants were over eleven times more likely to be at risk than related cohabitants.

A NONAGGRESSIVE TOY?

surement is similar to that of the second, correlation is high and we can assume that the measuring instrument is reliable. If correlation is low, we would know that the instrument is not very reliable.

To use our example of violent television programs, we might show the same set of movies of each child's behavior to a second panel of judges and compare the aggressiveness ratings given by the two panels. If the panels gave similar ratings, we can feel more confident that ratings taken from a panel of judges are reliable.

Validity* refers to whether we are measuring what we want to measure. Suppose we have a wooden ruler marked as 12 inches long, but it is really 24 inches long because each inch on the ruler actually measures 2 inches. In this case, we could measure the tabletop many times, and the ruler would indicate 11 inches every time. We have a reliable measuring instrument, but, of course, the measurement is wrong because we claim that we are measuring in inches when in fact we are not. Thus, we also need to know if our measuring instruments are valid—that is, if they measure in the same units as a standard measuring device known to be valid.

In establishing our operational definition of aggressiveness, for example, suppose we had decided to measure the percentage of time each child spent playing with aggressive versus nonaggressive toys. If our stopwatch were working correctly, this measurement would probably be reliable, because we would get about the same reading when we timed the behavior a second time. However, people might argue that our measure is not a valid measure of aggressiveness. They might claim that children tend to play with toys that they already know how to use. Because they have seen guns and tanks

*For a more detailed discussion of types of validity, see Chapter 8.

and knives used on violent television programs, they choose those toys to play with. Or they might claim that children can use trucks and tools and dolls in aggressive ways as well as nonaggressive ways. To convince them that your measure is valid, you must compare it to some standard that you both agree is a valid measure of aggressiveness. If your measuring instrument agreed with the standard, you could call it a valid instrument.

Directly Observable Dependent Variables

The closer you can come to directly observing the behavior you are interested in, the less controversy there will be over your measure. However, if your interest is in determining the workings of the human mind, you should recognize that all dependent measures are in a sense indirect. For example, suppose you are interested in memory and want to compare two ways of presenting material to be remembered. After a week you wish to measure how much your subjects remember. What should you measure?

That's easy; just ask them what they remember. But suppose they cannot recall any of the material in either presentation condition. Could you then conclude that they remember nothing? You might have given them a recognition test instead and determined their accuracy at distinguishing previously presented material from new material. Or you could have had them relearn the material and measured the percentage of time saved by having learned it before. Each of these methods might give you different answers to your question: How much do subjects remember? I hope you can see from this example that dependent variables, even those that at first appear to be directly observable, may be linked only indirectly to the behavior you are interested in.

Single dependent variables   Suppose we want to know whether a subject will respond more quickly to a bright light than to a dim light when pushing a button. We would probably start a clock when the light occurred and stop the clock when the button was pressed. We should recognize that only one characteristic of the response is being measured. We could have chosen any number of other characteristics—how subjects press the button, for example. Does one subject move her finger from the side of the button on one trial and from directly over the button on the next? On one trial, does she miss the button on the first try? On another trial, does she hit the button lightly at first and then mash it down? From this diverse set of responses, we chose to measure only one characteristic of the response: time from light onset to button depression. In other words, we selected a **single dependent variable.**

Any single dependent variable we choose may or may not be the appropriate measure to take. For example, suppose we ask a subject to use a pencil to trace the outline of a star while looking at the star in a mirror. Because the mirror reverses everything, most subjects find this task very tough on the first few trials. Suppose we want to measure a subject's

improvement from Trial 1 to Trial 10 on this task. What dependent variable would best reflect this improvement?

The standard dependent variable used in these experiments is the number of times the subject's tracing crosses the outline of the star. Figure 4-1 shows the tracings from two fictitious subjects that we will sagaciously call Subject 1 and Subject 2. On Trial 1, Subject 1 crossed the boundary 20 times; on Trial 10, 6 times. For this subject, the dependent variable reflects the expected improvement in performance. But look at Subject 2. This subject crossed the outline 14 times on each of the two trials. Our dependent variable indicates that Subject 2 did not improve in mirror-tracing performance. Do you believe this conclusion?

The basic problem is that even when a directly observable dependent variable such as number of border crossings is used, we must be concerned with validity. Border-crossing behavior is only one possible measure of mirror-tracing performance. Is it a valid measure? Other dependent variables might better reflect overall mirror-tracing performance. As an alternative, we could have measured the total length of the tracing and determined what percentage fell within the borders of the star. Or we could have measured the area between the border and the tracing for each trial. Or we could have timed the subjects to find out whether they were tracing the star more quickly by the tenth trial.

Multiple dependent variables   One way to improve the chances of using a valid dependent variable is to use **multiple dependent variables.** In fact, in some areas of experimental psychology, it is considered quite inappropriate to report only one dependent measure. For example, many types of research use choice reaction time as a dependent measure. **Choice reaction time** is the time it takes a subject to give one of several responses when one of several stimuli* occurs. Naturally, if subjects wish to make as

---

*Because I haven't used the term *stimuli* before, I should point out that **stimulus** is singular and **stimuli** is plural. It is time to expand your chant: "This stimulus is, this datum is; these stimuli are, these data are." Got that?

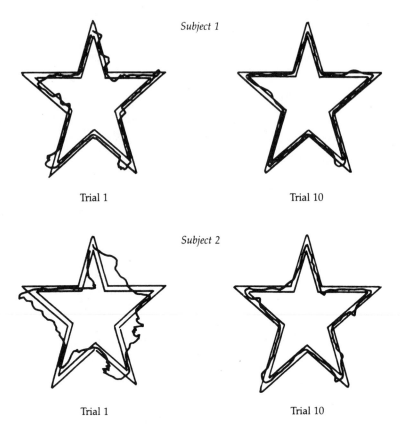

Figure 4-1. Star-tracing performance of two subjects on Trials 1 and 10.

few errors as possible, they must respond rather slowly. If they are willing to be less accurate, they can respond more quickly. This speed-accuracy tradeoff makes it necessary that both speed and accuracy be reported as dependent variables. If we are interested in a subject's overall level of performance, one measure is useless without the other. For this reason, the better journals will not accept articles that report only speed or only accuracy of a choice-reaction-time response.

Composite dependent variables   Although it is generally a good idea to report as many aspects of the subject's behavior as possible, this practice can make interpreting the results much more difficult. Suppose we have four dependent variables: one measure shows great improvement across conditions, two stay the same, and one decreases slightly. To say anything about the overall change in behavior, we need a way of combining our single dependent variables into a **composite dependent variable** that will give some indication of overall performance.

A number of areas in experimental psychology use composite dependent variables. One area is intelligence testing. The Wechsler Adult Intelligence Scale is an example of a composite dependent variable. The IQ (intelligence quotient) is a composite of two subscales—a verbal scale and a performance scale. The score on each of these is a composite made up of subtests. For example, the verbal score is derived from the scores on the following tests: general information, digit span, vocabulary, arithmetic, comprehension, and similarities. The idea behind intelligence testing is that it is useful to have a single measure that characterizes intelligence in general. Not all psychologists agree that a single number does adequately represent intelligence, of course, but the use of composite dependent variables is traditional in the psychology of testing.

A second type of composite dependent variable combines several instances of a single measure. These instances are taken at different times or under different conditions. **Percent savings** is one such dependent variable used in memory research. Suppose, for example, that one group of subjects learned to ride a bicycle when they were young and then did not touch a bike again until they were 40 years old. We could have them relearn bike riding, practicing for a number of trials until they could stay on for a minute without touching the ground. Suppose it takes them seven trials to do this. We could compare this number to the number of trials it takes a second group of 40-year-olds who had never ridden a bike to stay on for a minute. Suppose it took this group an average of 14 trials. We could then calculate the percentage of trials saved by having learned to ride at an earlier age:

$$\% \text{ saved} = \frac{\text{Number of trials to learn} - \text{Number of trials to relearn}}{\text{Number of trials to learn}} \times 100$$

In our example:

$$\% \text{ saved} = \frac{14 - 7}{14} \times 100 = 50\%$$

Through this type of composite dependent variable, you can use a single number to show the effect of a change caused by the independent variable (past bike-riding experience).

It may not be clear to you yet how these composite dependent variables are derived or why they are appropriate measures, but you will become familiar with many others if you do research in certain areas of psychology. You may even find yourself making up your own composite variables someday.

Indirect Dependent Variables

It is sometimes impossible to directly observe the behavior you are interested in, yet we know that the ROT (repeatable, observable, testable) test of science requires that the behavior we are studying be publicly observable.

How then can we do scientific research in such areas as emotion, learning, or intelligence? We need an indirect variable that changes along with the internal behavior we are interested in.

Physiological measures Probably the most popular type of indirect variables are **physiological measures,** which are based on the idea that if the behavior is a private event, such as an emotion, perhaps the physiology of the body will change along with the private event. Since modern technology allows us to observe changes in the physiology of the body, experimenters use these changes to infer what the private event must have been.

Of course, when we use physiological measures to infer internal states, we are assuming that a unique physiological pattern accurately reflects an internal state. For example, a polygraph or lie detector measures four physiological processes—respiratory rate, heart rate, blood pressure, and galvanic skin response.* The operator uses these measures to determine whether the accused is telling the truth. Some people doubt whether the assumption behind using physiological measures is correct. For this reason, the results of a lie-detector test are admissible evidence in most courts only if both the plaintiff and the defendant agree to their use. And recently, federal law has severely restricted the use of polygraph tests in employment screening.

Other physiological measures have become popular as researchers claim that they give an indication of some emotional state. They then lose favor as other investigators show that they can get the same type of physiological change with a different internal state. For example, an investigator named Hess at one point claimed that the diameter of a person's pupil increases when he or she is thinking pleasant thoughts and decreases when the person is thinking about unpleasant things. For a while, the Madison Avenue advertising tycoons were so impressed that they used pupillary responses to choose magazine advertisements. Other investigators have since found that the diameter of the pupil is perhaps a better indication of the amount of information the person is processing rather than the emotions the person is feeling (Johnson, 1971). Pupillometricians are no longer welcome on Madison Avenue.

Recently investigators have claimed that the characteristics of a person's voice can be used for "psychological stress evaluation." By tape recording a voice, slowing it down, and measuring certain aspects of vocal frequencies, these investigators believe that they can tell when a person is under great stress, such as they would be when lying. These claims have not been supported by research, and this measure is now considered worthless by many researchers.

---

*In case you are not familiar with the term **galvanic skin response,** it is not a rash caused by handling too many garbage cans. It is a measure of how well the skin will carry a small electric current. Although not technically accurate, the reasoning goes something like this: because wet skin carries electric current better than dry skin, a person who is "in a sweat" has a different galvanic skin response from one who is "cool and calm."

SOME STIMULI BRING ABOUT A CHARACTERISTIC BRAINWAVE.

Measurement of brainwave activity in the form of electroencephalo-graph (EEG) recording has been possible for some time now. It would seem that this measure might offer a way to directly assess cognitive behavior. The general pattern of activity, however, is not very useful other than for determining a person's overall level of arousal. Recently, researchers have been able to present a particular stimulus a number of times and average the brainwave activity from time of stimulus presentation. In this way a brainwave is produced that has consistent characteristics. Certain parts of the averaged wave appear to be related to stimulus dimensions or to the cognitive activity associated with the stimulus. But although these results indicate that in the future we may be able to "read" brainwaves to infer internal states or cognitive activity, EEGs, along with most other physiological measures, as yet offer only murky glimpses into the human mind.

Behavioral measures   Some **behavioral measures** can also be used as indirect dependent variables. As with physiological measures, changes in the way a person performs a behavioral task can reflect the person's internal state.

Indirect behavioral measures have become particularly important in the study of cognitive psychology. Researchers in this area are interested in determining what goes on in the "black box" of the human mind during cognitive tasks such as reading or problem solving. Because all they really have to work with are the inputs to (stimuli) and outputs from (responses) the box, they have had to devise clever ways to infer what must be happening in the box. Suppose, for example, that we want to know how much information is processed in completing a particular task. If we assume that there are limited resources available in the brain for processing cognitive information, one way to determine how much information is being processed is to measure how long it takes to make a response: the more information processed, the longer will be the response time. However, response time would give us only a single measure for the entire task and would tell us little about the processing required of subtasks such as encoding or response selection.

Dual-task methodology offers an indirect way of determining the processing requirements of a task while it is being performed. In this case, while the task of primary interest is being performed (the primary task), a second task (the secondary task) is also presented to the subject. The subject is instructed to do the primary task as well as possible and to use whatever resources are left over to do the secondary task. We can then measure performance on the secondary task and infer what the processing requirements of the primary task were. The better the performance on the secondary task, the fewer resources the primary task must have required. For example, the primary task might be to read a sentence. While the sentence is being read, tones are presented to the subjects and they are instructed to press a button as quickly as possible whenever they hear a tone. We would infer that the slower the response to the tone, the more processing the sentence must be requiring at that time. With several trials, it would be possible to plot response times to the tones at various times while the sentence was being read and thus get a profile of processing resources required by the sentence (Martin & Kelly, 1974).

As with all indirect behavioral measures, the measure is only as good as the assumptions that underlie it. In the case of dual-task methodology, the primary assumption is that a single pool of processing resources provides resources for all cognitive tasks. Some researchers have questioned this basic assumption (Wickens, 1984; Navon & Gopher, 1979). Indeed, there is now pretty good evidence that there are multiple pools of resources and that the type of pool used depends upon whether the task is visual or aural, spatial or verbal, and so forth (Wickens, 1984). These findings cast some doubt on the general usefulness of the dual-task methodology.

Other indirect behavioral measures do not necessarily make the same assumptions as dual-task methodology. However, in general, the more indirect the measure, the more elaborate the underlying assumptions have to be, and the less confident we can be of our inferences. The advantage of indirect measures is that they do offer a way of investigating experimental questions for which we have no direct measures. As long as we are aware of the assumptions we are making when using indirect measures, they can be a valuable tool for helping us get an idea of the nature of otherwise unobservable events.

Summary

In choosing an independent variable for your experiment, you must first specify an **operational definition** of the variable so that other experimenters will be able to go through the same operations when they conduct similar experiments. It is also important to choose the levels of your independent variable so that the **range** is large enough to show the experimental effect but small enough to be realistic. A trial run, or **pilot experiment,** will sometimes help you in this decision.

The dependent variable must also be operationally defined. In addition, we must be able to show that the dependent variable is **reliable** and **valid.** It is reliable if the same result is obtained every time a measurement is taken. It is valid if the measurement agrees with a commonly accepted standard. **Directly observable dependent variables** are relatively easy to measure, but deciding which **single dependent variable** to use is sometimes difficult. Some areas of research require that **multiple dependent variables** be reported or that dependent variables be combined to form a **composite dependent variable. Indirect dependent variables** are used when the behavior we are interested in is not publicly observable. **Physiological measures** may provide an indication of the subject's internal state, but they are often difficult to interpret. **Behavioral measures** such as **dual-task methodology** also offer the possibility of determining a subject's internal state.

References

Daly, M., & Wilson, M. (1988). *Homicide.* Hawthorne, N.Y.: Aldine de Gruyter.

Garner, W. R., Hake, H. W., & Eriksen, C. W. (1956). Operationalism and the concept of perception. *Psychological Review, 63,* 149–159.

Johnson, D. A. (1971). Pupillary responses during a short-term memory task: Cognitive processing, arousal, or both? *Journal of Experimental Psychology, 90,* 311–318.

Martin, D. W., & Kelly, R. T. (1974). Secondary task performance during directed forgetting. *Journal of Experimental Psychology, 103,* 1074–1079.

Navon, D., & Gopher, D. (1979). On the economy of the human processing system. *Psychological Review, 86,* 214–255.

Wickens, C. D. (1984). Processing resources in attention. In R. Parasuraman & D. R. Davies (Eds.), *Varieties of attention.* New York: Academic Press.

5

How to Decide on a Within-Subject
Versus Between-Subjects Design

> Humorist Robert Benchley once divided the world into two groups: those who
> divide the world into two groups, and those who do not.*

Now you have chosen an independent variable to manipulate and a dependent variable to measure. If everybody were exactly alike, you would need to take only a single subject and do your experiment on that one person. Fortunately, for the sake of having an interesting world, but unfortunately, for your task as an experimenter, we are not all alike. Because we are individually different, you will have to use a sample of subjects and try to minimize the subject variability by doing statistical tricks such as taking means. However, you have some choice about what to do with the variability caused by subject differences, depending on how you choose to assign subjects to the levels of your independent variable.

There are two basic ways to assign subjects: you can expose each subject to all levels of the variable or you can expose each subject to only one level. The first method is called a **within-subject design** because the independent variable is manipulated within a single subject; the second is called a **between-subjects design** because the variable is manipulated between at least two subjects.[†] Table 5-1 (page 68) illustrates the two methods of subject assignment for an experiment that has two levels of an independent variable. In the top case each of the ten subjects is assigned to both levels, while in the bottom case a different set of ten subjects is assigned to each level.

Suppose we wanted to do an experiment to determine whether taking rest breaks improves studying. In one condition we have subjects study certain material continuously for two hours. In the other condition, subjects study for a total of two hours but take a five-minute break after every half hour. In either case they take a test at the end of the study period. Now, we could use a within-subject design, in which case the same group of subjects would study different material under each study condition. Or we could use a between-subjects design and have a different group of randomly selected subjects assigned to each study condition. If we use the same subjects, we know that, while there are still individual differences in study-

---

*Time, May 17, 1976, p. 51.
[†]Others have called within-subject designs **Treatment × Subject designs** or **repeated-measures designs** on the same subjects. Between-subjects designs are sometimes called **separate groups.**

BETWEEN-SUBJECTS DESIGN: EACH
SUBJECT IS EXPOSED TO ONLY ONE LEVEL.

ing ability between subjects, there should be no overall difference in studying ability between the groups—they are the same people. If we use different people in the two groups, we not only have individual differences within the groups, but also a possible overall difference between groups. Let's consider some of the advantages and disadvantages of the two types of designs in more detail.

Within-Subject Experiments

Although, as you will see later in this chapter, within-subject designs are by no means the best choice for all experiments, they do offer a number of advantages.

Practical Advantages

One practical advantage of a within-subject experiment is immediately obvious from Table 5-1: fewer subjects are required. If N subjects* are required to give you an adequate number of data points for a within-subject experiment, then $N \times 2$ are required for a two-level between-subjects experiment, $N \times 3$ for a three-level between-subjects experiment, and so on.

In many cases, increasing the number of subjects also substantially increases the total time required for an experiment. For example, if your experiment requires that you pretrain subjects to do a basic task before you expose them to the experimental manipulation, you will have to pretrain twice as many subjects in a two-level between-subjects experiment as in a within-subject experiment. Suppose you want to know if requiring subjects to remember a certain number of words will interfere with their ability to perform a complex tracking task, which in itself takes several hours to learn.

*I am using N here to refer to any given number of subjects, such as 10 or 20, for a particular experiment.

Table 5-1.
The Assignment of Subjects for a Within-Subject Experiment and a Between-Subjects Experiment.

Within-subject	*Independent variable*	
	Level 1	*Level 2*
	Subject 1	Subject 1
	Subject 2	Subject 2
	.	.
	.	.
	.	.
	Subject 10	Subject 10

Between-subjects	*Independent variable*	
	Level 1	*Level 2*
	Subject 1	Subject 11
	Subject 2	Subject 12
	.	.
	.	.
	.	.
	Subject 10	Subject 20
	10	

If you add levels to your independent variable (number of words presented for memory), you add no more pretraining time in a within-subject experiment. But in a between-subjects experiment, you increase the number of subjects and thereby the pretraining time.

It is common to conduct several practice trials at the beginning of an experiment, a practice that also adds time to an experiment the more subjects you have. These practice trials are designed to minimize warm-up effects—that is, a fast improvement during the first few trials as the subject gets into a state of general readiness.

In addition to the inconvenience of using a large number of subjects for a between-subjects experiment, at times the number of subjects available to you will be limited, especially when the subjects must meet certain requirements. For example, you may need pilots, race-car drivers, or ballet dancers for certain experiments. Or you may want subjects to be afflicted with some disorder like psychosis, color blindness, or left-handedness.* In such cases, you may not be able to find enough subjects who meet these requirements to use a between-subjects design, and you will need to rely on a within-subject experiment.

---

*Just kidding, lefties.

Statistical Advantages

In addition to their greater efficiency, within-subject designs can be preferable for statistical reasons. We will take a brief look at statistics in Chapter 9, but I will mention a few concepts here.

In an inferential statistical test, experimenters attempt to infer whether any differences they find among the data samples collected at the various levels of the independent variable are due to real differences in behavior of some larger population or due to chance. To make this inference, most of these tests compare the differences between the average performance at the two levels with an estimate of how variable the performance is within each of the levels. A statistical test is more likely to call a difference *real* if the difference between levels is large or if the estimated variability within levels is small. An example will show you how logical this principle is.

Suppose a track-shoe manufacturer wanted to know whether to sell shoes with 7-mm spikes or 13-mm spikes* to the 100-yard dash[†] runners on a men's track team. To test these shoes, the manufacturer could randomly choose ten men from a college campus to wear one type of shoe and ten additional men from the same campus to wear the other type. The men in the two groups would probably be variable in their times to run the dash—from the 300-pound, 38-year-old ex-bartender to the 125-pound, 19-year-old halfback. Their scores might look something like those in Table 5-2. If you calculate a mean[‡] for the two groups, you find that those wearing 7-mm spikes average 0.5 seconds faster than those wearing 13-mm spikes. Examining the times for the two groups, would this difference convince you that the shorter spikes were better for running the 100-yard dash?

Now suppose the manufacturer decided to do a second experiment using members of the track team as subjects and randomly assigning them to the 7-mm and 13-mm groups. Their scores might look something like those in Table 5-3. Again there is a 0.5-second average advantage for the runners wearing the shorter spikes. Would these data convince you that the shorter spikes were better?

Undoubtedly, you would be more likely to accept the difference found in the second experiment as being a real difference. Because the scores in the second experiment were less variable, you probably feel that the difference found there is less likely to be due entirely to chance variation.

Most of the variability in the first experiment's scores was apparently due to large individual differences in the subjects' ability to run the 100-yard dash, regardless of the shoes. In the second experiment, much of the variability due to individual subject differences was eliminated by choosing subjects that were more alike.

How could we make the subjects even more alike in the two groups? By using the same subjects! You should be able to see why a within-subject

---

*0.276 in. and 0.512 in.
[†]91.44 m.
[‡]As will be discussed in more detail in Chapter 9 and Appendix A, a mean is the sum of the individual scores divided by the number of scores that were added.

Table 5-2.
Individual Times to Run the 100-Yard Dash for Two Groups of Randomly Chosen Men.

Subjects wearing 7-mm spikes	Time (in seconds)	Subjects wearing 13-mm spikes	Time (in seconds)
Mike	11.7	Don	15.7
Bob	18.2	Hector	13.4
Homer	12.2	Ron	18.0
George	15.4	Tom	12.8
Harry	15.8	Steve	13.6
Gordon	13.2	Dale	19.0
John	13.7	Pete	16.2
Bill	19.1	Juan	11.9
Randy	12.9	Dan	14.6
Tim	16.0	Paul	18.0

Mean for 7-mm subjects = 14.82 sec. Mean for 13-mm subjects = 15.32 sec.
Mean difference = 0.5 sec.

experiment gives you a statistical advantage here: it is the ultimate way to minimize the individual differences between subjects. By using a within-subject design, both you and statistical tests are more likely to be convinced that any differences in performance found between the levels of the independent variable are real differences.*

Disadvantages of Within-Subject Experiments

Because there are so many practical and statistical advantages to using within-subject designs, why should we ever use between-subjects designs? Unfortunately, the within-subject design also carries some rather serious disadvantages. Although their position is controversial, some experimenters would go so far as to say these disadvantages make within-subject experiments next to worthless. Poulton (1973) has said: "The day should come then when no reputable psychologist will use a within-subject design, except for a special purpose, without combining it with a separate groups [between-subjects] design."

The basic problem is that once subjects are exposed to one level of the independent variable, there is no way to change them back into the people they were before being exposed. The exposure has done something irreversible, so we can no longer treat the subject as a pure, uncontaminated, naive person. How is the subject changed?

One way a subject can change is to learn. Suppose we wanted to know whether it takes someone longer to learn to type on a manual typewriter

*Those among you with a bent toward statistical rigor may have shuddered and blanched at my attempt to make the logic of inferential statistics intuitively palatable. I'll be a little more rigorous in Chapter 9. But not much.

Table 5-3.

Individual Times to Run the 100-Yard Dash for Two Groups of Randomly Chosen Track-Team Members.

Subjects wearing 7-mm spikes	Time (in seconds)	Subjects wearing 13-mm spikes	Time (in seconds)
Art	10.6	Rob	10.8
Simon	10.3	Frank	11.0
Nick	10.3	Walt	10.8
Daryl	10.2	Gary	10.6
Ralph	10.4	Ken	10.8
Will	10.0	Bryan	10.7
Reuben	10.2	Dick	10.6
Ed	10.1	Stan	10.7
Fred	10.3	Rich	10.7
Wayne	10.4	Mark	11.1

Mean for 7-mm subjects = 10.28 sec.   Mean for 13-mm subjects = 10.78 sec.

Mean difference = 0.5 sec.

or an electric typewriter. We decide that because there are likely to be large individual differences in typing ability, we will use a within-subject design. We take ten subjects and find out how many hours they have to practice to type 30 words per minute on a manual typewriter. We then switch them to an electric typewriter and find out how many hours they have to practice to type 30 words per minute on it. We find that it takes them an average of 45 hours of practice to reach the criterion on the manual, but only 2 hours on the electric. Can we conclude that the electric typewriter is that much easier to learn on? Obviously not.

During the first part of the experiment, in addition to learning the specific skill of using a manual typewriter, the subjects were also learning a general typing skill. The general skill is confounded with the specific skill. By the time the subjects typed on the electric typewriter, their general typing skill was undoubtedly at a higher level than when they started the experiment. Any time such an effect changes systematically across the trials, we must be careful to keep the effect of our independent variable from becoming confounded with it.

Counterbalancing

One way to minimize the effect of a systematic confounding variable like learning is to **counterbalance.** Essentially, when you counterbalance, you admit that a potential confounding variable is present. You also admit that you cannot control it or randomize it out of existence. So you attempt to distribute an equal amount of the confounding effect to each level of your independent variable. In this way you hope that the effect will counterbalance itself and not bias any effect that is due to the independent variable.

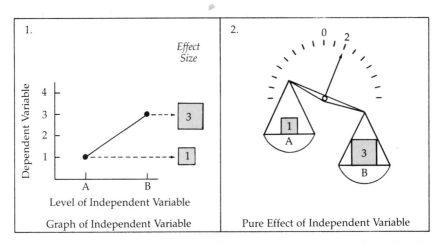

Figure 5-1. The graph in panel 1 shows the effect of the two levels, A and B, of the independent variable on the dependent variable. The scales in panel 2 indicate that the pure unconfounded effect of the independent variable is 2 units.

To illustrate the concept of counterbalancing I will use scales as shown in Figure 5-1. For a moment let us pretend we are omnipotent and know the actual size of effects due to the independent variable and the confounding variable. If we carried out a perfect experiment presenting two levels of our independent variable, A and B, we might find the result illustrated in the graph in panel 1 of Figure 5-1. We are assuming that no variables are affecting the result other than the independent variable. The size of the effect on the dependent variable is 1 unit for level A and 3 units for level B. Because these quantities will be put on the scales, I have converted them to weights. By placing the weights on the scales in panel 2, we see that the pure unconfounded effect of the independent variable is 2.

Now because we are using a within-subject design and we cannot present both levels of the independent variable at the same time, we obviously must have several trials. Suppose that some confounding effect, like learning, increases with each trial as shown in panel 1 of Figure 5-2. As you can see on trial 1, the effect of the confounding variable is 1 unit on the dependent variable, and by trial 4, it is 4 units. Again the effect size is converted to weights. What we wish to do is distribute these weights so that the scales are counterbalanced. In this way, the scales will show no bias when the independent variable is added.

One of the more frequently used counterbalancing schemes is called **ABBA counterbalancing.** The A and B, as in our example, stand for the two levels of any independent variable, and the sequence represents how the levels are assigned to trials. Thus, level A would be presented on trial 1, B on trial 2, B on trial 3, and A on trial 4. Each subject receives all trials.

Panel 2 of Figure 5-2 illustrates what happens when the weights for trials 1 and 4 are placed on the A side of the scales and those for trials 2

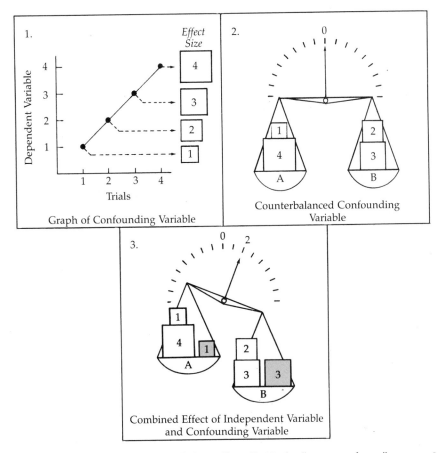

Figure 5-2. The graph in panel 1 shows the effect of a linear confounding variable on the dependent variable. The scales in panel 2 indicate that an ABBA ordering of the independent variable has successfully counterbalanced the confounding variable. When the weights representing the effects of the independent variable are added in panel 3, a correct net effect of 2 units is found.

and 3 on the B side. The scales are counterbalanced. When we also add the weights representing the effects of the independent variable, the net combined effect is 2, the original pure effect of the independent variable. Basically, this unbiased outcome is what we try to achieve with all counterbalancing schemes.

Before you wax too ecstatic over the beauty of counterbalancing, permit me to tell you that counterbalancing schemes are based on certain assumptions, and when these assumptions are violated, the beauty turns into a beast.

One assumption of ABBA counterbalancing is that the confounding effect is linear, that it forms a straight line. To illustrate what can happen when it is not, let's return to our weights. Suppose the confounding effect

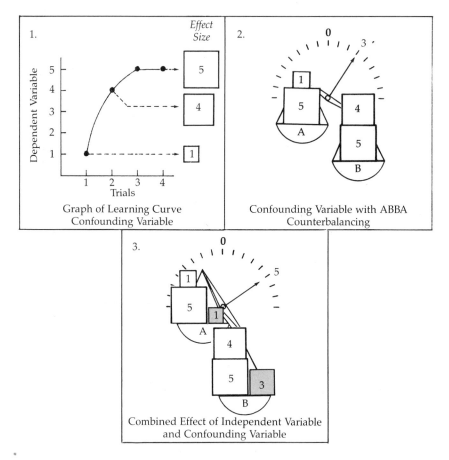

Figure 5-3. The graph in panel 1 shows the effects of a learning curve-type confounding variable on the dependent variable. The scales in panel 2 indicate that an ABBA ordering has not successfully counterbalanced the confounding variable; the scales are biased 3 units toward B. When the weights representing the effects of the independent variable are added in panel 3, the net effect of 5 units overestimates the effect of the independent variable by 3 units.

looks like that shown in panel 1 of Figure 5-3. In fact, learning is the most likely candidate for confounding, and most learning curves look a lot like this one; an initial large increase in performance is followed by progressively smaller changes. Converting to weights and stacking the weights according to an ABBA design, we can see in panel 2 that the scales are not counterbalanced. They are biased by 3 units toward the B side. When the weights representing the independent variable are added in panel 3, the net effect is 5 units rather than the 2 units we omnipotently know it should be.

Under certain conditions, ABBA counterbalancing not only fails to correct for a confounding variable but can compound the confounding prob-

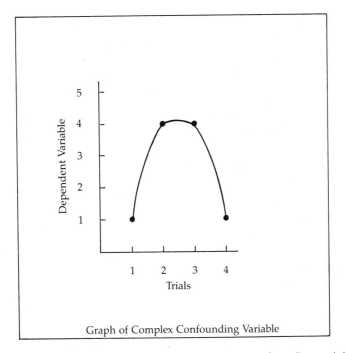

Graph of Complex Confounding Variable

Figure 5-4. A graph showing the effect of a complex confounding variable on a dependent variable. Such a function could be caused by learning and fatigue.

lem. An example of this is shown in Figure 5-4. The confounding effect first improves performance, then degrades it. Combining the effect of learning with the effect of fatigue could cause such a function. I will let you work out the size of the bias caused by the unbalanced confounding variable.

We have seen that ABBA counterbalancing can eliminate the effects of a confounding variable in within-subject experiments, but only if the confounding effect is linear. If the effect is nonlinear, we must choose a different counterbalancing technique or else design a between-subjects experiment.

An ABBA-counterbalancing technique attempts to counterbalance sequence effects in a completely within-subject manner: the same subject gets both the AB order and the BA order. Other counterbalancing techniques make order a between-subjects variable by counterbalancing order across subjects. In the simplest two-level case, one group of subjects would receive AB and a second group, BA. If you use this method, the confounding effect does not have to be linear. However, you are still making the assumption that the effect of having B follow A is just the reverse of the effect of having A follow B (Poulton & Freeman, 1966). This assumption is sometimes called an assumption of **symmetrical transfer.*** When this

*Sometimes it is called **nondifferential transfer.**

assumption is violated and you get asymmetrical transfer instead, this type of counterbalancing is not effective.

Consider an experiment in which asymmetrical transfer was found. The investigator was interested in the effect of noise on complex performance (Aldridge, 1978; Poulton, 1979). The subjects were first given a consonant-vowel-consonant trigram (for example, DOF) to remember for 16 seconds. While doing this memory task, they also listened to a series of "Bs," spoken one per second, to detect occasional "Ps." In the noise condition a loud, continuous, hissing noise was also present. To counterbalance for order effects, one group of subjects received a block of quiet trials followed by a block of noise trials (AB), while a second group received the reverse order (BA).

You can see the results of the experiment in Figure 5-5. The group exposed first to the quiet trials did well at remembering the trigrams. However, when transferred to the noise condition, their performance dropped drastically. The other group performed poorly in noise as expected. Notice, however, that their performance improved only a little when transferred to quiet. The magnitude of the effect was 31 percentage points for the quiet-first group and 10 percentage points for the noise-first group. We would expect the same size of effect if symmetrical transfer were present. What is the reason for the finding of asymmetrical transfer?

Apparently the two groups learned to do the task in different ways. The quiet-first group probably learned to use an **echoic store** to retain the words.* While this strategy worked well when it was quiet, the quiet-first group probably had to change to a new strategy when noise was added:

Echoic store is what the husband uses to dredge up a memory when he is reading the paper and his wife says, "Did you hear what I just said?"

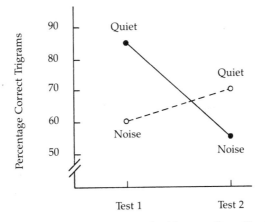

Figure 5-5. The effect of noise on memory for trigrams. The effect illustrates asymmetrical transfer.
Adapted from "Levels of Processing in Speech Perception," by J. W. Aldridge, 1978, Experiment 4, *Journal of Experimental Psychology: Human Perception and Performance, 4,* 164–177.

using an **articulatory store*** and repeating the trigram more frequently. Their performance dropped. The noise-first group apparently learned the task using the articulation strategy. When switched to quiet, they probably maintained this less efficient strategy, and their performance improved a bit without the noise. Although this explanation is somewhat speculative, some additional data I am not bothering you with support the speculation. The point is that the asymmetrical transfer was caused by differential learning in the two groups. When you get such asymmetrical transfer effects, no form of counterbalancing can save a within-subject design.

As you add more levels to your independent variable, you increase the complexity of a complete counterbalancing procedure. In a completely counterbalanced design, every level has to occur an equal number of times and also follow every other level an equal number of times. Table 5-4 shows completely counterbalanced designs for two-, three-, and four-level experiments. As you can see, **complete counterbalancing** can become a monumental task when you have a large number of levels or many independent variables. You can sometimes use a technique called **partial counterbalancing** in which you randomly choose only some of the orders while making sure that each level occurs the same number of times in each position. With large experimental designs, you can also assign levels **randomly** or **randomize within blocks** as described in Chapter 1.

You have seen that a counterbalancing technique is often necessary to minimize the sequential confounding effects found in some within-subject experiments. At this point, you should also be aware of the assumptions underlying the technique you are using and should try to use a counterbalancing technique that allows you to meet the assumptions.

*Essentially mumbling to yourself.

Table 5-4.
Completely Counterbalanced Design for Two-, Three-, and Four-Level Independent Variables. A, B, C, and D Represent the Levels.

Two levels of independent variable		Three levels of independent variable	
Number	*Order of levels*	*Number*	*Order of levels*
1	AB	1	ABC
2	BA	2	ACB
		3	BCA
		4	BAC
		5	CAB
		6	CBA

Four levels of independent variable			
Number	*Order of levels*	*Number*	*Order of levels*
1	ABCD	13	CABD
2	ABDC	14	CADB
3	ACBD	15	CBAD
4	ACDB	16	CBDA
5	ADCB	17	CDAB
6	ADBC	18	CDBA
7	BACD	19	DABC
8	BADC	20	DACB
9	BCAD	21	DBAC
10	BCDA	22	DBCA
11	BDAC	23	DCAB
12	BDCA	24	DCBA

However, in some experiments, such as those having asymmetrical transfer, it may be impossible to meet the assumptions, and you will have no choice but to use a between-subjects design. One other potential disadvantage of within-subject designs cannot be corrected by counterbalancing and may force you to use a between-subjects design—**range effects.**

Range Effects

Suppose you are the purchasing agent for a widget factory and you are ordering a new set of working tables for widget assembly. You must choose the height of the tables and you want to make sure that the tables are the right height to maximize production. You decide to do an experiment to determine the correct height. You take one group of workers, Group A, and have them sit at tables of varying heights while you count how many blocks they can turn over during a 3-minute period. The table heights you choose are -10, -6, -2, $+2$, $+6$, and $+10$ inches from elbow height. Having read this book, you realize that you could have a problem with sequential-ordering effects, so you carefully counterbalance the order of table heights.

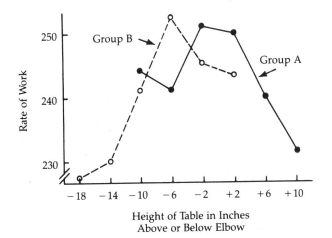

Figure 5-6. The effect of the range of table heights presented on the number of blocks turned during 3-minute trials. The range effect due to this within-subject design is seen in the superior performance at the middle heights for each group. SOURCE: From "Series Effects in Motor Performance Studies," by J. E. Kennedy and J. Landesman, 1963, *Journal of Applied Psychology, 47*, 202–205. Copyright 1963 by the American Psychological Association. Reprinted by permission.

After you have completed the experiment, your boss suggests that she would like to see you test some tables of even lower height. You design another experiment just like the first, except this time you have Group B use tables of the following heights: −18, −14, −10, −6, −2, and +2 inches from elbow height.

Figure 5-6 shows the actual results of this experiment. The startling thing about the results is that the best table height is different for the two groups. Group A performed best at about elbow height and Group B at 6 inches below elbow height. Why is this? In learning a task like turning over blocks at a table of a given height, subjects also learn a skill that is useful for other tasks, like turning over blocks on a table of a different height. The more alike the two table heights, the better the subject can transfer the skill from one height to the other. This is simply a basic principle of learning. So, if we consider the block-turning experiment to be a learning experiment, we would expect subjects to perform best at the table height that is most like all the other table heights used in the experiment. Table 5-5 shows the average number of inches difference in height between each table height and the other five heights presented for each group. For example, the difference between the +10 condition for Group A and the −10 condition is 20, between +10 and −6 is 16, etc. Adding all difference scores between +10 and the other five conditions for Group A and dividing by 5 produces a mean of 12. Now, if we expect the highest rate of work for the task that is most similar to the other conditions presented in each experiment, we could do a fairly good job of predicting Figure 5-6 from Table 5-5. You can now see why it is called a range effect; subjects tend to have the highest level of performance in the middle of the range of levels presented because

Table 5-5.

Average Number of Inches Difference Between Each Table Height and the Other Five Heights Presented.

			Table height					
	−18	−14	−10	−6	−2	+2	+6	+10
Group A			12	8.5	7.2	7.2	8.5	12
Group B	12	8.5	7.2	7.2	8.5	12		

transfer of learning is highest in the middle of the range. Range effects can result from a within-subject experiment whenever stimuli or responses can be put in a consistent order. Poulton (1973) has noted examples of range effects throughout most areas of experimental psychology.

Although range effects caused Poulton and others to warn against within-subject experiments, other investigators argue that in many cases within-subject experiments should be used. Greenwald (1976), for instance, has pointed out that a range effect is simply a **context effect.** The subject comes to the experiment with a context already established. In the table example, for instance, people are already experienced at using certain table heights. He suggests that repeatedly presenting a subject with only one level of the independent variable, as in a between-subjects experiment, will not eliminate context. As repeated trials are given at a single level of the independent variable, a new context develops—the context of the single level. For these reasons, Greenwald claims that context effects cannot be avoided by using either type of design. He suggests that a more important question to ask in choosing a design is to what situation you plan to generalize your results.

For example, in our violent-television experiment, it could be more artificial to repeatedly expose a child to one level of violence (a between-subjects design) than to expose the child to several different levels. Because we would like to generalize the results to a real-life situation having many levels, perhaps we should choose a within-subject design. That is, the range used in the experiment should approximate the range found in the situation to which we are generalizing. As an experimenter, then, although you should be aware that range effects could alter the outcome of your experiment, you should choose the design that allows you to generalize your results to the appropriate situation.

Between-Subjects Experiments

For the most part, I can just turn around the arguments for the advantages and disadvantages of within-subject designs to arrive at the disadvantages and advantages of between-subjects designs. However, there are some additional practical reasons for doing between-subjects experiments.

Because each subject performs under only one level of the independent variable in a between-subjects experiment, we can collect more data at that level during a single experimental session. Because subjects are likely to get tired or lose interest in what they are doing, it is easier to keep the total experimental time short for each subject. You can also avoid bringing subjects back for more than one experimental session, which is an advantage because the number of subjects who actually complete an experiment tends to decrease dramatically with each additional session required.

Randomization

When between-subjects designs are used, subjects are usually assigned to the groups in a random fashion. This assignment can be done in a number of ways, such as using slips of paper drawn from a hat, tossing coins, or selecting from random-number tables. People who have little experience with psychological experimentation or statistics seem to have little confidence in random processes. They often think that randomization is the equivalent of being haphazard or sloppy, and they believe that even with large groups there are likely to be sizable differences in behavior. With experience and an increased understanding of statistical sampling, researchers come to have considerably more confidence in random assignment of subjects. For although randomness may seem like the ultimate in lack of orderliness, it is at least unbiased. So it allows you assign subject variability to the groups in an unbiased fashion. Especially for large groups of subjects, the likelihood that the groups are quite different on any behavioral dimension is rather small. On top of that, the statistical tests that you do in analyzing your data take potential differences due to random assignment into account. Random assignment of subjects for between-subjects experiments is actually quite effective in removing potential bias among groups.

Matching

One way to gain the advantages of a between-subjects experiment yet avoid some of the problems of individual differences between groups of subjects is to use a **matched-groups** design. This simply means that an attempt is made to have the same kind of subjects assigned to each level of your independent variable. In the typical between-subjects experiment, you hope that the subjects at each level are pretty much alike, and you have randomization on your side. Random assignment of subjects makes it likely that the groups will be essentially equivalent, and this becomes more likely the larger the groups. However, because this is a random process, occasionally the subjects assigned to each group will be quite different and you may incorrectly attribute differences in their behavior to the independent variable. That is, your experiment may be confounded by subject differences. By matching groups of subjects, you can minimize this possibility. On what basis can you match the groups?

MATCHED-GROUPS DESIGN

You must match your groups on a variable that is highly correlated with the dependent variable. In our track-shoe experiment, it would have been a waste of time for us to match the two groups of runners on the basis of IQ scores. Fast minds are not related to fast feet. However, we could have had each subject run the 100-yard dash in tennis shoes first and then make up pairs of subjects: the two fastest, the two next fastest, and so on. We could then flip a coin to assign one member of each pair to each of the track-shoe conditions. In this way, we know that the groups are somewhat equivalent in running speed prior to introducing the independent variable. In this experiment, we are assuming a large correlation between tennis-shoe running times and track-shoe running times, because the lower the correlation between the matching variable and the dependent variable, the less we gain by matching.

Through matching, we decrease the probability of being wrong when we say that the independent variable caused a change in behavior. Matching can also provide a statistical advantage in that when matched groups are used, a statistical test is more likely to say that a given difference in the scores of the dependent variable is due to the independent variable rather than to chance. That is, the tests are more sensitive to any difference associated with the independent variable.

To illustrate this principle, the column on the left of Table 5-6 again lists the randomly chosen subjects who ran the dash in track shoes with 7-mm spikes (from Table 5-2). In order to match subjects, suppose we also had these people run the race in tennis shoes. The tennis-shoe scores are in parentheses. To get a matching group, we now have many more people run the dash in tennis shoes, and we choose as subjects those who have the same times as the subjects in our original group. These new subjects are listed in the column on the right, along with their tennis-shoe times in parentheses. Note that we have been able to eliminate any differences in groups for tennis-shoe scores; the scores are exactly the same. Now we have the new group run the race in 13-mm spikes and find that, as in our previous examples, there is an average 0.5-second increase in the mean running time. Would you be more likely to believe that the difference in

Table 5-6.
Individual Times to Run the 100-Yard Dash for Two Groups of Matched Subjects.

Subjects wearing 7-mm spikes	Time (in seconds)		Subjects wearing 13-mm spikes	Time (in seconds)	
Mike	(12.2)	11.7	Vic	(12.2)	12.2
Homer	(12.8)	12.2	Jack	(12.8)	12.6
Randy	(13.5)	12.9	Barry	(13.5)	13.5
Gordon	(14.0)	13.2	Larry	(14.0)	13.8
John	(14.3)	13.7	Jess	(14.3)	14.2
George	(16.1)	15.4	Stuart	(16.1)	15.8
Harry	(16.7)	15.8	Harvey	(16.7)	16.2
Tim	(17.0)	16.0	Sid	(17.0)	16.6
Bob	(18.7)	18.2	Pat	(18.7)	18.7
Bill	(19.7)	19.1	Joe	(19.7)	19.6

Mean for 7-mm subjects = 14.82 sec.   Mean difference = 0.5 sec.
Mean for 13-mm subjects = 15.32 sec.

length of spikes caused the 0.5-second average difference in running times in the original random-groups experiment or in this matched-groups experiment? Statistical tests make decisions in much the same way you do.

One disadvantage in doing matched-groups experiments is that it takes longer to match the groups, so that experiments sometimes require two sessions, one for the pretest and one for the experiment itself. If you are planning to use many subjects anyway, the chances of getting large differences between groups using random assignment are small, and the hassle of matching might not be worth the effort.

A final consideration is that the matching process itself may cause some problems. We assumed in the example that the tennis-shoe pretest did not differentially affect the spiked-shoe test. Suppose, however, that the tennis-shoe test taught the subjects a smooth-shoe running technique that they could transfer to a later test. We might predict that the smoother the shoes on the later test, the faster the subjects will run. Because the shorter spikes are more like smooth shoes, they will cause faster times. In this case, the pretest would differentially affect the subjects' performance at the two levels of the independent variable.

Thus, matched-groups designs can be valuable under certain conditions, but they can also cause more problems than they solve. You should weigh the pros and cons of using a matched-groups design for your own experiment.

Table 5-7 summarizes the advantages and disadvantages of the designs discussed in this chapter. Obviously, you will want to consider these pros and cons within the context of any experiment you are considering doing.

Table 5-7.

A Summary of the Advantages and Disadvantages of Using Within-Subject and Between-Subjects Designs.

Within-subject experiments	
Advantages	*Disadvantages*
Fewer subjects	Transfer between conditions
Shorter experimental time	ABBA counterbalancing assumes lin-
Smaller variability between groups	ear confounding effect
	All counterbalancing assumes sym-
	metrical transfer
	Range effects can cause problems

Between-subjects experiments	
Advantages	*Disadvantages*
Transfer effects between conditions not possible	Differences between groups are possible
Counterbalancing not required	Requires more subjects
Matching can reduce variability between groups	Requires more experimental time
Random assignment of subjects elimi- nates bias	Matching takes time and effort and assumes no transfer from matching operation

Summary

There are two basic ways to assign subjects to the levels of the independent variable: you can assign different subjects to each level or assign the same subject to all levels. The first method gives you a **between-subjects experiment** and the second, a **within-subject experiment.** The practical advantages of a within-subject design include using fewer subjects and minimizing training and instruction time. There are also statistical advantages in that you can eliminate variability due to individual differences in subjects. A disadvantage of within-subject designs is the necessity to **counterbalance** sequence effects. An **ABBA counterbalancing** can control for sequence effects within a subject, but you must be able to assume that the sequence effect is linear. **Complete counterbalancing** of order across subjects is also possible, but you must still make an assumption of **symmetrical transfer** between conditions. In large experiments where complete counterbalancing is not possible, one can use **partial counterbalancing, random assignment,** or **randomization within blocks.** Even counterbalancing will not overcome **range effects** in experiments where the stimuli or responses may be consistently ordered.

While between-subjects experiments require more subjects and have increased variability due to individual differences in subjects, they do offer the advantage of allowing shorter experimental sessions and making counterbalancing unnecessary. Individual differences between the subjects in the groups assigned to each level of the independent variable can be reduced by using a **matched-groups procedure.**

References

Aldridge, J. W. (1978). Levels of processing in speech perception. *Journal of Experimental Psychology: Human Perception and Performance, 4*, 164–177.

Greenwald, A. G. (1976). Within-subjects designs: To use or not to use? *Psychological Bulletin, 83*, 314–320.

Kennedy, J. E., & Landesman, J. (1963). Series effects in motor performance studies. *Journal of Applied Psychology, 47*, 202–205.

Poulton, E. C. (1973). Unwanted range effects from using within-subject experimental designs. *Psychological Bulletin, 80*, 113–121.

Poulton, E. C. (1979). Composite model for human performance in continuous noise. *Psychological Review, 86*, 361–375.

Poulton, E. C., & Freeman, P. R. (1966). Unwanted asymmetrical transfer effects with balanced experimental designs. *Psychological Bulletin, 66*, 1–8.

6

How to Plan
a Single-Variable Experiment

A carefully conceived and executed design is of no avail if the scientific hypothesis that originally led to the experiment is without merit.[*]

... instead of studying a thousand rats for one hour each, or a hundred rats for ten hours each, the investigator is likely to study one rat for a thousand hours.[†]

In this chapter I will discuss the design of single-variable experiments. Investigators usually use two approaches in designing such experiments. By far the most traditional are **single-variable group experiments,** which I have used in most examples so far. In this chapter I will go beyond two-level experiments and also talk some about multilevel experiments. The second, less traditional approach is called **single-subject** or **small-N baseline designs.** These designs have achieved some prominence in the areas of operant conditioning and behavior modification. The use of baseline designs to evaluate the success of clinical techniques and psychopharmacological interventions (drugs) is also increasing.

Single-Variable Group Experiments
Two-Level Experiments

In the simplest group experiment, there is one independent variable having two levels. Some investigators like to call the groups exposed to these levels the **experimental group** and the **control group.** In some cases it is obvious what the control condition should be: no application of a treatment. For example, if you were interested in the effects of a particular drug on a behavior, the control group would not receive the drug and the experimental group would. The control group here would also be valuable just to show that being in the experiment was not causing the observed effect. In other cases, especially where there are several levels of the independent

---

[*]Kirk, R. E. (1968). *Experimental design: Procedures for the behavioral sciences.* Pacific Grove, CA: Brooks/Cole, p. 1.
[†]Skinner, B. F. (1966). Operant behavior. In W. K. Honig (Ed.), *Operant behavior: Areas of research and application.* New York: Appleton-Century-Crofts, p. 21.

variable, it is not clear which one should be called the control level.* For this reason, I will generally stick to the term *level* to describe the independent variable. In any case, we must use at least two levels to have a real experiment. Otherwise, it would be impossible to say that a change in the independent variable caused a change in the subject's behavior, because no comparison is possible.

Until the last 35–40 years, the typical experiment reported in the psychological literature was a single-variable, two-level experiment. Because our science was very young, investigators were more concerned with finding out whether an independent variable had any effect at all than in determining the exact nature of this effect. In addition, they had not yet developed some of the statistical tests required to analyze the more complex experimental designs. In some cases, tests existed but generally were not well known by the average investigator.

Nowadays editors frown on experimenters who submit a single two-level experiment to their journals. Psychology has advanced far enough as a science that an experiment demonstrating only that an independent variable has some effect is considered but a first hesitant step toward specifying the exact relationship between the variable and the behavior. Nevertheless, you may wish to choose a simple design for your first experiment so that you can get your feet wet without drowning.

Advantages   Actually, two-level experiments do have several advantages over more complex designs. They offer a way of finding out whether an independent variable is worth studying. If an independent variable has no effect on a person's behavior, you obviously would be wasting your time doing a more complex experiment to determine the exact nature of the effect.

The results of a two-level experiment are also easy to interpret and analyze. The outcome is simply "Yes, the variable did have an effect; the behavior changed in this direction," or "No, the variable had no effect." To determine whether any effect is real or due to chance variation, you usually have to do a statistical test, and tests for two-level experiments are easy to do. They may involve no more than counting pluses and minuses, for example. Once you know which test to use, it should take you only a few minutes of hand (or a few seconds of computer) calculation to statistically analyze your data.

Finally, in some cases you need no more information than a two-level experiment will give you, especially in applied research. If you want to pit two pieces of industrial equipment against each other and only two are available that can do the job, a two-level experiment gives you all the infor-

---

*For example, if we decided to vary sex (not how much you get, but which one you are) as the independent variable in an experiment, should we call men or women the control group? Feminists and masculinists could argue for days over this issue, so why not avoid it altogether and assign the groups to Level 1 and Level 2?

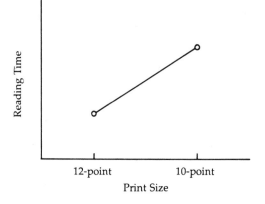

Figure 6-1. Possible results from an experiment measuring the time to read paragraphs typed in 12-point or 10-point print.

mation you need. The same principle holds if you are investigating two therapeutic techniques, two educational systems, two training programs, two drugs, two sexes, or two levels of any variable when only two levels are important.

Disadvantages   Although a straight line is the shortest distance between two points, it is not the only line between two points. In other words, you are at a disadvantage in a two-level experiment because it will tell you nothing about the shape of the relationship between the independent and the dependent variables.

Suppose we did an experiment to find out what size of type this book should be printed in so that you would have to spend as little time as possible struggling with my periphrastic prose. We might decide to use a word processor to print several paragraphs. Some of the paragraphs would be printed in a large 12-point type and the others in a smaller 10-point type. We could then measure the time it takes subjects to read the paragraphs printed in each size type. Of course, we would pretest the paragraphs for comprehensibility, counterbalance order, and do all the good things we have learned in this book.

Figure 6-1 shows fictitious results for this experiment. The arbitrary straight line drawn through the two data points indicates that the smaller the print, the longer the reading time. Thus, the experiment has answered our question, 12-point type makes for speedier reading. However, if we really wanted to know the best print size out of all possible sizes and we chose the two sizes used in the experiment because they were our best guess, we don't have enough information to make a decision. Our results give no indication whether a straight-line relationship between type size and reading time is true for any sizes other than 12-point and 10-point.

Figure 6-2 shows a number of other relationships that could also be the actual underlying relationship. You can see that not knowing the shape of

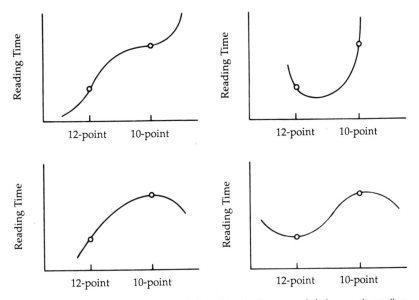

Figure 6-2. A number of possible relationships between print size and reading time. All the functions pass through the same two data points.

the relationship makes interpolation questionable.* We cannot correctly conclude that a print size halfway between 12-point and 10-point would give a reading time halfway between those sizes.

Extrapolating from two points is even more dangerous than interpolating. Most psychological functions have what are called **ceiling** and **floor effects.** A ceiling effect occurs when the dependent variable reaches a level that cannot be exceeded. Typical examples of ceiling levels are: accuracy of response, 100%; probability of response, 1.0; and confidence in a response, 100%. In each case, it is physically impossible for the subject to produce a response exceeding a particular value. (You can't be more accurate than 100%, in other words.)

A floor level is a value below which the subject cannot respond. A subject cannot respond in fewer than zero seconds, for example, or give fewer responses than none. If we take our two data points and extrapolate to values above a ceiling or below a floor, we won't be in the attic or basement; we'll be in hot water! And sometimes it is not obvious where a ceiling or floor should be. To avoid these problems, you should make it a rule in a two-level experiment not to interpolate or extrapolate beyond the levels used in the experiment.

Two-level experiments are also of limited theoretical value. We agreed in Chapter 1 that science is built on relationships and that scientists use theories to explain the relationships found in experiments. Each theory

---

Interpolation is an estimate of intermediate values within a known range; **extrapolation** is an estimate of values beyond a known range.

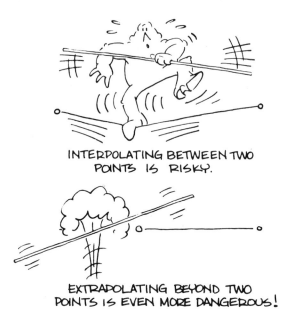

INTERPOLATING BETWEEN TWO
POINTS IS RISKY.

EXTRAPOLATING BEYOND TWO
POINTS IS EVEN MORE DANGEROUS!

competes with other possible theories until an experiment is done that supports one theory to the exclusion of the others. Because many theories predict that a change in a particular independent variable will cause the dependent variable to change in a particular direction, the outcome of a two-level experiment will often fail to distinguish among competing theories. In some cases, in which opposing theories predict changes in opposite directions, or one predicts a change while the other does not, a two-level experiment can be theoretically useful. However, theory testing usually requires more complex experimental designs.

Multilevel Experiments

Multilevel experiments are single-variable experiments presenting three or more levels of the independent variable. They are also called **functional experiments** by some investigators because they allow you to get some idea of the shape of the function relating the independent variable to the dependent variable.

CEILING EFFECT

FLOOR EFFECT

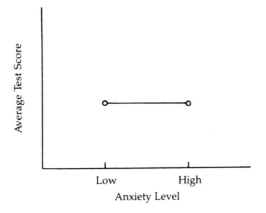

Figure 6-3. Imaginary results from a two-level experiment varying the anxiety level of students and measuring their average test score.

Advantages The major advantage of a multilevel experiment is that the results allow us to guess the nature of the experimental relationship. Even if an experiment has only three levels, it still provides us with a much better idea of the relationship than a two-level experiment does.

Suppose we wanted to know how a student's anxiety level influences test scores. We decide to use two introductory psychology classes* and a two-level, between-subjects design. In Class 1 the instructor spends five minutes before each major exam haranguing the students about the importance of grades for success in school. She makes it clear that students with the best grades get the best jobs, that students with college degrees earn a far larger salary, and that the university is a bit overcrowded at the moment.

In Class 2 she also gives a five-minute talk before each exam. In this talk, she reminds the students that making a good grade is not as important as learning the material. She tells them that ten years from now they won't remember what grade they got on this test anyway. We are careful to control as many potential confounding variables as possible, such as grade level, test difficulty, and class instruction. Thus, we decide that the difference in test scores can be attributed to the anxiety produced by the talk. Assuming that the first speech causes a high level of anxiety in the students and the second, a lower level, we might get the results shown in Figure 6-3.

At this point the best guess we could make is that there is no relationship between anxiety level and average test score; a straight line drawn through the two points is flat. Suppose, however, that we had decided on a multilevel design and added a third anxiety level, a neutral level in which the instructor gives a five-minute speech simply reminding the students of

---

*Because here we are using two classes that already exist rather than assigning students to the classes in a random manner, this example is not really an experiment but uses a quasi-experimental design that will be discussed in Chapter 8. I hope you noticed this difference.

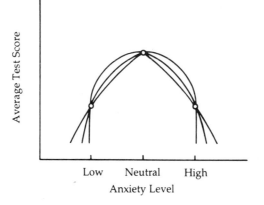

Figure 6-4. Imaginary results from a three-level experiment varying the anxiety level of students and measuring their average test score.

some procedural details. Figure 6-4 shows imaginary results for this multilevel experiment.

When we graph the third data point, we see that there is, in fact, an important relationship between anxiety level and test scores,* although some doubt exists about the exact shape of the function. Any of the three shapes shown in Figure 6-4 seem to be good possibilities; and, because most psychological functions do not take sharp turns or change directions rapidly, we know that not many other relationships are possible. As you can see, the third data point allows us to get a much better idea of the shape of the experimental relationship. As we add progressively more levels to our experiment, we can make even better guesses about the true functional relationship between the independent and dependent variables. We can also interpolate and extrapolate from our data points with more confidence. In this example the neutral group that we added could be considered to be a control group because the teacher was not trying to influence anxiety at all. Another control group, in which the teacher said nothing, could have been added to determine whether saying anything at all affects behavior. Multilevel experiments give this kind of flexibility.

This example also illustrates a second advantage of a multilevel experiment: generally the more levels you add, the less critical the range of the independent variable becomes. As you recall from Chapter 4, we determined that, while the range should be realistic, it should also be large enough to show a relationship if one exists. Obviously both of these requirements become easier for us to satisfy as more levels of the independent variable are represented in the experiment.

---

*If you have had a course in motivation or attention, you may recognize this function as a form of the Yerkes-Dodson law, in which an inverted U describes the relationship between arousal and learning. Good for you!

Disadvantages   From a practical point of view, the major disadvantage of a multilevel experiment is that it requires more time and effort than a two-level experiment. Recall that every time we add a level to a between-subjects experiment, we increase the number of subjects needed. In within-subject experiments, additional levels do not increase the number of subjects needed, but they do increase the total time of the experiment and make counterbalancing schemes more ponderous.

The statistical tests required to analyze multilevel experiments are also a bit more difficult to do. They take more time, and it is harder to interpret the data in light of the statistical test.

In weighing the advantages and disadvantages of two-level versus multilevel designs, these slight additional costs of adding levels to the independent variable are usually more than offset by the value of the information gained. This benefit is especially valuable for the first few extra levels added to the design. At some point, of course, adding more levels will do little to increase our knowledge of the experimental relationship.

Single-Subject and Small-N Baseline Designs
Individual Versus Grouped Data

Some investigators claim that the way the majority of psychologists do experiments is at best misleading and at worst pointless. The loudest revolutionary in this group has been Sidman (1960), who claims that the kind of traditional experiments you have been learning about in this chapter tell us little about an individual's behavior. Sidman points out that experiments usually tell us about the behavior of some imaginary average subject who does not accurately reflect any real individual subjects. He claims that most experimenters use groups of subjects and pretend that the behavior of individual subjects in the group resembles the average behavior of the group. He argues that there are times when no subject in the group may behave anything like the average group behavior.

To illustrate this point, consider an experiment designed to find out how quickly a person can learn a simple analogy by being exposed to examples. The first item might be: *edit* is to *tide* as *recap* is to _____ . The answer is *pacer*, because *pacer* is *recap* spelled backward. The next item might be: *pets* is to *step* as *tool* is to _____ . Again, the answer is *tool* spelled backward, or *loot*. We give each subject three seconds to solve an item before presenting the next item. We might expect learning to occur in an all-or-nothing fashion. That is, we assume that at some point the subject will cry "Aha!" or "Eureka!" and from then on get every item correct.

Figure 6-5 shows fictitious individual results for ten subjects; Figure 6-6 shows a group curve representing the average subject. You can see that the group curve in Figure 6-6 does not represent any of the individual curves in Figure 6-5. The group curve might cause us to conclude that subjects learn the solution gradually; however, every subject actually appears

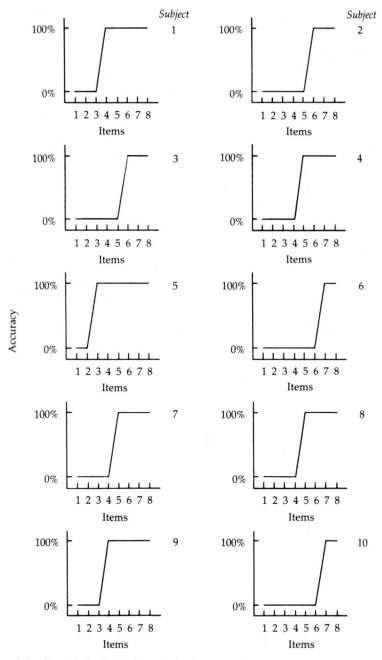

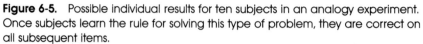

Figure 6-5. Possible individual results for ten subjects in an analogy experiment. Once subjects learn the rule for solving this type of problem, they are correct on all subsequent items.

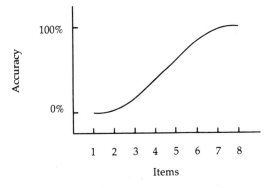

Figure 6-6. The group curve for the subjects shown in Figure 6-5. Note that the group curve is a poor representation of any individual subject.

to have gone from solving none of the items to solving all the items on a single trial.

Because of such discrepancies, Sidman believes that group performance seldom tells us much about how individual subjects perform. Psychologists decided to use groups in the first place because the behavior of single subjects is so variable and because an individual subject's variability is likely to be canceled out by other subjects who happen to vary in the opposite direction. Sidman, however, says that variability is not inherent in the subject but is caused by a failure of the experimenter to control all the variables affecting that subject. Once experimenters gain adequate control of the subject's behavior, they should no longer find it necessary to use large groups of subjects. The way for experimenters to demonstrate that they have gained this control is to do a baseline experiment.

Baseline Procedures

To illustrate a Sidmanian **baseline experiment,** let's consider an experiment designed to find out whether punishment can be used to change the behavior of a person with cerebral palsy. Suppose a therapist is working with a cerebral-palsied patient who wishes to improve his interview skills.* Cerebral-palsied individuals often have problems controlling their head movements and so tend to lose eye contact. As an attempt to increase the amount of eye contact, which is one aspect of a successful interview, the therapist decides to devise a procedure whereby the patient gets a mild electric shock each time eye contact is broken. The patient, wishing to improve his social skills, agrees to the shock procedure.[†]

---

*I wish to thank David A. Sachs of Las Cruces, New Mexico, for this particular example. He devised the technique described, although the results I will report are fictitious.
[†]The patient's agreement is a necessary although not always sufficient ethical requirement.

THE FIRST STEP IS TO
ESTABLISH A STEADY STATE...

The first step in this type of experiment is to establish a **baseline**—that is, a **steady state** at which the response rate changes very little. One of the nagging problems in baseline experiments is determining how much "very little" is. The methods for determining whether the baseline has reached a steady state vary from a statistical criterion such as "no more than 3% change in the response rate from one session to the next" to a simple visual inspection of the data for obvious fluctuations or trends. Once a baseline has been established, the experimenter begins the experimental manipulation.

In our example, the therapist might have the patient report every day for a half-hour simulated interview. During the interview, the therapist throws a hidden switch whenever the subject's eyes do not maintain contact. The switch is connected to a clock so that total time of eye contact during each half-hour session can be determined. After a number of sessions, when the therapist is satisfied that a stable baseline performance has been reached (that is, a fairly consistent time of eye contact per session), the therapist begins the shock procedure. Whenever the patient breaks eye contact and the experimenter throws the switch, the patient gets a short electrical shock to the forearm. The experimenter then tries to determine whether the amount of eye contact changes from its baseline rate.

Figure 6-7 shows a possible result for this experiment: The therapist decided that a stable baseline had been achieved after Session 5 and began shocks on Session 6. Once the shocks were begun, the subject's eye contact increased dramatically. By Session 10, the subject's eye contact had reached a stable **transition steady state,*** and the experimenter discontinued the shock. By Sessions 12 to 14, the subject returned to the original baseline behavior.

An experimenter must carry out each of the operations described to have a true baseline experiment: establish a stable baseline; apply the experimental manipulation and establish a stable transition steady state; then show **reversibility** by recovering the original baseline when the experimental manipulation is removed.

---

*The transition steady state is sometimes called the **treatment** or **modification state** in clinical work.

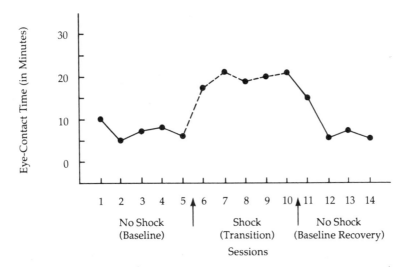

Figure 6-7. Possible results of an experiment in which eye-contact time for a cerebral-palsied patient was measured during 30-minute simulated interviews. The first five sessions provided a baseline. Shock was administered on Sessions 6–10, and baseline recovery occurred during Sessions 11–14.

The logic of the method is that, once a baseline has been obtained, an uncontrolled confounding variable is unlikely to suddenly begin to affect the subject's behavior on the same trial in which the experimental manipulation is made. Even if this unlikely event happened, the chances that a confounding variable then ceases to have an effect on the same trial in which the experimental manipulation is discontinued would be extremely small.

To be even more convincing, an experimenter could do an **intrasubject replication,** repeating the procedure with the same subject one or more times. That is, the experimenter might again shock the subject on Session 15, continue until a stable transition steady state is achieved, discontinue the shock, and recover the original baseline. Each time the effect can be repeated, our confidence that the change in behavior was caused by the experimental manipulation rather than an uncontrolled confounding variable increases. Even though this is a single-subject design, it would also increase our confidence in the result to do an **intersubject replication**—that is, to repeat the experiment with a few additional subjects. We would still evaluate the results by looking at the data from individual subjects rather than at grouped data. However, being able to do such intersubject replication strengthens our conclusion.

Advantages The major advantage of a baseline experiment is that it gives us a powerful way of looking at a single subject's behavior. For instance, if the results shown in Figure 6-7 were actual data, they would go a long way toward convincing me that eye contact can be controlled by contingent shock. You would be convinced too, wouldn't you?

The results are also easy to interpret. In fact, they are so easy to interpret that baseline experimenters use no statistical tests. They say that if you need a statistical test to convince other investigators that the effect you found is a real effect and not due to chance variation, either the effect is not strong enough to bother with or else you need to refine your techniques to get better control over the subject's behavior (eliminate unwanted variability).

In a traditional group experiment, if you use a large number of subjects in each group, you may find an effect that is statistically significant but of little importance. That is, you may have chosen an independent variable that has an effect on the subjects' behavior, but the effect may be small compared to other, more important variables. A baseline experimental procedure, however, is not sensitive to such unimportant effects. The variability due to the more important independent variables blankets such real but small effects. A baseline procedure, then, guarantees that any effect found is large enough to be of potential importance.

Another advantage of a baseline procedure is the flexibility it allows you in deciding when to impose a level of an independent variable and which level to use. Prior to doing a standard experiment, the investigator must choose the number of trials to present to each subject and which levels of the independent variable to use. Because most statistical tests require it, the investigator then needs to collect an equal number of data points for each level of the independent variable. However, investigators who use baseline designs can decide at any point in the experiment to collect more data at the present level or to change to a new level. For instance, in our example if the therapist had felt the need for more data under the shock condition, the therapist had the flexibility to continue that condition for more sessions before attempting to recover the baseline.

The therapist also could have decided to use an additional level of the independent variable after the experiment was under way. Suppose the change in behavior was not particularly convincing at the specific shock intensity chosen. After recovering baseline and reaching stable performance, the investigator could choose to try a more intense shock on the next block of trials. Thus, the investigator is not required to use predetermined levels of the independent variable.

In addition to the advantages of easy interpretation, the elimination of statistical tests, the guarantee of finding only fairly large effects, and flexibility, baseline experiments can also be used with only one subject. Therapists with only one cerebral-palsied patient or experimenters with individual subjects having unusual disorders, training, or talent could not use a traditional experimental design to study these single subjects. However, they could use a baseline procedure.

Disadvantages Although baseline experiments offer so many advantages, most experimenters still stick to traditional experimental group designs because they cannot meet the assumptions of baseline experiments. For example, the assumption that experimental effects can be reversed requires that the subject return to the original level of behavior at the end of the

SOME PROCESSES ARE
NOT REVERSIBLE.

experiment. We saw in the previous chapter that many potential sequence and ordering effects require counterbalancing when a within-subject design is used. A baseline experiment is a special kind of within-subject design in which effective counterbalancing is impossible. Thus, any kind of systematically changing confounding variable prevents us from recovering the original baseline. And unless the subject's behavior returns to its former state when the experimental manipulation is removed, we do not know whether to attribute the transition-state behavior to the manipulation or to some confounding variable.

For this reason, many traditional areas of psychology cannot be investigated by baseline procedures. Some obviously inappropriate areas are life span, memory, and some areas of learning. Most of the changes that take place during experiments in these areas cannot be reversed. ("Now forget all the words you have learned.")

A second disadvantage is that baseline designs may not allow us to discover small but important effects. Suppose you work for a telephone company and your job is to find out whether the time it takes a directory-assistance operator to find a number is improved by using a computerized search system rather than a standard telephone book. You decide to use a baseline design and, as each request comes in, you record the length of the call. You have the operator first use the standard telephone book until you achieve a baseline. Then you have the operator switch to a system in which the information is keyed into a computer and the computer provides the numbers. Finally, you have the operator return to the book.

Figure 6-8 shows some possible results. A visual inspection of the figure would probably not convince you or me that there is any difference between using the computerized system and using the standard telephone book. In other words, the transition state does not look any different from the baseline. However, the average call under the computerized system is three seconds shorter than the average call under the book system. If we had done a standard experiment, a statistical test might show such a difference to be significant. But, would this be an important effect? Yes, it would be, because each second saved on an average directory-assistance call cumu-

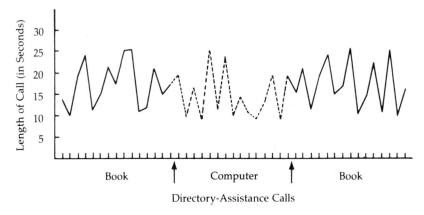

Figure 6-8. A fictitious baseline experiment measuring the length of each directory-assistance call when the operator was alternately using a standard telephone book and a computerized system.

latively saves telephone companies millions of dollars. That's certainly important to them!

Baseline design proponents may argue that variability is the experimenter's fault, and they may have a point with respect to rats in a sterile laboratory environment. However, I have a difficult time conceiving of how the telephone company scientist could have gained better control of the behavior being measured. In this case the behavior seems to be driven largely by the customer rather than by the operator. In some situations, variability is simply intrinsic to the setting. In this case, small but important effects can be blanketed by this variability, and baseline designs may not be appropriate.

A final disadvantage of baseline experiments is that it is difficult to determine how general any effect we find may be. Because different subjects may respond differently to experimental manipulations, our one subject may be an oddball. This criticism can be overcome by redoing the experiment using additional subjects. However, the tradition in baseline experiments is to use as few subjects as possible.

Thus, baseline experimental designs can be a valuable tool for some areas of experimental psychology. When the assumptions of the design can be met, a baseline experiment offers a way to convincingly show the effects of important experimental manipulations. Unfortunately, the assumptions are usually so rigorous that baseline designs must be restricted to only a few areas of experimental psychology.

Summary

Once you have decided on a research problem worth investigating, you must choose an experimental design. The simplest design you can choose presents only two levels of a single independent variable. This design provides a way to quickly determine if the independent variable has any effect at all on the subject's behavior. Such experiments are also easy to interpret and analyze; for some applied problems, they provide all the information necessary. However, these simple experiments can tell you nothing about the shape of the experimental relationship, so both **interpolation** and **extrapolation** are risky and the result is of limited theoretical value. Adding more levels to the independent variable will give you a better idea about the functional relationship between the independent and the dependent variables. It also makes choosing a range for the independent variable less critical. A disadvantage of such **multilevel experiments** is that they require more time and effort. They are also a bit harder to interpret and analyze.

A **baseline experiment** is a special type of single-variable experiment that can show experimental effects using data from only one subject. After establishing a **steady-state** rate of responding called a **baseline,** the investigator initiates the experimental manipulation until the rate of responding changes to a new **transition steady state.** The investigator then demonstrates **reversibility** by recovering the original baseline. An advantage of baseline designs is that they offer a convincing way to show important changes in a single subject's behavior. The experimenter can also be flexible in choosing when to manipulate the independent variable, and which level to change it to. These results are also easy to interpret. However, some assumptions of baseline experiments, such as reversibility, cannot be met in many areas of psychology. It is also sometimes difficult to show small but important effects and risky to generalize the findings to other subjects.

References

Sidman, M. (1960). *Tactics of scientific research*. New York: Basic Books.

Suggested Books on Baseline Designs

Hersen, M., & Barlow, D. H. (1976). *Single-case experimental designs*. New York: Pergamon Press.

Robinson, P. W., & Foster, D. F. (1979). *Experimental psychology: A small-N approach.* New York: Harper & Row.

7
How To Plan a
Multiple-Variable Experiment

I have yet to see any problem however complicated, which, when you looked at it the right way, did not become more complicated.*

So far we have been pretending that all experiments have only one independent variable. However, this restriction has been more for the purpose of discussion than it has been a reflection of the real world. Most of the experiments that you will want to do will use more than one independent variable. In this chapter I will discuss some of the general strategies used in designing progressively more complex experiments.

The most frequently used design in experimental psychology is a **factorial design.** To understand the results of most experiments published in psychology journals, you must understand the logic of factorial designs.

Factorial Designs

The usual way to combine several variables is in a factorial combination that pairs each level of one independent variable with each level of the second and the third and so on. The independent variables in such a design are also called **factors.**[†]

As an example of a factorial experiment, suppose you wanted to know whether a group with a leader is faster at reaching a consensus than a leaderless group. You need to decide which circumstances you will control and which you will let vary: Should all the subjects be of the same sex or not? Should communication be structured or free? Should you give the group an easy or a hard problem to solve? You may find it unsatisfactory to control or randomize all these factors. For example, you might feel that the effect of a leader on a group's efficiency might depend on the size of the group, in which case you might choose to vary both leadership and group size as factors. Suppose that you chose two levels of leadership—with and without—and four levels of size—3, 6, 10, and 20 members.

---

*Paul Anderson, from author's notes.
[†]Some investigators also call them **treatments,** which leads to the term *treatment combinations.* In building our science, we emulate the biblical folk building the Tower of Babel; no one can agree on the language. It's enough to make a new investigator a babbling idiot!

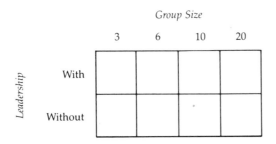

Figure 7-1. A schematic representation of a 2 × 4 factorial design. One factor, leadership, has two levels: with and without. A second factor, group size, has four levels: 3, 6, 10, and 20 members.

Figure 7-1 shows the usual way of representing such a factorial experiment. A **matrix** is formed with one factor on each side. The boxes within the matrix are called **cells.** As with the simpler experiments, subjects are assigned to the various cells in a random manner. In the example, the upper left cell would have subjects assigned to groups with three members, one of whom is made the leader. You can see that any row or column by itself forms a simple single-variable experiment. The example we have chosen is called a **2 × 4* design,** because one factor has two levels and the other has four.

The number of factors represented in a factorial design is limited only by your imagination and the population of the world. Suppose we thought that group decision-making time differs not only with leadership and size but also with the sex of the members. We make sex a third factor having three levels. Three levels? Right—men, women, and mixed (approximately half men and half women). Figure 7-2 shows a schematic of this expanded design,† which would be called a 2 × 3 × 4 factorial design.

Advantages The major advantage of a factorial experiment is that we can study **interactions.** An interaction occurs when the relationship between one independent variable and the subject's behavior depends on the level of a second independent variable. For example, a group of three may make decisions easily with or without a leader, but as the group gets larger, we may find that leaderless groups take progressively longer to reach a consensus. Thus, the relationship between leadership and decision time depends on the size of the group. Figure 7-3 shows a graph of such an interaction. As you can see, the time to solve a problem is unaffected by whether or

---

*The "×" in this expression is read "by," not "times." Thus, an English (rather than algebraic) reading of this design would be a **two-by-four design.**
†Schematically representing more than three factors becomes a bit more difficult. Three-dimensional paper is hard to come by. Experimental designs, however, are not limited by three-dimensional space. They are just difficult to represent in a two-dimensional drawing.

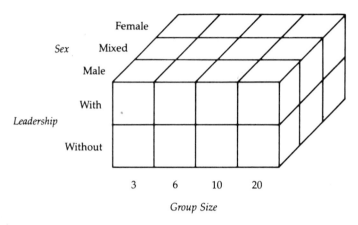

Figure 7-2. A schematic representation of a 2 × 3 × 4 factorial design. The factors are leadership (with and without), sex (male, mixed, and female), and group size (3, 6, 10, and 20 members).

not there is a leader for a group of three people. However, as the groups get larger, having a leader becomes important for minimizing solution time. Two single-variable experiments would not provide us with information about such interactions; they would simply allow us to see the general effect of either leadership or group size. Only a factorial experiment allows us to investigate interactions.

Remember in Chapter 1 when we talked about the infinite number of circumstances that could determine behavior? We decided that to do an experiment, we would have to pick one of these circumstances to be our independent variable. The other circumstances would either be controlled or be allowed to vary in a random fashion. Once we determined the effect of this circumstance on behavior, we could choose another circumstance to study. The problem with this approach is the naive assumption that, once we know the effects of each independent variable, we can simply add them together and account for the behavior. This assumption totally ignores interactive effects among the circumstances. The beauty of a factorial design is that the interactive effects are not ignored but evaluated.

Let's consider some of the experiments that we have used as examples and guess whether they might be influenced by interactions. Do you think that the effect of print size on reading speed would be different depending on the age of the reader? Would the effect of noise on memory depend on the strategy for storing the item? Would the effect of violent television programs on children's aggressiveness be different if children watched one hour, four hours, or eight hours of television at a sitting? In each of these cases, our single-variable experiment could not answer the question. We would have to do a factorial experiment.

In Chapter 1 we discovered that whenever a circumstance was made into a random variable, the experimental results increased in generaliza-

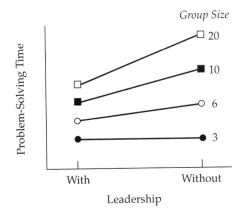

Figure 7-3. A graph showing a possible interaction of leadership with group size. Note that for the smallest group, problem-solving time is independent of leadership, but that for larger groups, leadership makes for shorter solution times.

bility but decreased in precision. On the other hand, choosing to make the circumstance into a control variable increased the precision of the outcome but decreased the generalizability. A factorial experiment gives us a third alternative: we can make the circumstance into another independent variable, thereby increasing the precision and generalizability of the result. We can generalize the outcome to a larger set of circumstances, because more circumstances have been made into factors, and we know precisely what the effect is at each level of these factors. Thus, we have the best of all possible worlds, although every time we choose to make another circumstance into a factor, the experiment gets progressively more complex.

A third advantage of factorial experiments is a statistical advantage. Recall from Chapter 5 that most inferential statistical tests compare the size of any difference found between the levels of the independent variable to an estimate of how variable the data are. A difference is more likely to be declared significant by the test if either that difference is large or the variability is small. In a factorial design, when a circumstance that otherwise would add variability to the data is instead made into a factor, the amount of estimated variability in the data decreases. Thus, the more circumstances we can make into factors, the smaller the estimate of variability. The smaller this estimate, the more likely it will be that any difference we find is declared statistically significant.

Disadvantages With all these good things going for factorial designs, you know that they must also have some drawbacks. They do. The major disadvantage of a factorial experiment is that it is time-consuming and costly. Suppose that, as in Chapter 1, you are again working for General Nosedive of the air force. You are working with a team of engineers who are designing the cockpit of a new aircraft. Because you are a psychologist and know all

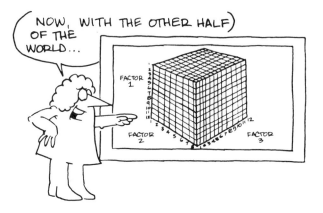

about humans, they expect you to tell them how to design the displays and controls and where to place them.

You are aware that some variables might interact with other variables, so you choose a factorial design. For example, you know that the location of the airspeed indicator might affect the best altimeter location. The first factor you select is the length of the pointer on the altimeter. You find that four standard lengths are currently in use, so you assign four levels to this factor. You also have a choice of five possible places to put the altimeter, so you select altimeter location as a second factor and assign it five levels. Your third factor is the size of the airspeed indicator with three levels. Because there are six possible locations for this instrument, you have a fourth factor. The fifth factor is the size of the joystick grip,* which has four possible diameters and five possible lengths. We have only started to consider the important variables for cockpit design, and we already have a $4 \times 5 \times 3 \times 6 \times 4 \times 5$ factorial experiment. So far the design has 7200 cells. If we assign ten subjects to each cell, we will exceed the number of pilots in the air force!

As you can see, whenever you add another factor to a factorial experiment, you increase the number of cells in the design by a multiple of the number of levels in that factor. At this rate, the size of factorial designs can get out of hand quickly. Because each additional cell calls for more time and effort, you must be careful not to choose an unrealistic number of factors or levels within each factor.

If you do not have the resources to do a large factorial experiment, how do you get an answer for the general? One way is to do several smaller experiments. For instance, in the example you could do 4×5, 3×6, and 4×5 experiments. The problem with this solution is that you are assuming that the independent variables appearing in separate experiments (such as altimeter location and airspeed indicator size) do not interact. And you have no way of verifying this assumption without combining the variables into

---

*You nonfliers can stop snickering now. A joystick is the steering lever on an aircraft.

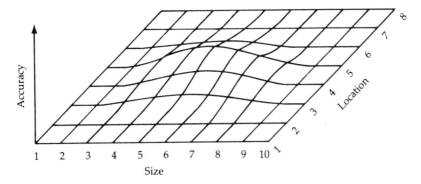

Figure 7-4. A possible response surface describing the accuracy with which subjects read altimeters as size and location are varied.

one experiment. Nevertheless, this is the way most psychologists who have to find answers to such questions go about doing so in the real world.

A second, more sophisticated way of getting an answer would be to use a technique called **response-surface methodology.** This technique was developed by a chemist (Box & Hunter, 1957), but psychologists now use it to make good guesses about the combined effects of many factors without having to use all possible combinations (Clark & Williges, 1973).

Response-surface procedures are complex mathematically and far too advanced for this book. However, I believe that I can give you a feel for the logic underlying the technique. Consider just two variables: altimeter size, with ten levels; and altimeter location, with eight levels. Suppose we put pilots in aircraft simulators and give them one second after a tone sounds to look at the altimeter and read the setting. We can then measure the accuracy of their readings. We might want to do a complete 10 × 8 factorial experiment, with 80 cells assigned to ten pilots each. However, we may not be able to afford an experiment with 800 subjects. The true relationship of altimeter size and location can be described by a response surface that in this case plots accuracy as a function of both altimeter size and location. Figure 7-4 shows such a response surface. Note that this is a three-dimensional graph, with the two independent variables on the horizontal axes and the dependent variable on the vertical axis.

For any experimental question having more than one continuous quantitative variable, such a true underlying response surface exists. When we carry out experiments, we are really attempting to get some idea of what a map of this surface looks like. In a complete factorial experiment, we systematically sample as many points as possible. These points are equally spaced on the surface and form a grid like that shown in Figure 7-4.

For some purposes it might be important to know as much about the shape of the surface as possible. However, in many applied settings such as the example we are considering, we really do not care what the entire surface looks like. All we want to know is where the highest point is because the levels at that point are the ones to use in designing the cockpit. In the example, knowing that the maximum accuracy occurs at size 5 and location 5 answers our question. Response-surface techniques allow you to determine maximum points and areas without having to map the entire surface.

Imagine a mountain climber, Hans Kold. Hans's calling in life is to find the highest mountain in the Alps. Unfortunately, because of eye trouble, Hans can neither read a map nor see distant mountain peaks. However, Hans is no fool; he knows certain rules of climbing such as:

1. One is more likely to find the peak by going uphill than downhill.
2. One is more likely to find a high peak when on a ridge than in a valley.

When you use a response-surface methodology, you use similar rules in an attempt to find maximum points. In fact, some of the terms would sound familiar to Hans, such as method of steepest ascent and method of ridge analysis. Basically the methodology makes it possible to use selected points from the response surface to estimate the complete relationship. You may select these points prior to the experiment or add them as the experiment proceeds, depending on the methodology you use. Investigators have found that a response-surface methodology allows them to make a very good estimate of the shape of a response surface with far fewer cells than would be required for a complete factorial experiment (Myers, 1971). This estimate is certainly adequate for answering the kind of question posed here: which combination of conditions gives the best performance?

Although the words *response surface* suggest that you must be able to plot the relationship in three-dimensional space, the methodology is mathematical in nature rather than physical and is not limited to three dimensions. For example, a response-surface methodology would be appropriate for the six-factor cockpit experiment we have been discussing. We should keep in mind that the technique is available and that it helps to overcome a major drawback of factorial designs.

A second possible difficulty with factorial experiments is interpreting the results. The statistical procedure used to analyze most factorial experiments and all factorial experiments having more than two factors is **analysis of variance.** This procedure requires you to make certain assumptions about the type of variability in your data. One assumption is that the variability is normally distributed in that familiar bell-shaped curve that approximates many real-world distributions. If the underlying variability in your data does not approximate a normal distribution, an analysis-of-variance statistical test is not appropriate.* Unfortunately, you often do not know whether you can meet this assumption until after you have completed your experiment, which is too bad, because other statistical tests presently available for analyzing complex interactions are inadequate (Bradley, 1968). In such cases, you are left with the unpleasant alternative of using a questionable statistical test or doing no statistical analysis at all. Fortunately, most factorial

---

*Bradley (1968), in his book *Distribution-Free Statistical Tests,* has a good discussion of the kinds of errors you can make when you fail to satisfy this assumption.

experiments produce distributions that are fair approximations of a normal distribution, thereby allowing you to use analysis of variance. (We will discuss analysis of variance in more detail in Chapter 9.)

Even when you can satisfy the assumptions of the statistical analysis, interpreting the results of complex factorial experiments is sometimes difficult. The interactions mentioned so far are two-way interactions in that the relationship between one factor and the dependent variable depends on the level of a second factor. However, you could also have three-way interactions in which the type or size of two-way interaction depends on the level of a third factor. By the time you get into four-way and five-way interactions, you will no longer find it obvious how to interpret your results. We will discuss interpreting interactions in more detail in Chapter 9.

We have seen that factorial experiments can offer many advantages over simple single-variable experiments. They allow you to investigate interactions, give you a statistical advantage by decreasing unwanted variability, and permit you to increase the generality of your results without decreasing the precision. However, you pay for these advantages in the time and effort expended and in the difficulty of interpreting the results. Is there a way to get some of the advantages of multiple-variable experiments without these difficulties? Yes. (Read on.)

Converging-Series Designs

Most journal articles report the results of a series of experiments because many experimenters choose to do a **converging series** of experiments. I use this term to refer to any set of experiments that progressively home in on a solution, rather than tackle a problem in one fell swoop. Most series of experiments are made up of single-variable or small factorial experiments.

In one type of series, we may simply have an applied problem that is too big for a single factorial experiment, like the cockpit-design example. In this case, we might decide to do a series of smaller factorial experiments, because higher-order interactions (three- or four-way interactions or larger) are of little interest. Once we find an optimal level for a particular factor in one experiment, we make the factor into a control variable in subsequent experiments. We then can vary other important factors until we have successively manipulated all the independent variables that might reasonably be expected to affect the subject's performance. In this way, we can progressively approach the optimal solution to our overall practical problem.

Converging operations A more exciting form of converging-series design than those used in practical problems is one that tests psychological theories by converging on a single experimental hypothesis that will explain an observed psychological behavior. This type of experimentation has been called a **converging-operations** approach (Garner, Hake, & Eriksen, 1956). We start out the series with a number of possible hypotheses that could explain the behavior being examined. Each experiment we do will help to eliminate one or more of our initial hypotheses until only one remains at the end of the series that can account for the data.

To illustrate a converging-operations technique, let's look at an experiment that investigates whether it takes longer for subjects to perceive vulgar words than nonvulgar words. Suppose the experimenter presents words to subjects using a tachistoscope, an apparatus that exposes visual material for very brief controlled periods. The experimenter presents four words, two vulgar and two nonvulgar, and instructs subjects to say the words aloud as soon as they recognize them. The experimenter finds that longer exposures are required for subjects to report the vulgar words and concludes that this finding supports the hypothesis that people unconsciously suppress the perception of vulgar material. This perceptual-defense hypothesis maintains that longer exposures are required to overcome this suppression.

Being an outstanding experimenter, you think of a number of other hypotheses that could explain this same finding. First, specific characteristics of the words may have made the nonvulgar words easier to read with short exposures. Second, subjects may have perceived all four words equally well but involuntarily suppressed their response on the vulgar words until they could no longer avoid it. Third, subjects may have been aware of the words and known what response to make but voluntarily withheld the response until they were positive of being correct. Thus, we have at least four possible hypotheses that can account for the results of the experiment. These are listed in Figure 7-5. We now need to do a series of experiments that will converge on one of these hypotheses and exclude the rest.

The first experiment you might do distinguishes between the word-characteristics hypothesis and the other three. You could repeat the original experiment using two different vulgar and nonvulgar words. If you again find that the vulgar words require longer exposures, you are on your way to eliminating the word-characteristics hypothesis.* If subjects did not require longer exposure times to say the vulgar words, your confidence in the word-characteristics hypothesis would increase.†

---

*Actually a single experiment seldom eliminates a hypothesis from further consideration. For example, we may have been unlucky and selected two additional vulgar words that were still harder to read than the nonvulgar words. Or we may have failed to consider a subset of this hypothesis. For example, the effect might be due to vulgar words having a lower frequency of usage than nonvulgar words. And we recognize higher-frequency words more quickly. To conclusively exclude a hypothesis, the converging operation must be completely independent of any other possible operation. By changing the specific words, we have not made word frequency completely independent of word vulgarity; therefore we cannot totally eliminate this hypothesis.

†This sentence was carefully worded, because we would not really have provided strong evidence supporting the word-characteristics hypothesis. In experimental psychology we design our experiments to show a difference in the dependent variable due to a manipulation of the independent variable. Showing that an independent variable caused no change in the dependent variable is weak evidence for the proposition that it *cannot* cause a change. There are a number of other reasons for finding no change in the subjects' behavior. For example, they may have failed to follow instructions, fallen asleep, or died.

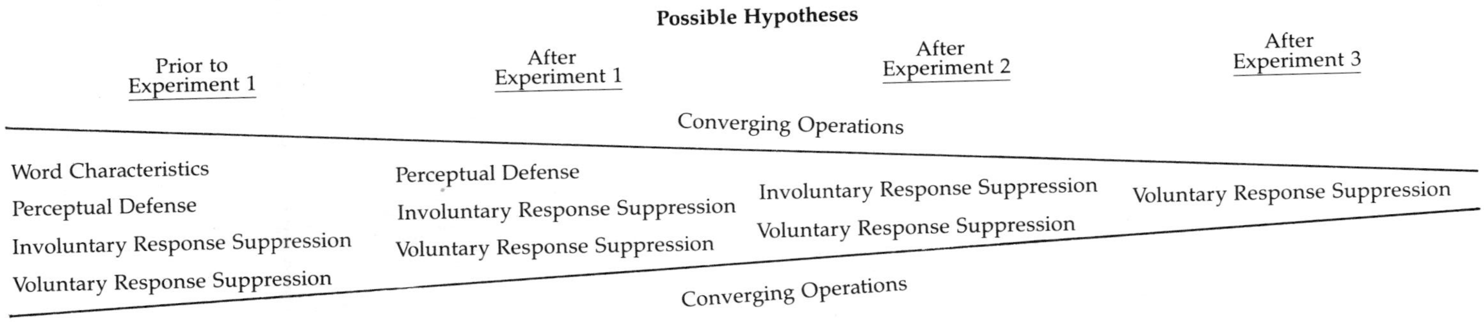

Possible Hypotheses

Prior to Experiment 1	After Experiment 1	After Experiment 2	After Experiment 3
Word Characteristics	Perceptual Defense	Involuntary Response Suppression	Voluntary Response Suppression
Perceptual Defense	Involuntary Response Suppression	Voluntary Response Suppression	
Involuntary Response Suppression	Voluntary Response Suppression		
Voluntary Response Suppression			

Converging Operations

Converging Operations

Figure 7-5. A schematic representation of the hypotheses in contention at each point during the three converging-operations experiments described in the text.

Assuming the word-characteristics hypothesis has been eliminated, you still must distinguish among the remaining three. In Experiment 2 we might try to determine whether subjects perceive the vulgar words at shorter exposures than they report them. We remember that a subject's galvanic skin response (GSR) gives an indication of his or her emotional response to stimuli. Thus, we decide to measure subjects' GSRs during presentation of the vulgar words to find out how long the words have to be exposed before they are perceived. The GSR can indicate whether subjects are perceiving a word, even though they may voluntarily or involuntarily suppress their response.

If you find that the GSR doesn't change until the exposure duration at which the subject reports the vulgar words, the perceptual-defense hypothesis receives some support. If, however, the GSR shows that the vulgar words are being perceived at the same exposure durations as the nonvulgar words, one of the two remaining hypotheses must be true.

To distinguish between voluntary and involuntary response suppression, you might look for an operation that causes subjects to voluntarily change the amount of suppression. You might anticipate that when the experimenter is the opposite sex from the subject, more voluntary suppression occurs than when both are the same sex. Thus, in Experiment 3, you attempt to determine if the difference in exposure time for detecting vulgar versus nonvulgar words is less when the experimenter and subject are the same sex. If so, the voluntary-response-suppression hypothesis is supported. If not, involuntary response suppression seems likely.

You can see how the converging operations in this example have allowed us to eliminate all but one hypothesis. The operations we used to zero in on one hypothesis were varied: a stimulus manipulation, a physiological measurement, and an interpersonal-relationship manipulation. We could have chosen other operations, but if the assumptions underlying our operations were correct, these other operations should converge on the same hypothesis. Every time a new operation converges on the hypothesis, we can have increased confidence in that hypothesis.

Actually, this discussion has been a bit idealized. You can seldom sit down before doing a converging series of experiments and detail every possible hypothesis and every operation that will be carried out to distinguish among the hypotheses. If you are like most experimenters, you will work on one experiment at a time. Only after seeing the results of one experiment will you decide on a new operation to get you closer to the true hypothesis.

As you complete more experiments in a series, you may also find that the number of hypotheses is increasing rather than decreasing. Although you can eliminate some old hypotheses, other new ones become obvious as the experimental problem is better understood. At this point it may seem that you are doing a diverging series of experiments rather than a converging series! In fact, you are still converging, but the set of potential hypotheses is simply much larger than you at first imagined it to be.

Advantages Most of the advantages of a converging-series approach are rather obvious from our discussion. You have a great deal more flexibility than you have in a large factorial experiment. In a large factorial experiment, you must decide on the factors and factor levels before starting the experiment, and you are then locked into this predetermined design. One bad choice can destroy a large investment of time and money. A converging series, however, gives you a number of choice points. You can choose new independent variables or levels at each of these points. You can also be much more efficient because you needn't waste time investigating factors and levels that have little effect on the dependent variable.

A converging-series design also has built-in replications. Every time you show an experimental result to be repeatable, it gains prestige in the scientific community. If you had done all three experiments in our vulgar-word example, you would have replicated or repeated the basic experimental result of vulgar words requiring longer exposures three times, providing convincing proof of the reliability of this result.

Disadvantages There are also some minor disadvantages of converging-series designs. It is difficult and sometimes impossible to determine how variables interact if the variables are manipulated between different experiments. Under certain circumstances, you can combine two experiments from a converging series to analyze them as a single between-subjects factorial experiment. However, if you are really interested in interactive effects, you should do a factorial experiment.

A second disadvantage is that when comparing the results of separate experiments in the series, you are always making a between-subjects comparison with all the accompanying disadvantages of between-subjects designs (see Chapter 5).

Finally, when you use a converging-series design, you must analyze and interpret the results of one experiment before you can begin the next. It often takes several weeks and sometimes months to complete such an analysis. For this reason, many investigators work on more than one series at a time so that they can do an experiment from one series while analyzing an experiment from another series.

Considering the advantages and disadvantages of converging-series designs, it is easy to see why the approach has become so popular in recent years. The converging-series approach offers a highly efficient and flexible way to investigate both applied and basic research problems.

Summary

The most frequently used multiple-variable experimental design is called a **factorial design.** In this design the independent variables, sometimes called **factors,** are combined so that the levels of each variable occur in combination with the levels of every other variable. These designs allow you to investigate **interactions.** Every time you add a factor, the generalizability and precision of the results increase, while the statistical variability decreases. However, complex factorial experiments can be time-consuming and costly. The design can become so large that a **response-surface methodology** is necessary to estimate the experimental effects. Interpreting the results can also be a problem, particularly when the statistical assumptions of **analysis of variance** cannot be met.

You can use a **converging-series design** in place of a complex factorial design. This design allows you to discover **converging operations,** which progressively eliminate hypotheses until only one remaining hypothesis can account for the data. Converging-series designs offer the advantage of flexibility and also provide built-in replications. However, evaluating interactions between factors varying across experiments is difficult. You must also manipulate these factors in a between-subjects manner, and you must analyze one experiment before beginning the next.

References

Box, G. E. P., & Hunter, J. S. (1957). Multifactor experimental designs for exploring response surfaces. *Annals of Mathematical Statistics, 28,* 195–241.

Bradley, J. V. (1968). *Distribution-free statistical tests.* Englewood Cliffs, N.J.: Prentice-Hall.

Clark, C., & Williges, R. C. (1973). Response surface methodology central-composite design modifications for human performance research. *Human Factors, 15,* 295–310.

Garner, W. R., Hake, H. W., & Eriksen, C. W. (1956). Operationism and the concept of perception. *Psychological Review, 63,* 149–159.

Myers, R. H. (1971). *Response surface methodology.* Boston: Allyn & Bacon.

8

How to Plan Quasi-Experiments

The task confronting persons who try to interpret the results from quasi-experiments is basically one of separating the effects of a treatment from those due to the initial noncomparability between the average units in each treatment group.*

It is not always possible to do the type of nice, neat experiment that you learned about in Chapters 1, 6, and 7. For practical reasons you may not be able to manipulate only the independent variable while making all other circumstances into either control or random variables. When you are forced to violate the rules of the basic experimental model, the simple conclusion that "the difference in the levels of the independent variable caused the change in the dependent variable" is more difficult to state with confidence. In this case you may choose to use a **quasi-experimental design** in your research. Quasi-experiments have independent, dependent, control, and some random variables but do not use random assignment of subjects to the levels of the independent variable. Instead, nonequivalent groups must be compared, and these may differ from each other in many ways other than in their exposure to different levels of the independent variable.

In this chapter I will first discuss why it is not always possible to use basic experimental designs. Then we will consider the reasons why violating certain rules of experimentation weakens the conclusions that you can draw. Finally, we will look at several types of quasi-experimental designs that can be used to strengthen your conclusions.

Situations Requiring Quasi-Experimentation

Recall from Chapter 1 that one of the options for assignment of circumstances is to turn them into random variables. In that chapter I also emphasized how important it is for true randomization to take place. If we cannot be sure that a truly random process has been used, a circumstance may vary in a systematic way along with the levels of the independent variable. That is a nice way of saying that you have allowed confounding to raise its ugly head.

*Cook, T. D., & Campbell, D. T. (1979). *Quasi-experimentation*. Chicago: Rand McNally, p. 6.

To illustrate this problem, consider an experiment in which researchers wish to study the effect of lecturer pace on student attentiveness. The lecturer presents material at one of three rates: fast, medium, and slow. Attentiveness could be measured in several ways, but that need not concern us here. The class used in the experiment meets on Monday, Wednesday, and Friday mornings. On which days should the three rates be used?

Suppose the experimenters decide that the lecturer will use the slow pace on Mondays, medium on Wednesdays, and fast on Fridays. Obviously, the levels of pace would be entirely confounded with the day of the week. "Blue Monday," "hump day," and "TGIF" might cause changes in attentiveness that would be falsely attributed to pace. For this reason the experimenters would probably choose to randomly assign level of lecture pace to days, perhaps with the constraint that each pace be represented an equal number of times on each day. In this way a potentially confounding variable could be changed into a random variable.

Now consider a similar problem in a different experiment. Suppose we wish to determine whether handing out "learning evaluations" (short noncredit quizzes) at the end of each lecture improves class performance on the major tests in a particular college course. We know from our basic experimental model that we must use at least two levels of the independent variable—probably "learning evaluations" versus "no learning evaluations." Some circumstances will become control variables. For example, we would probably choose to use the same major tests to evaluate the performance of both groups. However, because we cannot clone students and using a within-subject design is not feasible, we will have to make the subjects assigned to each group into a random variable. Ideally we could put the names of all students in the university who had not taken the course into a hat and draw out 100 students to assign to each of two classes. One class would then be given learning evaluations and the other would not.

Unfortunately, we would probably not be allowed to force these students to take a particular class; in the real world, students are allowed to choose the classes they wish to take. We might have to use two classes that already exist, perhaps a morning class and an afternoon class, and assign them to the levels of our independent variable. Do you suppose that there are any differences between the type of students who choose to take morning classes and the type who take afternoon classes? Can you imagine dimensions in which these students differ that might be related to class performance?

Suppose the classes were both morning classes, but one met on Monday, Wednesday, and Friday and the other for longer classes on Tuesday and Thursday. Can you imagine dimensions related to days of the week or lecture duration that might affect performance?

An even more likely problem would develop if the instructor taught only one section of this particular course each semester or each year. How many dimensions do you suppose vary between fall and spring students or between students from one year to the next? So while we can avoid turning some circumstances into confounding variables by using control or randomization, we do not have the option of control for subject assignment.

In most applied field settings we do not have the option of making subject assignment a random variable. When random assignment of subjects is not possible, it is often possible to use a quasi-experimental design. However, before we can evaluate the limitations of such designs, it is important to understand some of the problems that we can have if we fail to completely randomize subject assignment.

When Random Assignment Is Not Possible

Before we can specify the problems that arise when subjects cannot be randomly assigned to the levels of the independent variables, the types of validity and the subtle distinctions among them should be understood.

Types of Validity

In Chapter 4 you were introduced to the term **validity** when we discussed dependent variables: "Validity refers to whether we are measuring what we want to measure." Here we will expand the use of this term to indicate the validity of experimental conclusions about cause. For example, we might ask how valid a particular experiment is in determining the truth of the conclusion "Violence on television causes aggression in children."

Cook and Campbell (1979) have described four types of validity. Concern with **statistical conclusion validity** is expressed when you ask if there is a real relationship between the independent and dependent variables as well as a statistically significant relationship. Some concerns about statistical conclusion validity will be mentioned in Chapter 9, such as what happens when certain assumptions underlying statistical tests are violated.

A second type of validity is **internal validity.** In this case, the question that the investigator asks is, "Given that there is a relationship between the independent and dependent variables, is it likely that the former caused the latter?" Any time that you violate the principles of the basic experimental model, you may have threatened internal validity. Failing to randomly assign subjects is one way of violating those principles. The major concern in this chapter is internal validity, and the threats to internal validity will be discussed in more detail later in this section.

Construct validity refers to whether the constructs used to talk about a causal relationship are appropriate. For example, we might be confident that we used an appropriate statistical test to show that there was a causal relationship between watching either a James Bond film on television or *Wild Kingdom* and the types of toys children play with, such as guns and knives or tractors and dolls. However, someone could readily challenge whether we had shown that violence on television causes aggression in children. The challenge might be that more than the construct of violence is being manipulated in comparing the two shows, or that choice of toys does not adequately tap the construct of aggression.

The fourth type of validity is **external validity.** Suppose that you are confident that you have demonstrated a causal relationship from one well-defined construct to another. You might still be concerned with how well you can generalize this relationship across persons, settings, and times. Threats to external validity might occur if you use a limited subject sample, such as college sophomores, when you wish to generalize to all humans of any age or intelligence. Or you might have done a highly controlled laboratory experiment when you wish to generalize to real-world work settings. Generally, the more tightly controlled your experiment, the less likely your conclusion is to suffer from threats to internal validity, but the more likely it may suffer from threats to external validity. However, in this chapter we have the opposite concern. Because we want to have good external validity, we may choose to do research in an applied field setting, and this choice may threaten the internal validity of our conclusions.

Threats to Internal Validity

Because the major concern when doing quasi-experiments is internal validity, let's discuss some of the threats to internal validity. Remember that internal validity refers to how valid the statement is that the change in the independent variable caused the change in the dependent variable. The validity of this statement may be challenged because subjects were not assigned to groups in a truly random fashion. Thus, the change could have been caused by a confounding variable due to subject assignment rather than by the independent variable.

History

In laboratory experiments, one usually can collect data at all levels of the independent variable over a relatively short time. In this case, any change in the dependent variable is unlikely to have been due to **history**: that is, some event that takes place between the testing of the levels of the independent variables.

Consider, however, the learning-evaluation experiment mentioned earlier in this chapter. Suppose that the particular course in which you wish to manipulate the use of learning evaluations is taught only once per year. For practical reasons you decide to implement the use of evaluations in this year's class and compare the grades of this class to those of last year's class. If you find that the overall grades are better for this year's class, you might be correct in attributing the improvement to the use of learning evaluations. However, some historical event could have caused the change. For example, the school could have tightened admission standards, thereby changing the academic quality of students in the class. Or perhaps the college of engineering has decided to require that all senior engineering students take the class, again changing the class composition. Or perhaps the world has undergone an increase in interest for the subject matter being taught, sim-

ilar to what occurred in science courses after the Soviets sent Sputnik into space. Or perhaps, at a local level, a fraternity has acquired a copy of last year's test and has made it available to certain students in the class. To have much confidence in the conclusion that the change in grades between the classes was due to the use of learning evaluations, you must rule out these historical events as well as any others that might threaten the internal validity of the conclusion.

Maturation

Maturation is a threat to internal validity caused by the subjects growing older or perhaps more experienced. Obviously, maturation is more of a threat with young children than with adults, such as when one is investigating the effects of preschool educational programs. However, even for adults, maturation can be a problem in long-term experiments or when the subjects are undergoing rapid change—for example, when an employee is first assigned managerial duties.

Selection

Selection can be a threat whenever subjects are assigned on other than a random basis, particularly when subjects are self-selected. Mention was made of selection when students who chose to take a morning class were being compared to those taking an afternoon class. Experimenters who use college students as subjects are familiar with the potential differences between early-semester volunteers* and late-semester volunteers. However, the worst kind of selection threats are those that are directly linked to the independent variable, such as comparing the performance of workers who volunteer for a new training program to the performance of those who do not volunteer or comparing the recovery rates of people who choose a new type of therapy to that of those who refuse it.

*The term *volunteer* is a euphemism that psychology instructors sometimes use to describe students who flock to sign-up sheets to keep from having their grades docked—that is, to fulfill a course requirement.

Mortality

When subjects drop out of an experiment, **mortality*** can also be a threat to internal validity. Fortunately, in most experiments, these subjects die only with respect to their life in the experiment, not with respect to life in general. Overall mortality is not really a problem; differential mortality is a problem. This occurs when more subjects or different kinds of subjects drop out of the groups assigned to various levels of the independent variable. For example, suppose a company decides to try a new training program to inoculate newly promoted middle managers against socially stressful situations. They randomly choose half of their new managers to expose to one hour a day of simulated personal confrontation with employees. The other managers are not exposed to such training. For five years after the conclusion of training, the number of stress-related health complaints of the two groups is counted. It is found that the stress-inoculated group has reported fewer complaints and the company concludes that the program was a success. Was it?

Among the questions that you should ask is: How many managers dropped out of each group during the training program?† It is likely not only that more managers would have dropped out of the stress group, but that these would be the managers who are most sensitive to stress. The success of the training group might have little to do with the inoculation procedure but be due entirely to mortality changing the characteristics of the groups.

Testing

The act of **testing** a group of subjects can change their behavior independent of any other manipulation. Testing can be a threat to internal validity when a pretest or multiple-test design is used. Suppose you were interested in whether a new advertising campaign would increase the public's awareness of your company's brand of shaving cream. You pick a large random sample of consumers and send them a questionnaire. The questionnaire asks a number of questions about various brands of shaving cream and the commercials associated with the brands. Three months later, after launching a new series of commercials touting your brand, you again send the questionnaire to the same people and discover that they are now much more familiar with your brand of shaving cream. You declare the advertising campaign a success. Are you right?

One problem with this conclusion, that the campaign caused a change in awareness, is that instead the pretest may have caused the change in awareness. The test may have sensitized this particular group of people to noticing shaving cream brands in general. During the following three months,

---

*Mortality is also referred to as *attrition* by some experimenters.
†In addition to the threat to internal validity of mortality, which is being emphasized here, you should be able to find other potential threats. For example, the training program might harbor demand characteristics (see Chapter 13) that bias these managers against reporting stress-related health problems. Or conversely, the training may have sensitized the managers to be more aware of stress-related health problems.

THE THREAT OF
DIFFERENTIAL MORTALITY

they may have watched all the shaving cream commercials more closely, and now they are able to tell you more about each of the brands regardless of whether new advertising campaigns were started.

In addition to sensitizing the subjects, testing can also help create demand characteristics (Chapter 13) by informing the subjects of the experimenter's topic of interest or even the experimental hypothesis. A pretest can also provide information to subjects, increasing their knowledge of a topic or knowledge about how that topic is tested so that scores on a posttest will be higher, independent of any experimental manipulation.

Statistical Regression

Perhaps the most subtle threat to internal validity is **statistical regression.** This term refers to the fact that when subjects are chosen on the basis of having scored very high or very low on a particular test, their scores tend to move toward the mean on a second test. It is not immediately obvious why regression toward the mean should occur. Perhaps an example would help.

Suppose that you have devised a program that you claim will increase the IQ scores for preschool children who have been classified as mildly retarded (IQ of 53–68). You give an IQ test and choose 30 children who score within the mildly retarded range. After one year in your program, the children are given the test again. You discover that the mean IQ of the group has increased by 7 points and that this change is statistically significant. You declare your program to be a success. Is it?*

How could statistical regression have caused or contributed to this result? Imagine that the IQ pretest was composed of two separate components: a

---

*At this point you should be able to identify a number of potential threats to internal validity other than regression. The problem with maturity over a one-year period for preschool children is obvious. Testing could be a problem as well. The IQ pretest was probably the first test of any kind that these children were exposed to. They may have learned something in general about taking tests. They may also have remembered specific items from the pretest and learned the answers over the year.

"true" IQ that a perfect test would measure and "error." The perfect test is, of course, perfectly reliable (Chapter 4) and yields exactly the same score for a particular child every time you give it. If you could use such a test, statistical regression would pose no problems. But, alas, the IQ that you measure also has an error component.

This error may be due to a number of unpredictable variables. For instance, the child may have been lucky and guessed the correct answers to several items on the pretest, or unlucky and guessed fewer correct answers than chance would predict. Or perhaps the child got up on the wrong side of the crib that morning and had a difficult time concentrating on the pretest. Or perhaps the examiner was feeling particularly grouchy that morning and failed to establish good rapport with the child. Because we cannot predict the size or direction of this error component for any particular score,* we must treat error as if someone were drawing a random number out of a hat and adding or subtracting it from the true score.

When you chose the mildly retarded group on the basis of a low pretest score, you probably chose many more children who had error working against them than children who had error artificially inflating their true score. That is, the true scores of this group were, on the average, not really as low as the ones they received on the pretest. Because you chose children with low scores, you biased the group toward those with error working against them. However, on the retest one year later, we would expect a less biased error. We would expect as many errors that increase the true scores as decrease them. There is still an error component, but now it is not biasing the measured score away from the true score.

If you are not yet convinced, try a little demonstration. Pick some true score, say 100. Write the numbers from −10 to +10 on equal-sized slips of

---

*Testing psychologists can give you some idea of the general magnitude of the error component for a test, a number that characterizes the reliability of a test. The lower this number, the more we must be concerned with the effects of statistical regression.

paper and put them into a container. Draw a number from the container, add it or subtract it from 100, write down the result, and replace the number. After doing this 30 times, take the lowest five numbers and figure the mean (add the numbers and divide by 5). Now, follow the same procedure, drawing just five numbers and figuring the mean. Is the first mean lower than the second mean? You have just demonstrated statistical regression.

Interactions With Selection

Finally, variables such as maturation and history may have **interactions with selection.** For example, we might wish to compare the effects of an education program on nonequivalent groups such as middle- versus lower-class children. In this case, the middle-class children may learn more quickly owing to faster maturation. Or perhaps the middle-class children learn more quickly because they are more likely to have access to television and thus are affected by local history in the form of *Sesame Street*. In either case, the threat to internal validity comes not so much from selection or from maturation or history, but from a combination of selection with maturation or history.

Nonexperimental and Quasi-Experimental Designs

Now that you are aware of some possible threats to internal validity, what can you do to counteract these threats? Each of the designs that will be discussed next has some strengths for countering some threats, but none is able to give us complete assurance that we have eliminated all threats. In discussing quasi-experimentation it is useful to characterize the different designs using a notation system employed by Cook and Campbell (1979) in their classic book on the topic. In this system an "X" stands for a particular level of the independent variable (also called a treatment). An "O" stands for an observation during which the dependent variable is measured. The subscripts "1" through "n" refer to the order of presenting the treatments ($X_1 \ldots X_n$) or measuring the observations ($O_1 \ldots O_n$). A dashed line between experimental groups indicates that they were not randomly chosen.

Nonexperimental Designs

One-Group Posttest-Only Design

If you measure the behavior of a group that has been exposed to only one level of an independent variable, you are using a **one-group posttest-only design.** Using our notation system, this design looks like this:

X   O

When you have no other information to supplement the outcome, this design is essentially useless for determining the impact of the treatment.

For example, suppose a television network airs a program on the Holocaust and you are interested in how the show affected the population's awareness of the event. You send out a questionnaire to a group of people and discover that 76% are now aware of what happened during the Holocaust. What do you know about the impact of the telecast? Did it cause an increase in awareness? A decrease? Without knowing what the awareness level was before the show or what the level is for an equivalent group not exposed to the show, your result is useless for answering these questions.

This design is similar to the case-study approach discussed in Chapter 1. However, some important differences generally make case studies more useful. In a case study the researcher typically knows a great deal about the context in which the behavior is being observed. For this reason, while there may be no direct measure of preobservation behaviors, these can often be inferred. In addition, more than one behavior is usually being observed. These behaviors may form a pattern that provides much more information than is provided by a single dependent variable measured in a more sterile laboratory setting.

Posttest-Only Design With Nonequivalent Groups

If we add a posttest done on a nonequivalent group to the design we have been discussing, it looks like this:

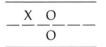

By nonequivalent, we mean that the group was chosen using a different selection mechanism than was used to choose the group exposed to the treatment.

In the Holocaust example, suppose we discovered that because a local sports team was playing, the telecast was not shown in Miami, Florida. We might decide to use a randomly selected sample from Miami as the nonequivalent group and send them the questionnaire. If we now find a difference between groups, can we attribute this difference to the television show? Miami has a large Jewish population. Do you think that being Jewish could affect your awareness of the Holocaust?

The basic problem with a posttest-only design using nonequivalent groups is that any observed difference could be due either to the treatment or to selection differences between the groups. The more equivalent the groups, the more convincing the conclusion.

One way of strengthening the conclusion in the absence of a formal pretest is to have informal pretest information by which the two groups can be compared. This pretest information is more useful the more highly correlated it is with the dependent variable. Thus, we might compare our two samples in terms of age, sex, social class, race, and religion. This comparison could give us an idea of how equivalent the groups are. However, the basic design is still weak, and great care must be taken in interpreting the results of any posttest-only nonequivalent-groups design.

One-Group Pretest-Posttest Design

Again taking the basic one-group posttest design, consider what would happen if we also gave that group a pretest. This one-group pretest-posttest design looks like this:

$$O_1 \quad X \quad O_2$$

This design has widespread usage in applied field settings and is an improvement over the nonequivalent-groups design in its selection. Obviously, the same people are selected for both observations. However, we buy this improvement at some cost, because other threats to internal validity can blindside us.

Again, using the Holocaust example, what effect do you think giving a pretest that asks about awareness of this event would have on a posttest assessing awareness of the event? You can see that the threat of testing is a problem in this case. If we decided to minimize the testing problems by giving the pretest well in advance of the treatment, say one year, we could well run into other threats. History might conspire against us in that some Holocaust-related event besides the telecast, such as the capture of a war criminal, might change the group's awareness. Or, particularly if we were using schoolchildren, maturity could have an effect. If we were using the pretest to select a group, regression could also cause problems. Thus, while the pretest design may solve the selection problem, great care must be taken in interpretation because of the other threats to internal validity.

Quasi-Experimental Designs

The three designs discussed in the previous section are called nonexperimental designs because there is no way to assess many of the threats to internal validity when these designs are used. The designs discussed in this section are called **quasi-experimental designs** because, although they do not meet the strict requirements of the basic experimental model, most of the threats usually can be assessed. It is not within the scope of this book to exhaustively cover all quasi-experimental designs. Instead I will mention several that illustrate the two major classes of designs. For more detail, refer to Cook and Campbell's (1979) excellent book.

Nonequivalent Control Group Design With Pretest and Posttest

This design uses a nonequivalent control group not exposed to the treatment in addition to a treatment group. Each group is given both a pretest and a posttest. The notation for the design is

$$
\begin{array}{ccc}
O_1 & X & O_2 \\
\hline
O_1 & & O_2
\end{array}
$$

This design is probably the most widely used in social science field studies. It allows us to assess most of the simple threats to internal validity.

How much we have to worry about certain threats depends to some extent upon the particular experimental outcome. If there is essentially no difference in the pretest scores of the groups, we can have some confidence that the groups are relatively equivalent, and the possibility of a selection or a regression threat is minimized. If the scores of the control group are the same at pretest and posttest, the threats of history and maturation are minimized. Because both groups receive the same tests, differential effects of testing should also be minimal. If the number of participants that drop out of the two groups between pretest and posttest is different, mortality could be a problem. However, the design allows this threat to be assessed. The most serious potential problem when using this design is having a threat that interacts with selection. Again, if the two groups score equivalently at pretest, the threat of a selection interaction is reduced but still possible. For example, while school A is receiving a particular treatment and school B is not, school A may also employ a new principal who requires new standards of the teachers. This history-selection interaction could threaten our conclusions.

We must be even more concerned about interactions with selection when the two groups have very different scores on the pretest. For example, suppose we want to determine whether paying assembly-line workers by the piece increases productivity. We request volunteers who will have their salary lowered but will receive extra money for piecework. At the pretest we discover that the volunteers are more productive, but we figure that we can compare the size of this initial difference to the size of the posttest difference. Sure enough, at posttest the difference is even larger. Both groups improved their productivity, but the piecework group improved the most. We conclude that paying by the piece improves productivity. Are we right?

Because there was a pretest difference in productivity, the volunteers in the treatment group not only may have been better at that point, but also may have been maturing (learning, becoming more experienced) at a faster rate. Workers are seldom stable, and we know these workers were not because even the control group improved. When everyone is improving, we should not be surprised that the better workers improve more rapidly. The basic design does not allow us to determine the size of this potential maturation–selection interaction. We might subdivide the treatment group by pretest to get some idea of the effect. That is, we would expect the less able workers from the treatment group to improve more slowly than the more able workers. However, we then have a different design. The point is that even when you use a nonequivalent-control-group design with both pretests and posttests, your findings may still be subject to threats such as selection interactions.

Variations Rather than exhaustively detailing each variant of non-equivalent-control-group designs, I will just mention a few possibilities. Sometimes when it is not possible or practical to use the same test for the pretest and posttest, a **proxy pretest** is used. That is, a pretest measure is taken of some variable or variables that should correlate with the posttest. For example, if you wished to evaluate the effects of a new method for teaching algebra, you might expose one class to the new method while a second is taught by the traditional method. Rather than give a pretest assessing algebra achievement to classes that have yet to learn algebra, you might give them a proxy pretest assessing general mathematical aptitude.

A proxy pretest can be used if it is not possible to give a pretest, such as when the treatment consists of some unpredictable historical event affecting a portion of a population. Alternatively, even when it is possible to give a pretest, testing may be a threat to internal validity, and a proxy test can be used to avoid exposing the participants to the test that will be used as a posttest. In other cases, when novel responses are called for, using the same test as the pretest and posttest could be nonsensical. For example, it would not make much sense to give a final exam for an introductory psychology course to two classes prior to their taking the course.

If testing is a threat, one may use **separate pretest and posttest samples.** Rather than draw a single sample for each group that will receive both the pretest and the posttest, two samples are drawn for each group—one to receive the pretest and one the posttest. For instance, if an educational program is to be given to one class and not the other, the two classes could be randomly subdivided with half of each given the pretest and the other half given the posttest later. The obvious weakness of this design is that it hinges entirely on the comparability of the pretest and posttest groups. If one believes that the groups differ along a dimension related to the treatment, the design is considerably weakened.

Another way of strengthening the basic nonequivalent-control-group design with pretest and posttest is to add **pretest observations at more than one time interval.** Adding one or more pretests can help us assess the effects of two possible threats. Remember when we were discussing how "the able get more able" and how this might cause a maturation-selection interaction? If we had given an earlier pretest, we could have determined whether the scores on that test fell on the trend line for each group. If they did, we would have a strong case for concluding that a maturation-selection interaction rather than the treatment caused the posttest difference. That is, the two pretests would have established a maturation trend, and the posttest would have been interpreted as nothing more than a continuation of this trend. An additional pretest can also help us assess the effects of statistical regression. If the groups were selected on the basis of the first pretest, regression effects should show up in the scores of the second pretest as well as in the scores of the posttest.

Other variations that are used less frequently include those in which there is a pretest, the treatment is imposed, there is a posttest, the treatment is removed, and there is another posttest. This design can also be expanded by reinstating the treatment, giving another test, ad infinitum (or possibly ad absurdum). These designs are much like the baseline designs described in Chapter 6. However, unlike quasi-experiments, baseline experiments typically use very few subjects and the data are examined for individual subjects, usually without the aid of statistical analysis.

In some cases one group can be given a treatment that is expected to change the dependent variable in one direction, and a second group can be given a treatment expected to have the opposite effect. For example, suppose two groups of workers are paid partly by the hour and partly by the piece. We might impose a treatment whereby we pay one group entirely by the hour and the second group entirely by the piece. If we predicted that paying by the piece increases productivity, we would expect a decrease for the first group and an increase for the second. An outcome supporting our predictions is strong support for our hypothesis.

We have discussed only a few possible variations of the basic nonequivalent-control-group design. These are also shown in Table 8-1. Others are possible, and you will find information about these in the books listed at the end of the chapter.

Interrupted Time-Series Designs

The second major class of quasi-experimental designs is called **interrupted time-series designs.** A basic time-series design requires that a single group be observed multiple times prior to treatment and then multiple times after treatment. The notation for one such design looks like this:

$$O_1 \ O_2 \ O_3 \ O_4 \ O_5 \ X \ O_6 \ O_7 \ O_8 \ O_9 \ O_{10}$$

The most interpretable outcome for such a design is an instantaneous, permanent change in the level of an otherwise flat line. For example, if we employed a new payoff scheme for workers and found an immediate 10% increase in productivity and this change was maintained over the course of the study, we can have considerable confidence that the new payoff scheme caused the change. Even given this ideal outcome, however, we still need to be wary of possible threats such as history or mortality. Some historical

Table 8-1.

Procedures for Conducting Various Types of Nonequivalent-Control Group With Pretest and Posttest Designs. Note that Groups 1 and 2 were not randomly assigned to the treatment and no-treatment conditions and are therefore considered nonequivalent.

	Time 1	Time 2	Time 3	Time 4
Basic non-equivalent control group with pretest and posttest	Test Group 1	Apply treatment	Test Group 1	
	Test Group 2		Test Group 2	
With proxy pretest	Proxy Test Group 1	Apply treatment	Test Group 1	
	Proxy Test Group 2	No treatment	Test Group 2	
Separate pretest and posttest samples	Test first half of Group 1	Apply treatment	Test second half of Group 1	
	Test first half of Group 2	No treatment	Test second half of Group 2	
Pretest observations at more than one time interval	Test Group 1	Test Group 1	Apply treatment	Test Group 1
	Test Group 2	Test Group 2	No treatment	Test Group 2

event could have coincided with the introduction of the treatment. It is also possible but probably unlikely that at exactly the time the treatment was introduced, some unknown event caused a number of participants to drop out of the study.

Other potential threats to internal validity can be excluded or assessed using interrupted time-series designs. For instance, selection and interactions with selections are not problems because the same group is used throughout the experiment. Any effects of testing or statistical regression should have disappeared before the treatment was introduced. Generally, we should also be able to exclude maturity as a problem because the effects of maturity are typically sluggish; hence we would expect to see a trend line rather than a discontinuous change.

When the change in the dependent variable is delayed, temporary, or reflected in the slope of an increasing or decreasing trend rather than in

INTERRUPTED TIME SERIES

the overall level of a flat line, we usually state our conclusion with less confidence. In this case more sophisticated statistical techniques can sometimes help tease out treatment effects.

Variations   As with the first type of design, variations of the simple time-series design are possible. One variation that will add considerable strength to a conclusion is the **addition of a nonequivalent no-treatment control group time series.** That is, a second nonequivalent group is measured at each of the observation intervals, but no treatment is given during the series. The control group allows us to assess the effects of history as a threat, because both groups will probably be affected equally by an historical event. If the two groups are selected in a different manner, a history-selection interaction can occur. However, this threat is a problem only in the unlikely event that a unique historical event occurred coincidental with presentation of the treatment and only for the treatment group.

When treatment effects are expected to be reversible, an **interrupted time series with removed treatment** can be used. After the basic design is completed, the treatment is removed, and another series of observations is taken. This design is really an overlapping combination of two basic time-series designs—one series in which the presence of the treatment is the treatment and the other in which its absence is the treatment. Actually you might choose to add and delete the treatment as many times as you wish to produce **multiple replications.** Each replication would increase your confidence in the causal effect of the treatment. Again, this design is similar to the baseline designs discussed in Chapter 6.

Another way of building in replications is to use nonequivalent groups but introduce the treatment at different points in the series of observations for the two groups. Such a design is called an **interrupted time series with switching replications.** This design offers a way to counter or assess most of the threats to internal validity such as history and maturity. Also, by having a built-in replication on a sample from a different population, the design enhances the external validity of the experimental conclusion. Table 8-2 summarizes the interrupted time-series designs discussed in this section.

Statistical Analysis of Quasi-Experiments

Available techniques for doing statistical analysis of quasi-experimental data have undergone great advances in the past few years. Rather sophisticated statistical tests, which are well beyond the scope of this book, can be found in some of the books listed at the end of this chapter. I am sure you noticed that several of the designs presented here were similar to the baseline designs discussed in Chapter 6. However, an important difference between baseline and quasi-experimental designs is that while baseline experiments usually have so few subjects that statistical analysis is impossible, quasi-experiments typically can be analyzed with the same statistical rigor used for fully randomized experimental designs. Certainly, it is no longer the case that quasi-experimentation should be avoided because statistical analysis is difficult or impossible.

Commentary

Upon first reading, you may have found this chapter to be a bit discouraging. It may seem as though all sorts of problems are sure to crop up when we do research in applied field settings. None of the quasi-experimental designs is so clean that we need not worry about certain threats to internal validity. On top of that, they appear to be rather complex to implement. But there is good news in all of this, too. These designs allow us to do research that was not even possible before. Quasi-experimentation has provided a new bagful of tools to psychologists who are interested in social issues, clinical evaluation, and educational programs and wish to investigate these issues in real-world settings. And although care must be taken to determine whether there are threats to internal validity, at least we know what these threats might be, and the designs make it possible to evaluate most of the threats to see whether they are a problem.

The behavioral sciences have often been criticized for either doing sound research on simple but unimportant problems or doing unsound research on complex and important problems. The advances in quasi-experimental design have made it possible to do sound research on complex and important problems. Welcome to a new frontier!

Table 8-2.

Procedures for Conducting Various Types of Interrupted Time-Series Designs. Note that Groups 1, 2, and 3 were not randomly assigned to the treatment conditions and are therefore considered nonequivalent.

Time 1	Time 2	Time 3	Time 4	Time 5	Time 6	Time 7
Basic interrupted time-series design						
Test Group 1	Test Group 1	Test Group 1	Apply treatment	Test Group 1	Test Group 1	Test Group 1
With addition of a nonequivalent no-treatment control group						
Test Group 1	Test Group 1	Test Group 1	Apply treatment	Test Group 1	Test Group 1	Test Group 1
Test Group 2	Test Group 2	Test Group 2	No treatment	Test Group 2	Test Group 2	Test Group 2
With removed treatment						
Test Group 1	Test Group 1	Apply treatment	Test Group 1	Test Group 1	Remove treatment	Test Group 1
With switching replications						
Test Group 1	Apply treatment	Test Group 1	Test Group 1	Test Group 1	Test Group 1	Test Group 1
Test Group 2	Test Group 2	Test Group 2	Apply treatment	Test Group 2	Test Group 2	Test Group 2
Test Group 3	Test Group 3	Test Group 3	Test Group 3	Test Group 3	Apply treatment	Test Group 3

Summary

In applied field settings where random assignment of subjects to groups is often not possible, **quasi-experimental designs** can sometimes be used. Such designs require the investigator to be aware of threats to four types of validity. **Statistical conclusion validity** refers to whether a statistically significant relationship is real. **Internal validity** refers to whether any change in the dependent variable was caused by the independent variable rather than by a confounding variable. **Construct validity** refers to whether the constructs we use to talk about a causal relationship are appropriate. And **external validity** refers to how well a relationship can be generalized to other persons, settings, and times.

Threats to internal validity include: **history,** the occurrence of an uncontrolled event during the experiment; **maturation,** the change in age or experience of subjects during experimentation; **selection,** the biased assignment of subjects to groups; **mortality,** the nonrandom loss of subjects from groups; **testing,** the change in subjects due to the testing process; **statistical regression,** the movement of scores toward the mean for groups selected on the basis of extreme scores; and **interactions with selection,** the differential effect of a threat on nonequivalent groups.

Nonexperimental designs are difficult to interpret because of multiple threats to internal validity. These designs include: a **one-group posttest-only design,** in which the behavior of only one group is tested after exposure to a treatment; a **posttest-only design with nonequivalent groups,** in which a second group, selected in a different manner, is also tested but not exposed to the treatment; and a **one-group pretest-posttest design,** in which one group is tested before and after exposure to the treatment.

Quasi-experimental designs permit you to eliminate or assess most threats to internal validity. In a **nonequivalent-control-group design with pretest and posttest,** one group is tested before and after the treatment, and a second group, selected in a different manner, is tested at equivalent times but without being exposed to the treatment. Variations of this basic design include: using a **proxy pretest** to measure a variable correlated with the posttest when the use of a pretest is not possible; using **separate pretest and posttest samples** by subdividing the nonequivalent groups and testing half of each group before and half after exposure to the treatment; and making **pretest observations at more than one time interval** so that each group is tested several times before exposure to the treatment.

The second class of quasi-experimental designs is **interrupted time-series designs,** in which one group is tested multiple times before and after exposure to the treatment. Variations of this design include: the **addition of a nonequivalent no-treatment control group time series,** in which a second group, selected in a different manner, is tested at equivalent times but not exposed to the treatment; using an **interrupted time series with removed treatment,** where a third series of tests is given after the treatment is removed; and using an **interrupted time series with switching replica-**

tions, in which two groups selected in different ways are tested at many points in time but are exposed to the treatment at different points in the series.

References

Cook, T. D., & Campbell, D. T. (1979). *Quasi-experimentation: Design & analysis issues for field settings.* Chicago: Rand McNally.

Suggested Books on Quasi-Experimental Statistics

For the Beginning Student
Cook, T. D., & Campbell, D. T. (1979). *Quasi-experimentation: Design & analysis issues for field settings.* Chicago: Rand McNally.

For the Advanced Student
Box, G. E. P., & Jenkins, G. M. (1976). *Time-series analysis: Forecasting and control.* San Francisco: Holden-Day.
Campbell, D. T., & Stanley, J. C. (1966). *Experimental and quasi-experimental designs for research.* Chicago: Rand McNally.
Kidder, L. H., & Judd, C. M. (1986). *Research methods in social relations,* 5th ed. New York: Holt Rinehart.

9

How to Interpret Experimental Results

A well-wrapped statistic is better than Hitler's "big lie"; it misleads, yet it cannot be pinned on you.*

There are three kinds of lies: lies, damn lies, and statistics.   DISRAELI[†]

You should now be ready to collect some data. At this point make sure that you have made a note of all the information you will need when reporting the experiment, such as the exact levels of your independent and control variables and the way you counterbalanced other variables. You may think that you will easily recall all these facts after the experiment is finished, but you will be amazed at how quickly these facts merge into one undifferentiated lump. This lump usually locates itself in your throat about the time you want to write an experimental report. Never trust the details of an experiment to memory. If they're important, write them down.

You will need **response sheets** to record each subject's data. At the top of each sheet, you should have a place to write such information as a subject number, the subject's sex, the condition being presented, and any specific comments you might wish to note about the subject or experimental session. Under this information should be lines on which to write each subject's response values for each trial in order. If it has been necessary to counterbalance or randomize the order of some variables, you will later need to transfer the data to a **data sheet,** on which they can be arranged according to independent variables and levels.

Once you have the data on paper, you are still a long way from answering the experimental question: what effect did the independent variable have on the dependent variable? To answer this question, you need to know about several approaches to analyzing data and how to use them.

This chapter should give you an understanding of the logic underlying data analysis. It will not help you to do the statistics required to analyze an experiment. Should you need to do such calculations, you should first read this chapter and then look for an appropriate statistical operation in Appendix A. That appendix is not meant to be a substitute for a statistics text, but with your instructor's help, it should allow you to analyze most of the simple experimental designs discussed in this book.

---

*Huff, D. (1954). *How to lie with statistics.* New York: Norton, p. 9.
[†]Huff, D. (1954). *How to lie with statistics.* New York: Norton.

Plotting Frequency Distributions

Suppose you are interested in the difference between women who support the feminist movement and those who do not. In particular, you want to know whether these two groups of women differ in anxiety level. You decide to ask a number of women "Do you support the feminist movement?" Those who say "yes" will be assigned to the feminist group and those who say "no" to the nonfeminist group. After assigning ten women to each group, you give them a test that has been found to reliably indicate a person's overall anxiety level. The test scores for the two groups are your raw data.*

Table 9-1 shows some fictitious scores between 0 and 100. The larger the score, the more anxious the subject. Is there a difference between groups? Looking at individual scores in this case is like listening to individual notes from a song; it's difficult to tell what the melody is. We need some way to rearrange the raw data so that we can interpret them more easily. We can draw a **frequency distribution,** which is simply a plot of how frequently each score appears in the data. You may notice, however, that no score occurred more than one time. Thus, to make the distribution meaningful, we need to put the individual scores into categories. We want several data points in each of the more frequently occurring categories, so we make each category include ten scores (for example, 10–19). Figure 9-1 shows such a frequency distribution for each of our two groups. The vertical axis labeled

Table 9-1.
Fictitious Anxiety Scores for Ten Women Who Say That They Support the Feminist Movement and Ten Who Say That They Do Not.

Feminist		Nonfeminist	
Subject	Score	Subject	Score
1	62	11	55
2	56	12	42
3	67	13	61
4	91	14	58
5	53	15	70
6	87	16	47
7	51	17	62
8	63	18	36
9	46	19	74
10	71	20	51

*You will note that this example is not really an experiment but a correlational observation, because we are comparing two dependent variables: the behavior of saying "yes" or "no" to the question and the test score. It is also necessarily a between-subjects manipulation, because the same women cannot answer both "yes" and "no" to the question or score both high and low on the test.

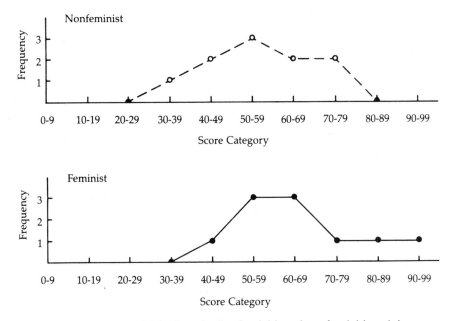

Figure 9-1. Frequency distributions for the feminist and nonfeminist anxiety scores listed in Table 9-1.

"Frequency" is simply the number of raw data points that fall into each score category.

Plotting a frequency distribution can be a useful first step in finding out whether there is a difference between conditions. Sometimes the experimental effect is strong enough that a visual inspection of the distributions will convince you that there is a difference. In this example, however, the distributions look very much alike.

Statisticians have given names to different types of distributions so that investigators can talk to each other in some common terms without having to show each other a plot of the entire distribution. We have already mentioned the properties of a **normal distribution,** shown in the upper left panel of Figure 9-2. To be normal, a distribution has to fit a complex mathematical formula. For our purposes, however, we can simply say that a distribution approximates a normal distribution if it looks something like the bell-shaped distribution shown in the figure. It is important to know whether your distributions are similar to a normal distribution because many statistical tests you will wish to use require that the data be approximately normal.

Some other types of distributions are also illustrated in Figure 9-2. A distribution that has two most-frequent categories rather than one is a **bimodal** distribution. The distribution of heights for a group composed of an equal number of men and women would often be bimodal. A distribution is **skewed** if it is asymmetrical through having more scores in one of the tails. A distribution of IQ scores for Ph.D.'s would be skewed because,

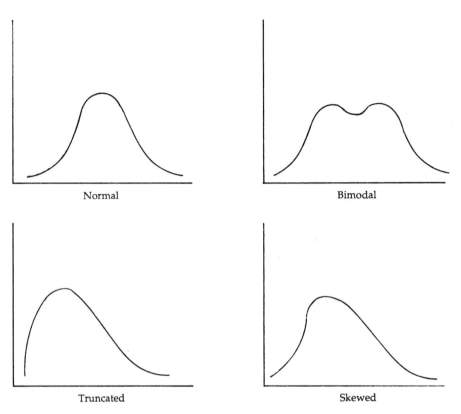

Figure 9-2. Four types of frequency distributions.

generally, few have low IQs. However, if a distribution looks as though one of the tails has been completely chopped off, it is said to be **truncated.** A plot of reaction times would form a truncated distribution because there is a limit to the speed with which a person can respond.*

Plotting a frequency distribution allows you to describe your data in a more orderly way than simply listing it in raw form, but it is still a rather cumbersome way to represent the results of an experiment. It would be nice to have a single number that represents how the subjects in each group performed. What we need is a way of calculating a descriptive statistic that will describe the data in this manner.

Statistics for Describing Distributions

Psychologists use basically two kinds of statistics: descriptive statistics and inferential statistics. A **descriptive statistic** is simply a number that allows the experimenter to describe some characteristics of the data rather than having to report every data point. Inferential statistics will be discussed later in the chapter.

---

*Remember ceiling and floor effects? They usually cause truncated distributions.

Central Tendency

One important descriptor of data is the location of the middle of a distribution. Psychologists call such a statistic an indication of **central tendency**; you probably call it an **average.** One way of comparing the two groups in our example is to calculate the average anxiety score for the feminists versus the nonfeminists.

There are three common ways to express an average. The **mode** is the easiest average to calculate, but it is usually the worst one to use because it ignores lots of data. The mode is simply the most frequently occurring score. In our example, there is no mode, because no score occurred more than once. After the data have been put into categories, a mode can be found. The mode for the nonfeminist group is the category 50–59, because it occurred with a frequency of 3. While this category seems to represent the central tendency of this distribution pretty well, note that if only one score were moved, the mode could change dramatically. For example, suppose subject 14 scored 71 instead of 58. Now the category mode would be 70–79 because there would be a frequency of 3 in that category. Do you think that this category would represent the central tendency of the distribution well?

The problem is that the mode uses only one property of the data—the most frequently occurring score—to describe average behavior. It ignores all the other scores. So when you use the mode, you are throwing out lots of information, such as the ordering and size of each number. With small samples, relying on a mode to describe your data can be risky.

A TRUNCATED DISTRIBUTION

PIE À LA MODE

The **median** is literally a middle score; it has an equal number of scores above it and below it. To calculate a median, list all the scores in order and then pick the middle score. If you have an even number of scores, the median falls halfway between the two middle scores. For example, in ordering the feminist scores, we find that the fifth score is 62 and the sixth is 63, so the median is 62.5. The median for the nonfeminist group is 56.5. The median does not reflect the size of the differences between scores, because it uses only order as its defining principle. Thus, we can change any score in the distribution without changing the median, as long as the position of the middle score in the list remains the same. Again, we lose some information when we describe our data in terms of a median.

The **mean** is a weighted average of the scores—that is, it is the sum of all individual scores divided by the number of scores that were added. For example, to find the mean for the feminist group, we add the 10 scores for a sum of 647 and then divide by 10, with the result of 64.7 for the mean. The mean for the nonfeminist group is 55.6. The mean is the center of gravity for the distribution. Thus, because the mean is an average that is affected by the size of the scores, it changes whenever any score in the distribution changes.

Which average best describes a distribution? As with all interesting questions, the answer is "It all depends." First, it depends on the shape of the distribution. If you have a normal distribution or any other unimodal symmetrical distribution, all three averages give you the same number. However, as a distribution becomes more skewed, the three averages get progressively farther apart. Figure 9-3 shows that the mean is most influenced by the size of the extreme scores in the right tail of the distribution. The median is influenced only because there are more scores to the right, while the mode is unaffected by these extreme scores.

You must use your judgment in deciding which measure to use. If you were to plot the incomes for a large group of people, you would probably get a distribution similar to the one in the figure. In this case a median would probably be the best average, because it would be influenced less than the mean by the few folks who make outlandish salaries. You can probably think of other more extreme examples in which a few very large or very small scores can distort the mean. Whenever you must choose a

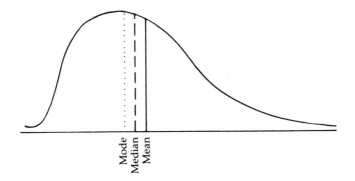

Mode
Median
Mean

Figure 9-3. The location of the mode, median, and mean for a skewed distribution.

measure to describe an average, you will simply have to examine the shape of the distribution, determine for what purpose the average will be used, and then use your judgment.*

Dispersion

An average tells you something useful about a distribution, but it describes only one special aspect of a distribution. A second statistic that helps describe a distribution is a measure of **dispersion,** or how spread out the scores are.

One measure of dispersion is the **range,** which we can calculate by subtracting the smallest score from the largest score. In our example for the feminist group, the range is $91 - 46 = 45$; for the nonfeminist group, the range is $74 - 36 = 38$. Although the range gives some indication of dispersion, because it is determined by only the smallest and largest scores, it is totally insensitive to scores in between. For this reason, a different measure of dispersion may be more useful.

As an alternative, we could subtract the mean from each score so that we have a number indicating the deviation of each score from the mean. To get a mean deviation, we could then add up these deviations and divide by the number of deviations. However, because the numbers cancel each other out when added, we will get a sum of zero, which doesn't help us much. We could ignore the sign of the deviations, add up the absolute values, and thus get an average deviation. But statisticians feel that a more useful indication of dispersion is found by squaring[†] each deviation (this also gets rid of the plus or minus sign), adding the squares, and then dividing by the number of squared deviations that were added. We then have a measure of dispersion called the **variance.** An even more useful

---

*I am assuming that you will read Chapter 14 and are trying to be fair with science. The books *How to Lie with Statistics* by Huff (1954) and *Flaws and Fallacies in Statistical Thinking* by Campbell (1974) give many humorous examples of how to make descriptive statistics like the mean into distorting statistics.

[†]Multiply it times itself.

measure is the square root* of the variance, a number called the **standard deviation.** Formulas for calculating these measures can be found in Appendix A.

You may find it helpful to view the standard deviation as a way of expressing the extent of error you are making by using the mean to represent the scores in a distribution. In reality, the mean is simply the best estimate you could make about any individual score; thus, the standard deviation indicates, on the average, how good an estimate you have made. If all the scores were the same, the standard deviation would be zero, indicating that the mean would never be in error. As the differences among scores get larger, the standard deviation increases, as does the error you would make by representing a score with the mean.

Plotting Relationships between Variables

The reason you do an experiment is to find out if there is a relationship between the independent and dependent variables. Although plotting frequency distributions is a good first step in analyzing your data, you will often find it useful to draw a graph to represent the experimental relationship. Graphs are not new to you. They have been cropping up from time to time in earlier chapters. To be complete, however, let's start by discussing basic concepts.

Drawing Graphs

A graph has two axes. The vertical axis (*y* **axis**) is called the **ordinate** and the horizontal axis (*x* **axis**) the **abscissa.**[†] When plotting experimental results, you plot the dependent variable on the ordinate and the independent vari-

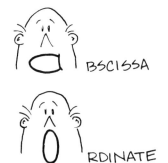

BSCISSA

RDINATE

---

*A number that, when multiplied times itself, gives us the variance.

[†]You may find it helpful to remember which term refers to which axis by noticing the shape your mouth takes when saying the first part of each word; "ab _____ " is said with a horizontal mouth, "or _____ " with a vertical mouth. That's the way I remember them!

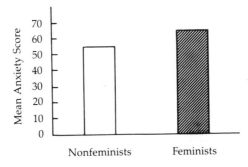

Figure 9-4. A bar graph showing the mean anxiety scores for the nonfeminist and feminist groups listed in Table 9-1.

able on the abscissa. If the levels of the independent variable cannot be represented by numbers, it is usually appropriate to use a **bar graph** to represent the data. Figure 9-4 shows a bar graph for the mean anxiety scores of the feminist and nonfeminist groups.

If the independent variable is continuous, then you can draw a **histogram** as shown in Figure 9-5. A histogram eliminates spaces between the bars of a bar graph. Figure 9-5 shows fictitious data relating the length of time patients are in therapy to their rating of self-image. Time in therapy is a continuous variable, because we could choose levels anywhere on the continuum of time.

A more common way of representing data when the independent variable is continuous is to use a **line graph** or **function.** Figure 9-6 shows the same results as those plotted in Figure 9-5, but is a line graph rather than a histogram. The individual data points are simply plotted and then connected by straight lines. Notice how this way of representing the data emphasizes the trends quite effectively. To use this type of graph, you must have data that lie on a continuum. By way of bad example, suppose that on

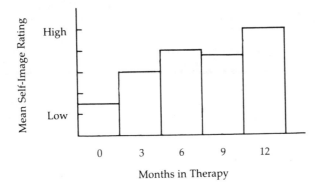

Figure 9-5 A histogram illustrating the results of a multilevel experiment relating a subject's perceived self-image to months spent in therapy (fictitious data).

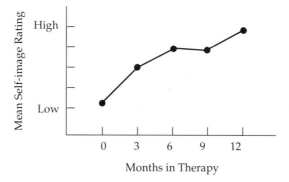

Figure 9-6.   A line graph illustrating the same data as those plotted in the histogram in Figure 9-5.

the abscissa of the figure, we had ethnic categories such as Hispanic, black, and so on instead of months in therapy. These categories obviously do not lie on a continuum; so the order of listing the categories would be totally arbitrary. Trying to find a trend in such data doesn't make any sense.

Line graphs are also best used to illustrate the results of a functional (multilevel) experiment rather than those of a two-level experiment. The problem with a two-level experiment is that you really do not know whether the relationship is linear, and yet you would be using a straight line to represent it. With a functional experiment, more than two levels of the independent variable are used, and it is possible to get an idea of the shape of the function even though the points are connected with straight-line segments. (For more on constructing figures for an experimental report, see Chapter 10.)

Describing Functions

Several types of graphed functions are illustrated in Figure 9-7. If changing the independent variable by one unit always causes the dependent variable to change in a given direction by a constant amount, the function is **linear**; any other relationship is **curvilinear.** If increasing the independent variable causes an increase in the dependent variable, the relationship is **positive**; if it causes a decrease, it is **negative.** A function that never reverses direction (that is, portions of the function are either all positive or all negative) is a **monotonic** function; otherwise, the function is termed **nonmonotonic.** If changes in the dependent variable get increasingly larger as the independent variable increases, the function is **positively accelerated**; if the changes get smaller, it is **negatively accelerated.** A negatively accelerated function eventually approaches a particular level and appears to flatten out. The curve is actually getting closer and closer to a straight line called an **asymptote,** although the curve and asymptote never touch. Such a function is said to be **asymptotic** or to approach an asymptote.

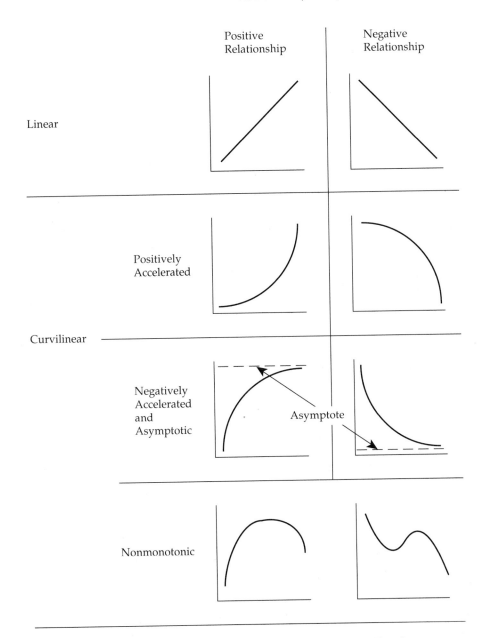

Figure 9-7.   Graphs illustrating some terms used to describe functional relationships.

If you are seeing these terms for the first time, you may be a bit confused. However, as you use them to describe psychological relationships, you will find that they become more familiar and allow you to discuss your results more efficiently.

Describing the Strength of a Relationship

The functions in the previous section either were idealized or were plots of a descriptive statistic rather than individual data points. However, rarely will you find every data point falling exactly on a smooth function. If you use raw data to plot an experimental relationship, you will most likely find some variability or spread around the functions. Such a plot is called a **scatterplot.**

Scatterplots

Figure 9-8 shows some examples of scatterplots. These plots could result from an experiment, in which case the relationships between independent and dependent variables are plotted, or from a correlational observation (Chapter 1), in which case dependent variables are plotted on both axes. If you observe the spread of the points in a scatterplot, you can get some idea of how strong the relationship is. However, visual observation is a rather

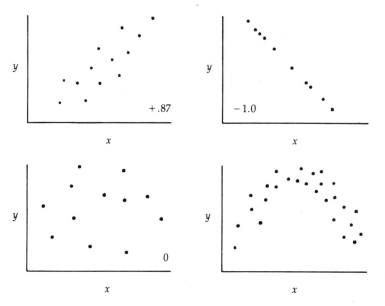

Figure 9-8. Four illustrations of scatterplots. Correlation coefficients are shown for three panels. No coefficient is given for the lower right panel because the relationship is curvilinear and a correlation ratio should be used.

SCATTERPLOT OF A
STRONG RELATIONSHIP?

crude way of estimating this strength. Fortunately, when the relationship is linear,* a descriptive statistic called a **correlation coefficient** can be used for this purpose.

Correlation Coefficients

A correlation coefficient is a number between $+1.0$ and -1.0, with the sign indicating whether the relationship is positive or negative and the size of the number indicating the strength of the relationship. A correlation of 1.0 ($+$ or $-$) indicates a perfect relationship, and 0 indicates no relationship.

Figure 9-8 shows the correlation coefficients for three sets of data. No coefficient is shown for the lower right panel since the function is obviously curvilinear and simple linear correlation is not appropriate. (There is, however, a way of describing a curvilinear correlation called a **correlation ratio** [Kirk, 1982]). You can find out how to calculate a correlation coefficient by reading Appendix A or by looking in any statistics text.[†]

Interpreting Results from Factorial Experiments

The results of factorial experiments are more difficult to interpret than those of other types of experiments, because they use more than one independent variable and require you to evaluate interactions. Figure 9-9 shows some fictitious results of our earlier experiment in which we measured the time it took subjects to read paragraphs typed in 12-point or 10-point print. In this case, however, assume that we used 8-year-old subjects in one group

---

*Actually, one form of correlation uses data that can only be ranked or ordered, in which case the term **linear** is meaningless. Such a correlation can be used for any monotonic relationship.
[†]Several statistics texts are listed at the end of the chapter.

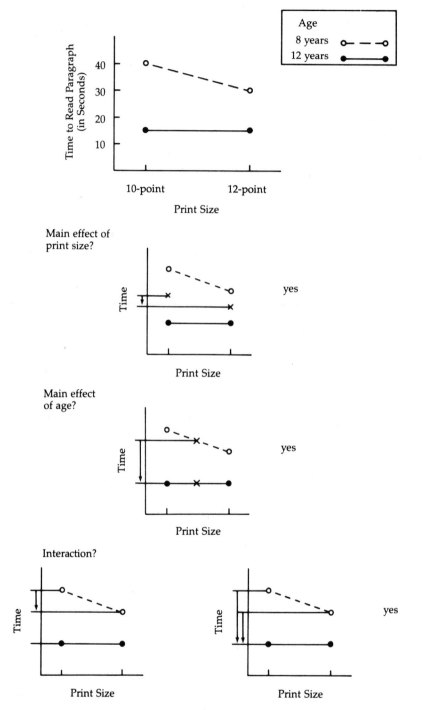

Figure 9-9. Analyses of a 2 × 2 factorial experiment for main effects and interactions.

and 12-year-olds in another. Notice that one independent variable (print size) has been plotted on the abscissa, while the other (age) is represented by a point and line code. We can no longer just ask whether the independent variable has had an effect on the dependent variable. We must ask three more specific questions: (1) Is there an effect of print size? (2) Is there an effect of age? (3) Does the effect of one variable depend on the level of the other? The first two questions refer to **main effects** and the third to an **interaction.**

Main Effects

To evaluate the main effect of an independent variable, we must average across the levels of the other variable. Thus, to determine the effect of print size, we need to find a point halfway between the two levels of age at each level of print size. On the first small graph in Figure 9-9, these points are indicated by an x. You can see that a change from 10-point to 12-point print caused a decrease in the dependent variable (time). In the second small graph, an x has been drawn for each age by averaging across print sizes. The dependent variable also decreases with increased age.

Interactions

To determine whether the independent variables interact, we can ask whether the effect of print size is different for each age or, alternatively, whether the effect of age is different for each print size. The answer to the first question is that going from 10-point to 12-point causes a decrease in reading time for 8-year-old children but no difference for 12-year-olds. The answer to the second question is that the difference between reading times for the two ages is larger for 10-point print than for 12-point. These effects are illustrated in the two bottom graphs of Figure 9-9.

Figure 9-10 shows some other possible results for this experiment. Using the same procedure we have been discussing, answer the three questions for each graph.

This discussion has been limited to the simplest type of factorial experiment. When each factor has more than two levels, or when more than two factors are used, interpreting interactions becomes even more difficult, although the basic procedures for interpreting your results remain the same.

Inferential Statistics

To discuss the general logic of inferential statistics, let's return to the anxiety test scores for the ten feminist and ten nonfeminist women. To find out whether the two groups differed in anxiety level, we plotted frequency distributions and calculated means for each group. We found that the mean for the feminist group was 64.7 and for the nonfeminist group, 55.6. Is this

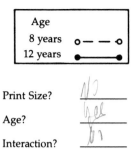

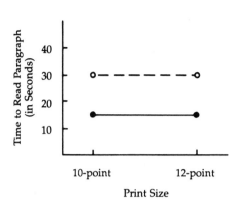

Print Size? _No_

Age? _yes_

Interaction? _no_

10-point   12-point

Print Size

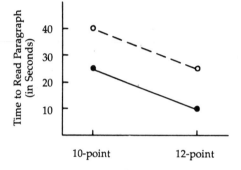

Print Size? _yes_

Age? _yes_

Interaction? _No_

10-point   12-point

Print Size

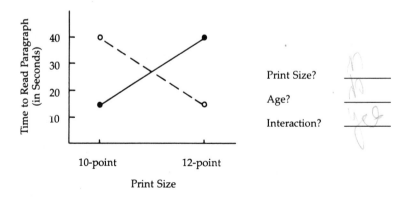

Print Size? _n_

Age? _no_

Interaction? _yes_

10-point   12-point

Print Size

Figure 9-10. Graphs of three possible outcomes for a 2 × 2 factorial experiment. Answer the three questions for each graph. (The answers can be found at the end of the chapter.)

a real difference? Of course it is, you say: how can a difference not be a difference? And for these two samples you are absolutely correct: any difference between samples is a real difference between samples. However, what a psychologist means by the question is not "Is there a real difference between the scores for the two samples that you happened to choose for this experiment?" but rather "Is it likely that there is a difference in anxiety level between the population of feminist women and the population of nonfeminist women who could have potentially been sampled?" The goal of the experiment is to say something about the two populations that could have been chosen, not just the particular samples that were.

Pretend that you are a bean farmer. You are not doing very well as a bean farmer because of bean blight. Bean blight is a mysterious bean disease that causes many beans to wither and shrivel. To find out whether you can get rid of bean blight, you plant a field with a new type of bean that may resist the blight. After harvesting a blighted field and the new field, you have two bean bins each containing 10 tons of beans. You want to know if both bean bins are blighted.* You obviously do not wish to examine every bean in the two bins, so you decide to take a sample of 100 beans from each bin. You find 12 withered beans in the sample from the bin you know to contain blighted beans and 7 in the other sample. Obviously there is a difference between the samples, but you want to know whether there is a difference between the entire populations of the two bins. An **inferential statistical** test can help you answer this question. The "infer" in "inferential" denotes that the test helps you infer whether there is a difference between the populations.

You, as a psychologist, face the same problem that you would face as a bean farmer. You have chosen a randomly selected sample of data from two potentially different populations (the levels of the independent variable), and you want to know whether the behavior of the populations differs.

Parametric Versus Nonparametric Tests

Many inferential tests are available to help you make this decision. The one you choose depends on your experimental design and what test assumptions your data can meet. (See Appendix A for worked examples of some inferential tests.) The most frequently used tests are called **parametric tests.** These tests assume that if frequency distributions were plotted for the populations of interest, they would be normal distributions. When this assumption cannot be met, you must use **nonparametric tests.**

Different inferential tests use somewhat different procedures for making inferences about populations. However, all tests that infer whether populations are the same provide a probabilistic statement about the likelihood that two or more samples could have come from the same population. In

*Say that quickly three times!

other words, such tests determine the probability that the observed difference among your data samples is due simply to chance variation. Any time that you randomly choose samples from the same population, it is possible, even though unlikely, to get a large difference. How unlikely must a difference be before you can conclude that the samples come from different populations?

Levels of Significance

Although it is probably unfortunate that we adhere to such a strict standard, most psychologists agree that, for a result to be significant, the likelihood of obtaining the observed difference in samples due to chance should be less than 1 in 20. Thus, if the samples really came from the same population distribution, you would expect to get a significant difference in only 1 out of 20 (or 5 out of 100) experiments. Some psychologists are even more careful to avoid saying that there is a difference between populations when there isn't. They will not accept a difference as a real difference unless the test indicates that it could be due to chance only 1 time in 100. These strategies are called testing at the **.05 level of significance** or at the **.01 level of significance.** When these probabilities are reached or exceeded, the result is said to be **statistically significant.**

When reading a journal article, you will see these levels of significance referred to as $p < .05$ or $p < .01$. This means that the test was found to be statistically significant at the .05 or the .01 level, so that you would expect this difference in the levels of the independent variable five times out of 100 or one time out of 100 if they actually came from the same population. Be sure to notice which way the sign is pointing; $p > .05$ means that the test was not found to be significant.

Inferential tests are obviously an important tool for evaluating the results of psychology experiments. In fact, the development of sophisticated statistical tests has been a major influence in making psychology into a respectable science. However, we must realize the limitations of inferential tests.

Misinterpreting Statistical Tests

Some experimenters believe that when a statistical test fails to show a significant difference in the levels of the independent variable, it has therefore shown that they are significantly the same. To avoid this error, we should keep in mind that inferential tests are designed to say something about the probability of getting a difference if the samples come from the same population; they tell us nothing about getting a sameness if the samples come from different populations. Consequently, negative results (ones that are not statistically significant) are seldom published in psychology journals. Our statistical tests are just not designed to tell us the probability that two samples would be this equivalent if they came from different populations; rather they tell us how probable it is that samples could come from the same population.

A second mistake some investigators make when using inferential tests is to act as though the .05 and .01 levels are chiseled in stone; they wouldn't be caught dead paying any attention to a .06 level. A more realistic approach to significance levels is to treat them for what they are—a way to help you make a decision. Whenever you make a decision in the face of uncertainty, you have to consider not only the probability of being right or wrong but also the values and costs of being right and wrong. In other decisions you do not ignore these factors. For example, if you are deciding whether to fly an airplane, you probably require a higher probability of fair weather than if you are simply deciding whether to carry an umbrella. The values and costs are far different. The .05 and .01 levels ignore such values and costs. Thus, you should consider the consequences of being right or wrong when you interpret the results of your experiments and not blindly test at the .05 level.

There is some controversy in psychology about whether the term *significant* should ever be modified—for example, by saying "highly significant." Some argue that the use of such modifiers is wrong because the tradition in psychology is to dichotomize results as *significant* or *nonsignificant* and, more importantly, that the use of modifiers mistakenly substitutes the size of importance of the effect for the probability of an effect (Harcum, 1989, Levenson, 1990). However, others argue that because probability is a continuum, there is nothing wrong with saying that one effect is more significant than another (Kanekar, 1990). Those on both sides of this argument would probably agree that the key is to avoid mistaking the level of statistical significance for practical significance, the issue we have just been discussing. For this reason, when reporting a positive result it is best to say that it is *statistically significant* to emphasize that you are not necessarily claiming practical significance. And when reporting a negative result say that it is *statistically nonsignificant* rather than insignificant. The term *insignificant* certainly does imply unimportant.

A third error you should avoid is confusing statistical significance with practical significance. Remember the fine old saying that a difference is a difference only if it makes a difference. Suppose you are an employer, and the owners of the Fast Finger Speed Reading School are trying to convince you that you should pay them to teach all your employees how to speed-read. They say that they have experimental evidence showing that people read significantly faster after taking their course. Being a skeptic, you ask how much faster. They admit that the study shows that their students read an average of half a word per minute faster, but they insist that this difference is statistically significant. They could well be correct. By using enough subjects and collecting enough data, even tiny differences between populations can be shown to be statistically significant. As an employer, though, you care more about practical significance than statistical significance. As a scientist, you should, too.

In the end, evaluating practical significance is a matter of judgment. The tools discussed in this chapter should help you determine when a result is important, but the tools do not establish the importance of the result. You, the experimenter, must do this by using logical arguments to convince other researchers that your differences make a difference.

Using Computers to Help Interpret Results

Computers can be used in many areas of psychological experimentation such as conducting literature searches, presenting stimuli, and recording responses. However, the most widespread use of computers is helping with statistical data analysis. Computers are particularly valuable for this task because they can quickly store and manipulate large sets of numbers. In recent years the cost of computer equipment has decreased and sophisticated statistical programs have become available. These changes have led to increased opportunities in colleges and universities for using computers to do data analysis.

Hardware

In computer terminology **hardware** refers to the actual machines that are used in the computing process, such as central processing units, disks, and printers. There are basically two types of hardware systems: mainframes and micro- or mini-computers. A mainframe is a large, high-speed machine, usually placed in a central location, that can be used to process "batches" of data, from small to very large sets. A number of formats can be used for entering data into mainframe computers, such as cards, tapes, disks, or terminals. While the actual time to do the data analysis for a typical psychology experiment on a mainframe computer is only a couple of seconds or less, the turn-around time can be considerably longer because your analysis might have to wait in line for a turn at the machine.

Many micro- or mini-computers, such as the IBM PC or Macintosh, now have the storage capability and speed to do statistical data analysis for a typical psychology experiment. While the time to complete an analysis will be longer on such a computer, the total turn-around time is often faster than for a mainframe because the computer is *dedicated* to one task at a time, and your job will not have to wait in line. Also, the smaller machines are more often set up in an *interactive* mode rather than in a *batch* mode. This means that the machine will execute commands immediately, provide the results, and sometimes prompt the user for additional instructions or data rather than requiring that all of the data and commands be entered in one batch. The interactive mode has the obvious advantage of allowing the user to immediately correct any errors and to quickly submit additional analyses if needed.

Software

Software refers to the computer programs that tell the hardware what to do with the data. While not all software can be executed on all machines, a particular software program usually can be run on a class of machines. There are so many software programs available for analyzing data and displaying it that any attempt to give a comprehensive list would be doomed to failure and would be quickly outmoded. The following list provides you with the names of software packages most frequently used in psychology:

> SPSS-X (Statistical Package for the Social Sciences)
> SAS (Statistical Analysis System)
> BMDP (BioMedical Computer Programs)
> Minitab
> Statement SIZT
> Statmarks
> Tadpole
> StatWorks
> SYSTAT

Some of these packages may be available either in your psychology department or your computer center. Also some of the smaller packages are affordable, particularly for students who have discounts available in their schools.

Entering Data

The amount of drudge work required to analyze data has certainly decreased through the years as paper and pencil computation has been replaced by mechanical and electronic calculators and then by computers. However, just because the manual effort necessary has been eased, do not be misled into thinking that the mental effort has also lessened. If you put your mind on hold and bumble your way through data analysis, all the computer will do is allow you to make a fool of yourself—with less effort. The old computer saying of "garbage in, garbage out" certainly applies here. When using a computer to analyze your data you must continue to remember the lessons about interpreting results that you have learned in this chapter. Also you need to know the assumptions and limitations of the various statistical manipulations that you might use (see Appendix A).

You should consult the appropriate user manual to find the precise steps necessary for signing onto your particular computer, entering data, and calling up the statistical programs you want to use. However, there are some steps that will be necessary regardless of the program you will be using. At some point, you will need to systematically enter the data that you have collected into the computer. The data, of course, will consist of the scores of a dependent variable. These must be arranged with respect to the levels of your independent variable or variables and your subjects. Suppose, for example, that you have completed an experiment in which 8- and 12-year-old children were asked to read four paragraphs printed in small (9-point) or large (12-point) type. Let us assume that you took proper precautions through counterbalancing or randomization to counteract possible confounding variables such as the order of presentation. You timed in seconds how long it took each child to read each paragraph and produced the following data set:

	8-year-olds			
Small Type	*Para. 1*	*Para. 2*	*Para. 3*	*Para. 4*
Subject 1	72 sec.	87 sec.	84 sec.	70 sec.
Subject 2	92 sec.	94 sec.	86 sec.	86 sec.
Subject 3	68 sec.	88 sec.	70 sec.	84 sec.
Subject 4	79 sec.	89 sec.	81 sec.	87 sec.
Large Type	*Para. 1*	*Para. 2*	*Para. 3*	*Para. 4*
Subject 1	83 sec.	80 sec.	88 sec.	95 sec.
Subject 2	87 sec.	98 sec.	95 sec.	92 sec.
Subject 3	75 sec.	72 sec.	86 sec.	87 sec.
Subject 4	92 sec.	90 sec.	99 sec.	85 sec.
	12-year-olds			
Small Type	*Para. 1*	*Para. 2*	*Para. 3*	*Para. 4*
Subject 1	56 sec.	59 sec.	67 sec.	62 sec.
Subject 2	65 sec.	62 sec.	72 sec.	68 sec.
Subject 3	73 sec.	61 sec.	65 sec.	62 sec.
Subject 4	48 sec.	56 sec.	55 sec.	58 sec.
Large Type	*Para. 1*	*Para. 2*	*Para. 3*	*Para. 4*
Subject 1	68 sec.	72 sec.	76 sec.	66 sec.
Subject 2	88 sec.	79 sec.	86 sec.	81 sec.
Subject 3	77 sec.	73 sec.	84 sec.	71 sec.
Subject 4	74 sec.	63 sec.	65 sec.	65 sec.

Obviously, the numbers from this data set will have to be entered into the computer one at a time. Thus, they will form a long number stream or **vector.** For example, if you started with the upper left and read downward, the number string would be: 72, 92, 68, 79, 83, 87, . . . Until you tell the computer how to interpret these numbers, it will not know how to put them into a **matrix** (such as the one shown on page 156) with the proper format. For some statistical packages you give the computer this information by specifying the order in which variables are being read. For our number string, which variable is being entered first? That is, for which variable do you read through the levels while holding the levels of the other variables constant? The first number, 72 sec., is for: Subject 1, small type, an 8-year-old, reading paragraph 1. The next one, 92, is for: Subject 2, small type, an 8-year-old, reading paragraph 1. Thus, subjects is the first variable being entered. After entering the numbers for the first four subjects, what variable is next in order? After 79—the reading time for subject 4, small type, an 8-year-old, reading paragraph 1—comes 83, for subject 1, large type, an 8-year-old, reading paragraph 1. So you have now moved to another level of type size—the second variable being entered. Examine the data matrix assuming that once the entire left column is completed, the column for paragraph 2 is read from top to bottom, and so on. You should discover that the order in which the variables are read is subjects, type size, age, and finally paragraph number.

While there are some variations, many computer programs require that you specify the order of the variables in a fashion similar to that in the example, so that a matrix can be set up exactly like the data set being entered. A small mistake here will make the entire data analysis useless. For instance, if you accidentally told the computer that the order of variables in our example was type size, subjects, age, and paragraph number, it would correctly interpret the first entry 72 to mean that it took 72 seconds for a small-type paragraph to be read by subject 1 who is 8 years old and reading paragraph one. However, it would then interpret 92 incorrectly to mean that it took 92 seconds for a large-type paragraph to be read by subject 1 who is 8 years old and reading paragraph 1. In fact, every number except the first (and last) would be misinterpreted and the analysis would, indeed, be garbage!

For some programs, rather than specifying the identity of each datum by telling the computer about the order of entry, a code is attached to each datum as it is entered. For example, as the number 72 was entered it might be identified by calling it 1, 1, 1, 1, meaning it represents subject 1, print size 1 (small), age level 1 (8-year-olds), and paragraph 1. The next number, 92, would receive the code 2, 1, 1, 1. In this way the computer would be able to arrange the numbers on the basis of any variable specified as long as the computer has been given the key to the code used.

You will also be required to tell the computer about the design of your experiment in order for it to know the proper analysis to select. For instance, in our example, the computer would not know whether subject 1 is the same person throughout the data set, or a different person; that is, whether you used between-subjects variables or within-subject variables. You may think it is obvious that subject 1 cannot be both 8 years old and 12 years old, but, while computers are great number crunchers, they have no common sense at all! Thus, in addition to telling the computer in what order to read your variables you must also inform it about which variables are manipulated between-subjects and which within-subject. Exactly how you do this will depend on the program you are using. In some cases, you can simply tell the computer the names of the variables that are within-subject and between-subjects. In other cases, you will be required to enter all within-subject variables before the between-subjects variables. If the program required the data to be identified by a code, then the computer must be told which code refers to one type of variable or the other.

Reading the Output

I remember the first time I picked up the output of a computerized data analysis. It was a fifty-page stack of perforated paper containing so many numbers that I didn't know where to begin searching for the result of the test. Part of my problem was that I was not familiar enough with the statistical test I was using to know what the outcome should look like. For this reason most instructors insist that their students calculate statistics by hand several times before turning to computers for help.

The output for an inferential data analysis will usually contain the following parts:

- a cover page or pages stating what program was run
- the set of instructions you gave the computer indicating the order of your variables and any information about the experimental design
- the data set
- some descriptive statistics, such as means and standard deviations for the levels of the various variables
- a table with the results of the statistical tests performed

Some of these parts can be suppressed with appropriate instructions, but you will probably want most of them for your records. It is okay to sneak a look at the final table to see if anything is statistically significant, but before you believe the table you should do some consistency checks to determine if the analysis was done properly.

Sometimes, to inexperienced users, computers seem to possess magical qualities that make them seem infallible. The computer takes all of those large sets of numbers, arranges them in various ways, waves a statistical magic wand, and presents the results printed in a neat orderly table. It doesn't seem possible that this pretty table may contain garbage. Actually, it is unlikely that the computer has made a mistake. It is much more likely that the source of any error has been a failure to communicate. The computer may have misunderstood the user (probably because the user failed to use the computer's strict little rules). The message here is that before you believe the output, make a number of checks to determine whether the computer did what you intended it to do.

Suppose we are checking the output for the data set in our paragraph-reading example. We have asked the computer to do an analysis of variance having the factors of age, print size, paragraph number, and subjects. (See Appendix A or a statistics book for a more detailed discussion of this test.) The result of an analysis of variance is an F value for each of the main effects and interactions. If you did the test by hand you would have to take the F value and compare it to numbers in a table to determine whether it is statistically significant. However, the computer will have already done this for you and will report not only the size of the F but also the value of p, the probability or level of statistical significance that has been exceeded. Assuming that we have followed procedures well enough that the program has run to completion, the first thing to check is whether the summary table contains the anticipated number of main effects and interactions. Next we might check to make sure that the numbers for the degrees of freedom for the test are appropriate. For instance, when using an F test, the first number in the degrees of freedom statement for a main effect should be the number of levels of the variable minus one (e.g., for four levels of paragraph, the first number in the degrees of freedom statement should be 3).

Next some of the descriptive statistics can be examined or plotted in a graph to see if the results are logical. For instance, in our example we would expect that the mean time to read paragraphs for 8-year-olds would be longer than for 12-year-olds. We would be wary of the analysis if such logical expectations were not upheld. As a final check we should calculate some means for a small part of the data by hand to see whether the result agrees with the computerized output. In the example we might decide to compute a mean for 8-year-olds reading paragraph 1 in small type by simply adding the numbers for the four subjects and dividing by 4. This result could then be compared to the one listed in the output. Several such small computations would require only a couple of minutes but would greatly increase our confidence that the output is correct.

I hope this general discussion of the use of computers for interpreting experimental results has put the role of computers in perspective. Computers and statistical packages are simply tools that can be used to make data interpretation easier. There is no reason why computers should strike fear in your heart. They are your *friends* and getting friendlier all the time. But, as with all complex tools, care should be taken to make sure that they are being used correctly. These computer friends are not at all flexible and require you to compulsively follow their rules. They believe what you say, even when you are wrong, and they have no common sense for determining when you are wrong. In order to stay out of trouble, you should understand their limitations as well as their capabilities.

Summary

Once you complete an experiment, you must interpret the data listed on the subjects' response sheets. A useful first step is to plot a **frequency distribution** illustrating the number of data points occurring within categories of the dependent variable. Sometimes these distributions are similar to a symmetrical bell-shaped distribution called a **normal distribution.** Others are **bimodal** with two most frequent categories, **skewed** by having more scores in one tail of the distribution, or **truncated** by having one tail of the distribution missing. Three commonly used statistics describe the central tendency or average of a distribution: the **mode** is the most frequently occurring category, the **median** is the middle score, and the **mean** is the center of gravity for the distribution. Two statistics are commonly used to describe the **dispersion** of a distribution: the **range** is the difference between the highest and lowest scores, and the **standard deviation** and sometimes the **variance** describe the dispersion of distributions that are approximately normal.

Graphs illustrate the relationship between the independent and dependent variables. The levels of the independent variable are put on the horizontal axis, the **abscissa,** while the values of the dependent variable are put on the vertical axis, the **ordinate.** A **bar graph** can be used to illustrate data points that represent qualitatively different categories. Either a **histogram** or a **functional line graph** can be used to illustrate continuous variables. In describing functions, you can indicate whether they are **linear** or **curvilinear, positive** or **negative, monotonic** or **nonmonotonic, positively accelerated** or **negatively accelerated,** or **asymptotic.** The strength of an experimental relationship can be illustrated in a **scatterplot,** or, if the relationship is linear, you can calculate a **correlation coefficient.**

To interpret the results of a factorial experiment, you must determine whether there is an effect of one factor on the dependent variable at an average value of the other factors. In addition to determining this **main effect,** you must also determine whether the effect of one variable is different depending on the levels of the other variables. Such differences are called **interactions.**

Inferential statistics are used to infer how likely it is that the difference between data samples is due to chance selection rather than due to a real difference in populations (levels of the independent variable). For an effect to be declared **statistically significant,** the probability that the difference is due to chance usually must exceed **.05** or **.01. Parametric tests** assume that population distributions are normal; **nonparametric** tests do not. Researchers sometimes misuse statistical tests by equating nonsignificant results with equivalence of conditions, by overemphasizing the .05 and .01 levels of significance, or by confusing statistical significance with practical significance.

Computers can often be used to help with the interpretation of experimental results through computerized data analysis. The **hardware** available on most campuses includes both mainframe computers and micro- or mini-computers. Many **software** packages or programs are available that calculate descriptive and inferential statistics on databases. Care must be taken when entering data to ensure that the computer converts the **vector** or number string into an appropriate data **matrix**. The output must be checked for internal consistency and accuracy before it can be accepted.

Answers to the questions in Figure 9-10:

Top graph:	Print size?	*no*
	Age?	*yes*
	Interaction?	*no*
Middle graph:	Print size?	*yes*
	Age?	*yes*
	Interaction?	*no*
Bottom graph:	Print size?	*no*
	Age?	*no*
	Interaction?	*yes*

References

Campbell, S. K. (1974). *Flaws and fallacies in statistical thinking.* Englewood Cliffs, NJ: Prentice-Hall.

Harcum, E. R. (1989). The highly inappropriate calibrations of statistical significance. *American Psychologist, 44,* 964.

Huff, D. (1954). *How to lie with statistics.* New York: Norton.

Kanekar, S. (1990). Statistical significance as a continuum. *American Psychologist, 45,* 296.

Kirk, R. E. (1990). *Statistics: An introduction.* Fort Worth: Holt, Rinehart & Winston.

Levenson, R. L., Jr. (1990). Comment on Harcum. *American Psychologist, 45,* 295–296.

Nelson, N., Rosenthal, R., & Rosnow, R. L. (1986). Interpretation of significance levels and effect sizes by psychological researchers. *American Psychologist, 41,* 1299–1301.

Suggested Books on Statistics

For the beginning student

Kirk, R. E. (1990). *Statistics: An introduction.* Fort Worth: Holt, Rinehart & Winston.

Hinkle, D. E., Wiersma, W., & Jurs, S. G. (1988). *Applied statistics for the behavioral sciences.* Boston: Houghton Mifflin.

For the advanced student

Keppel, G., & Zeddeck, S. (1989). *Data analysis for research designs: Analysis of variance and multiple regression/correlation approaches.* New York: Freeman.

Maxwell, S. E., & Delaney, H. D. (1990). *Designing experiments and analyzing data: A model comparison perspective.* Belmont, CA: Wadsworth.

Myers, R. H. (1971). *Response surface methodology.* Boston: Allyn and Bacon.

10
How to Report Experimental Results

Research is complete only when the results are shared with the scientific community.*

The [scientific] writer quite properly reacts to the pressure toward conformity with the writing practices of his group, but he errs if he succumbs abjectly. He needs to qualify and to define exactly, but the danger is that his sentences can become so impossibly larded with subordinate phrases and clauses that even his close associates cannot read them.†

We are all blind seekers after truth
Confused by the noisy rabble of words
Whether we shall ever say what we mean
Or mean what we say
We know not,
And only our doing
Will teach us in its hour.‡

There was a classic philosophical debate a few decades back that went something like this: If a tree falls in the forest and nobody is there to hear it, did it make a sound? The debate was whether a person had to hear a sound for the sound to be a sound. What do you think? In reporting research, we can ask a similar question: Is research research if nobody hears about it? The metaphysical answer to either question depends on how you want to define the terms; because we are concerned with a practical answer, we can at least say that unreported research might as well not have been done. The ultimate goal of research is not doing experiments but building a scientific body of knowledge. If other scientists do not know about your experiments, your results cannot be used as building blocks. The experimental report is the way to make your results public so that science can benefit from your research.

Because your experimental report is the product of your research, you should try to make it a high-quality product. While an elegantly written experimental report cannot save a bad piece of research, a poorly written

*American Psychological Association (1983). *Publication Manual of the American Psychological Association* (3rd ed.). Washington, D.C.: Author, p. 17.
†Schindler, G. E. Why engineers and scientists write as they do—Twelve characteristics of their prose. *IEEE Transactions on Engineering Writing and Speech*, 1967, EWS-10, p. 32.
‡Decker, B. (1967). Words about words, I. Pessimistic. *Journal of Creative Behavior, 1*, p. 34. Published by the Creative Education Foundation, Buffalo, NY. Reprinted by permission.

report can effectively destroy a good piece of research. I know researchers who, based on informal discussions of their research, seem to do well-thought-out experiments on important problems, but their ability to communicate on paper is so poor that their work is unknown. Much good research is probably lost this way.

Even instructors in writing courses have a difficult time teaching people how to write orderly thoughts. I do not have enough room in this chapter to teach you much about writing in general.* The most concise instructions I have seen for writing appeared in *The New York Times Magazine* (November 4, 1979, pp. 16–18), by William Safire. Here they are:

> . . . Remember to never split an infinitive. The passive voice should never be used. Do not put statements in the negative form. Verbs has to agree with their subjects. Proofread carefully to see if you any words out. If you reread your work, you will find on rereading that a great deal of repetition can be avoided by rereading and editing. A writer must not shift your point of view. And don't start a sentence with a conjunction. Don't overuse exclamation marks!!! Place pronouns as close as possible, especially in long sentences, as of 10 or more words, to their antecedents. Writing carefully, dangling participles must be avoided. If any word is improper at the end of a sentence, a linking verb is. Take the bull by the hand and avoid mixed metaphors. Avoid trendy locutions that sound flaky. Everyone should be careful to use a singular pronoun with singular nouns in their writing. Always pick on the correct idiom. The adverb always follows the verb. Last but not least, avoid cliches like the plague: seek viable alternatives.

The goal of this chapter is quite limited. I will describe the parts of a research report, and give you some suggestions for determining whether what you write is readable, and provide an annotated sample report.

Experimental reports should convey information efficiently. With this guideline in mind, the American Psychological Association (1983) has compiled a set of rules for writing an experimental report: the *Publication Manual of the American Psychological Association.* A well-thumbed copy of this publication should sit on every experimental psychologist's desk. Even if you are writing an experimental report as a class project, you should follow the general guidelines in the *Publication Manual.* While we obviously cannot discuss all of the topics covered in the 208 pages of the manual, I will mention the most important rules and point out where new investigators often make mistakes.

Parts of a Report

All experimental reports should contain certain standard sections in proper order. Otherwise we would have to be like the old minister who said of his sermons: "First I tell 'em what I'm gonna tell 'em, then I tell 'em, then I tell

---

*If you seem to have a difficult time with your writing you might find Strunk and White's book *Elements of Style,* 3rd edition helpful.

'em what I told 'em." Experimental reports all follow a standard pattern, so we do not need to use much space "telling 'em what we're gonna tell 'em." Not only does the standardized structure improve writing efficiency, but the consistent organization also allows the reader interested in only one section, such as the method or results, to quickly find that information. The parts of a report are listed in the following outline and described in the following sections:

I. Title page
   A. Title
   B. Author(s)
   C. Affiliation(s)
   D. Running head
II. Abstract page
III. Body of report
   A. Introduction
      1. Background
      2. Literature review
      3. Statement of purpose
   B. Method
      1. Subjects
      2. Apparatus/Materials
      3. Procedure
   C. Results
      1. Verbal statement of results
      2. Insert statements for tables and figures
      3. Descriptive and inferential statistics
   D. Discussion
      1. Relationship between stated purpose and results
      2. Theoretical or methodological contribution
      3. Future directions for research
IV. References
V. Author notes (if any)
VI. Footnotes (if any)
VII. Tables
VIII. Figure captions
IX. Figures

Title

During the first two months after publication, about half the research reports in major psychology journals are likely to be read by fewer than 200 psychologists (Garvey & Griffith, 1971). The people who do read a report have probably selected it because of the **title,** most psychologists regularly scan the title pages of several journals looking for current research that might interest them. Most of the key words used in a literature search (Chapter

3) are also chosen from the title. Thus, in some respects, the title is the most important part of your report; if your title conveys little information or the wrong information, you may lose most readers even before they know what you did.

The two most helpful suggestions for creating a title are contradictory: (1) Put in as much information as possible. (2) Make it as short as possible. Most titles should mention the major independent variables of interest and the dependent variable. You should also identify the general area of research if it is not obvious from the variables. The *Publication Manual* says that titles should be no longer than 12 to 15 words. Most titles should be considerably shorter than this.*

One way to create a title is to start with a long version and then eliminate words until you are absolutely unwilling to shorten it any further. As an example, suppose we needed a title for the print-size experiment discussed earlier. As a first step we might start with this: *An experiment examining the effect of the size of print on the time to read a standard paragraph for children of various ages.* Now let's shorten it. We can immediately eliminate "An experiment examining the effect of . . . ," because these words give the reader no new information. We can also eliminate most of the prepositions (of, on, to, for) by rearranging the words. In this case, it is also more efficient to identify the specific levels of the independent variable (8- and 12-year-olds) than to use a general descriptor (children of various ages). After a little work, the title might read: *Print size and reading speed of 8- and 12-year-olds.* This title contains most of the original information but is certainly much shorter.

The use of a colon in the title can often shorten it and allow words to be eliminated. If you examine the titles in the references at the end of every chapter in this book, you will find many examples of this. For example, at the end of Chapter 4 is a title by Johnson, "Pupillary responses during a short-term memory task: Cognitive processing, arousal, or both?" Without

---

*Although I have no evidence to back it up, it seems to me that, in general, the better known the article, the shorter the title. Perhaps this effect is due to the memory span of the reader, or maybe good writers work at creating short titles. Perhaps I should have called this book *Book*.

the colon it would be longer: for example, "Are pupillary responses during a short-term memory task an indication of cognitive processing, arousal, or both?" At the end of Chapter 5 is an article by Greenwald entitled "Within-subjects designs: To use or not to use?" He could have opted for "Should within-subjects designs be used or not?" In this case, the use of a colon does not shorten the title, but it does allow a more interesting, Shakespeareanesque version of the question.

Authors and Institution

After the title, list the **author** or authors, followed by the **institution** where the research was done. When there are multiple authors, list only those who have made substantial scientific contributions to the study. People who have simply helped collect or analyze some of the data should be acknowledged in a footnote rather than listed as authors. Generally, the person who took primary responsibility for the research will also write the research report and should be listed as the first author. When several authors have made equal contributions, the order is sometimes determined by tossing a coin. When several reports are produced by the same team of investigators, first authorships are often passed around.

Abstract

The **abstract** is the second most important part of the report. Once readers choose your paper because the title is of interest, they will next read the abstract, either in the journal or in *Psychological Abstracts*. Like a door-to-door salesperson, the title may get your foot in the door, but the abstract can get you an invitation into the house.

The abstract should be a condensed version of the complete report. Most investigators wait to write the abstract until the rest of the paper is finished, although it appears immediately after the title in the final report. In 100 to 150 words, you should introduce the problem, name the variables, briefly present the method, mention the important results, and discuss the

implications of the results. As you can see, you must cover a lot of information in only a few words. Again, you may find it useful to write a long first draft and then start eliminating unnecessary information and parts of speech. Make sure that the abstract is still comprehensible and contains complete sentences (unlike a title). If the abstract is still too long after this first editing, you will have to make some choices about the relative importance of the remaining information, eliminating the least important material until your abstract meets the length requirements.

Some investigators treat titles and abstracts as afterthoughts. They dash them off after having taken great pains with the body of the paper. In this discussion, I have tried to convince you that the title and abstract are the two most important parts of your experimental report. Give them your best effort.

Introduction

The **introduction** is used to describe the current state of the body of knowledge. Because it is always the first section of the body of the report, you don't need a heading. You should assume that the reader has some familiarity with your area of research, so you only need to mention the few experiments most relevant to the one you have done. When you cite an experiment, only give the author's name and date of the article in the report body and give the complete citation in the references section.* Describe these key experiments in just enough detail to set the stage for your experiment. A good introduction is a mini-literature review that leaves your readers with the feeling that they know what experiment should be done next—the one you did.

---

*A note about how to cite experiments: For one author, just give the author's name and the date of the article: "Jones (1967) found . . . " or "It was found (Jones, 1967) . . ." For two authors, use both last names: "Jones and Smith (1971) found . . . ," or "It was found (Jones & Smith, 1971) that . . ." For more than two authors, use all of the names the first time you cite the research and the first author's name followed by "et al." thereafter: "Johnson et al. (1972) also found . . ."

After reviewing the supporting literature, you should state the purpose or object of your experiment. This statement should specify the relationship between the independent and dependent variables that you investigated. For example: "The purpose of this experiment was to determine if print size would have the same effect on reading speed for 8-year-olds as for 12-year-olds." If you can predict the outcome of the experiment from the literature review or from a theoretical argument, do so here. You must explain the logic behind your prediction, however, because the purpose of predicting an outcome is to make the results easier to interpret later in the report. If your prediction is an unsupportable hunch, don't waste the reader's time.

Method

At this point, your readers should know why you did what you did. Now you must tell them what you did. The **method** section should contain enough detail so that the reader could replicate your experiment. However, you must use your judgment about which details are relevant to the experimental outcome. For example, in the print-size experiment, you would not need to specify the exact dimensions of the room in which the paragraphs were read, although you would certainly specify the dimensions of the paper each paragraph was typed on. Because it is impossible to mention each circumstance from the infinite set of circumstances, you should limit yourself to those that could logically have been expected to influence the results.

The method section is usually divided into several subsections. A typical report has three subsections, although you may wish to use additional subsections if your experiment calls for more.

Subjects The **subjects*** subsection should specify who the subjects were. Were they students, pilots, children? What sex were they? How many subjects did you use, and how did you select them? (Were they volunteers? Were they satisfying a class requirement? Were they paid?) If you eliminated the data for any subjects (see Chapter 14), you should indicate the basis for this decision. For animal subjects, be sure to report their genus and species along with their age and sex.

Apparatus/Materials The **apparatus/materials** subsection should describe the equipment or materials you used in your experiment. If you used a standard psychological apparatus, you need only give the general name, the manufacturer, and the model number ("A Scientific Prototype two-channel tachistoscope, Model 800-F, was used"). Describe any custom-built apparatus in enough detail so that the reader could construct a similar

---

*When reading experimental reports published prior to 1974, you will see the word **subject** abbreviated as **S** and **experimenter** as **E**. These abbreviations are no longer acceptable. In fact, you should try to use a more descriptive word than subjects if possible, such as "students," "children," or "rats."

apparatus ("The slides were back-projected on a Plexiglas panel 15 cm high and 20 cm wide, mounted vertically 30 cm from the subject").* Be sure to make a note of all the measurements at the time you do the experiment. Reconstructing these details after the experiment is often difficult and sometimes impossible.

Procedure The **procedure** subsection should specify exactly what happened to each subject during the experiment. When writing this section, imagine that your naive, innocent subject has just walked into the experimental room. What happens from that point on? What instructions were the subjects given? Usually these can be paraphrased unless they were a major part of the experimental manipulation. What events happened during a trial, in what order, and with what timing? How many trials were presented? Were they in blocks or sessions? Were trials randomized or counterbalanced? Exactly what was measured, and how was it measured and recorded? What type of experimental design did you use? Why did you choose to use the procedure described?

The procedure section is one of the most difficult sections to write well because you have become intimately familiar with each detail, and the procedure now seems so obvious and straightforward to you. By all means have someone who has no idea what you did read the procedure section and then tell you in his or her own words what you did. Then correct any false impressions and try it with someone else. Eventually the two accounts will correspond and at that point the procedure section is complete.

Results

You should report the results of most experiments using one or more descriptive statistics. Provide raw data only when illustrating a general finding or when showing the results of baseline experiments. Whenever you report a measure of central tendency, such as the mean, you should usually include a measure of dispersion as well, such as the standard deviation. If you mention only a few measures, you can include them in the text: "The response times for the 1-, 2-, and 4-sec foreperiods were 350, 362, and 391 ms, respectively." However, use a table or figure when you must report many measures.

Investigators typically use tables to show the results of main effects and to give exact values of the dependent variable when these are important. You should type tables on separate pages from the text, with the instruction "Insert Table 1 about here" typed in the text to indicate the approximate location for the table. The short sample report at the end of this chapter shows how a table should be organized. For specific problems, refer to the *Publication Manual*.

---

*Report all measurements in metric units. If the object was manufactured in nonmetric units, report them as such but insert the metric equivalents in parentheses ("The panel was 3 ft [0.91 m] in width.").

Use figures sparingly, for they are even more costly to draw and print than are tables.* As we saw in Chapter 9, however, figures are a great way to show interactions and to illustrate trends in the data. In most cases, figures are preferable to tables. Readers can generally extract and remember information better from figures than from tables. Here are some general rules to follow in drawing figures:

1. Label the abscissa and ordinate, and specify the units of measurement.[†]
2. Draw the ordinate about two-thirds as long as the abscissa.
3. Make 0 the smallest mark on the ordinate. If you must break the ordinate to save space (for example, if you have no response times between 0 and 0.3 second), indicate the break by a double slashed line at that point.
4. Use point and line codes (as in Figure 9-9) to indicate those independent variables not listed on the abscissa. Make these codes consistent throughout the report. Do not rely on different colors to make your distinctions. Colors should be used only in coloring books!
5. Draw your figures on pages separate from the text, and indicate the location of figures by putting "Insert Figure 1 about here" in the text.

These rules are designed to help you make your results clear and to minimize the possibility of distortion. You may find, however, that you will need to bend them occasionally to keep from distorting your data.

It used to be that figures submitted to journals for formal publication had to be prepared by a professional draftsperson. Now computer programs make it possible for researchers to produce neat figures on their own. But be sure, if you do your own figures, that you use a good printer and that the line sizes and letter/number sizes are appropriate even if the figure must be reduced for publication.

The results of inferential statistical tests are reported in a standard way. For example, if the result of a t test[‡] done on two groups of ten subjects was 4.7, which you found to be significant at the .01 level, you would report it as follows: "The difference between groups was found to be significant, $\underline{t}$ (18) = 4.7, $\underline{p}$ < .01."[§] Report other tests in the same way, first stating the symbol for the test statistic (underlined if not a Greek letter), followed by the degrees of freedom in parentheses, an equals sign, the result of the test calculation, a comma, a lowercase $\underline{p}$ underlined for italic, a < sign (or, for

---

*A figure is any visual representation of data that cannot be set in standard type. Graphs are the most common figures in experimental reports.

[†]New investigators commonly forget this step. To avoid this error, set a rule for yourself that you will never put in a data point until you have labeled the axes.

[‡]A t test is an inferential test that indicates whether the means of two samples are significantly different from each other. The result of a t test is a number. By comparing this number with other numbers listed in a table, you can determine if the means are statistically different at a particular probability level (for example, a probability level of .01, $p < .01$).

[§]The number in parentheses is the degrees of freedom for the t test. Most statistical tests have a degrees-of-freedom term, either a single number or two numbers. You will find out how to determine this number when you learn those tests.

nonsignificant results, a $>$ sign), and finally the testing level. When the results of a statistical test are complex, you may want to put them in a table.

No interpretation of the results, other than information needed for clarification, should be done in the results section. The results section should be used for stating *what* you found; the discussion section is for explaining *why* you think you found what you found, and, in the standard format, never the twain should meet. In some cases, if the information can be presented more clearly or efficiently, it is legal to combine the results and discussion sections. If you do that, be sure to clearly use this heading: Results and Discussion Section.

Discussion

In your introduction you described what the body of knowledge consisted of and where it needed to be expanded. Your results section then provided a new building block.* You now have to describe how the new block fits the structure and how the new structure differs from the old. Thus, the **discussion** section is the place where you update the body of knowledge with your results.

In most cases the introduction section will have identified competing theories or stated hypotheses about what the outcome of the experiment might be. In the discussion section you should briefly review these theories and hypotheses and discuss whether your results support or refute them. If more than one theory or hypothesis can explain your results, you might suggest ways of testing these in future experiments.

This section is also the place to qualify your results, if necessary, and to speculate on the reasons for unpredicted findings (as long as you keep your speculations short and identify them as such). However, you should not waste the reader's time explaining effects that were not statistically significant. Only in rare cases should negative results be interpreted as due to anything other than chance.

*Or, in some cases, your experiment may have blasted away part of the existing structure.

Particularly if you are doing applied work, you should use the discussion section to point out the practical value of your results—how and where they can be used and how they might change current applied procedures.

Finally, you can use the discussion section to make suggestions about the direction of future research. Now that you have discussed the new state of the body of knowledge, you may be able to suggest where new expansion should take place.

References

Your **reference** section should list only those references cited in the report and should be ordered alphabetically by the first author's name. The references listed at the end of each chapter in this book and in the sample report follow the proper style and should provide you with many useful examples. For unusual references, refer to the *Publication Manual*.

Writing Style

Experimental reports are not intended to be literary masterpieces or entertaining monologues. Thus, your general writing style should not get in the way of smoothly flowing thoughts, nor should it bring more attention to you than to your research. To meet these requirements, scientific writing has evolved a standard style.

Traditionally, scientific writers have used third-person passive voice rather than first-person active. Instead of writing "I did this experiment to. . . ," the investigator would write "This experiment was done to. . . ." While this style did keep the report from reading like a letter home, it also forced out much of its life. The prose became dull and monotonous and caused the reader more pain than pleasure. Today it is considered proper to use the pronoun "I" to a limited extent: for example, "I thought that . . ." rather than "It was thought that. . . ." You should, however, avoid excessive use of "I" to keep from drawing the reader's attention to you rather than to the research. You should also try to use an active verb form rather than a passive form, especially when there are no pronoun problems—for example, "A previous report described a new method" rather than "In a previous report, a new method was described."* Again the general rule is to use words that make the writing come alive without interrupting the smooth flow of thoughts.

The context of a sentence will usually tell you which verb tense to use. Most sentences in the introduction and method sections refer to past actions

---

*Some writers may object to this form on the grounds that a report cannot describe—an author describes. I suppose writing is largely a matter of personal preference. In this case, I prefer to trade a little accuracy for a lot livelier style.

["Boles (1972) reported . . ." and "The subjects recalled the words . . ."].
On the other hand, results "are" and theory "is" even after the experiment
is completed. That is, the body of knowledge exists in the present and so
should be discussed using present-tense verbs ("These data support an
interference theory of forgetting").

Finally, scientific writing should be concise. The limited resources of
time and space simply do not allow us the luxury of excess verbiage. For
instance, the style I have used in this book would not be appropriate for
scientific writing.* I have purposely used more words than necessary because
I have tried to do more than transfer information; I have tried to convince,
cajole, and convert you as well as communicate with you. In scientific writing, you should assume that the reader has already been convinced, cajoled,
and converted; your only job then is to communicate.

The most common problem new investigators have with report writing
is laziness. The investigator is not really lazy, of course, because lazy people
do not do experiments, but his or her writing style may be lazy. In writing
a report, the most important end of your pencil is the one without the
point. Extremely rare is the person who can write a good, concise report
the first time through. Most good scientific writers have to try a number of
alternative words and sentence structures before deciding on the best one.
Every word must say precisely what you want it to say, and every sentence
should flow smoothly into the next. Writing this way is hard work!

When writing a report, most investigators first produce a draft of the
best version they are capable of writing. Getting the report to this point
may take two or three attempts, because it is often easier to rewrite whole
sections than to make corrections on top of corrections. Once you come up
with a final draft you are satisfied with, you should give it to several people
to read. At least one of these people should be unfamiliar with your experiment, because you are probably so familiar with your own research that
you cannot judge how well the report describes it. Because you already
know what happened, your mind conveniently fills in all the gaps you leave
in the report. An uninformed reader can be a good gap detector.‡

It is also helpful to give the report to a reader who is familiar with what
you did so that he or she can tell you whether you did what you said you
did. This person can serve as your error detector. Finally, you should have
a reader who is familiar with scientific writing style and is a good writer.
This reader can tell you how you might improve the way you say what you
did.

---

*If I had written the book in scientific style, you would have been bored, I would have been
  bored, and the publisher would have been bored. My mother would have bought the
  only copy; she loves me even when I'm boring.
‡On the death of one of his scientific colleagues, one of my friends remarked to me: "I'm really
  going to miss him. He was one of my best enemies. Now I don't know who I'll send my
  reports to." It is often best to have someone read your report who will be critical without
  fearing that he or she will break up a social relationship. Friends are often too nice to be
  good critics.

AN ENEMY MAKES THE BEST CRITIC.

After getting comments from these readers, you are ready to write a final version of the report. This copy should be neatly typed and proofread before you submit it.

Some of you may find that if you follow the procedure described here, your reports will be more readable; others may find that another procedure works best. Writing is an art; what works for one writer may not work for another. However, the major point we have been discussing is valid for any procedure: the report is the final product of your research and deserves at least the same effort you give to all other aspects of your research.

A Sample Report

Please ignore the contents of this sample report. It is not only fictitious, but the writing style suffers because I have attempted to illustrate as many instances of American Psychological Association style as possible in a short report. The marginal comments contain shortened versions of some style rules, with an arrow pointing to an example in the report. The definitive word is still the *Publication Manual*.

Your instructor may ask you to violate some of these rules. For example, when a report is not actually going to be submitted to a journal for publication, I prefer to have students incorporate figures and tables into the body of the report. That way the reader has easy access to them while reading the text. Your instructor may have similar preferences.

For a more detailed coverage of APA style you should, obviously, order a copy of the *Publication Manual of the American Psychological Association, Third Edition*. And if you wish to become truly proficient at APA style you could also order a book titled *Mastering APA Style* from the American Psychological Association. This is a workbook that has exercises on various aspects and features of APA style including grammar, punctuation, spelling, referencing, headings, and statistical and mathematical notation.

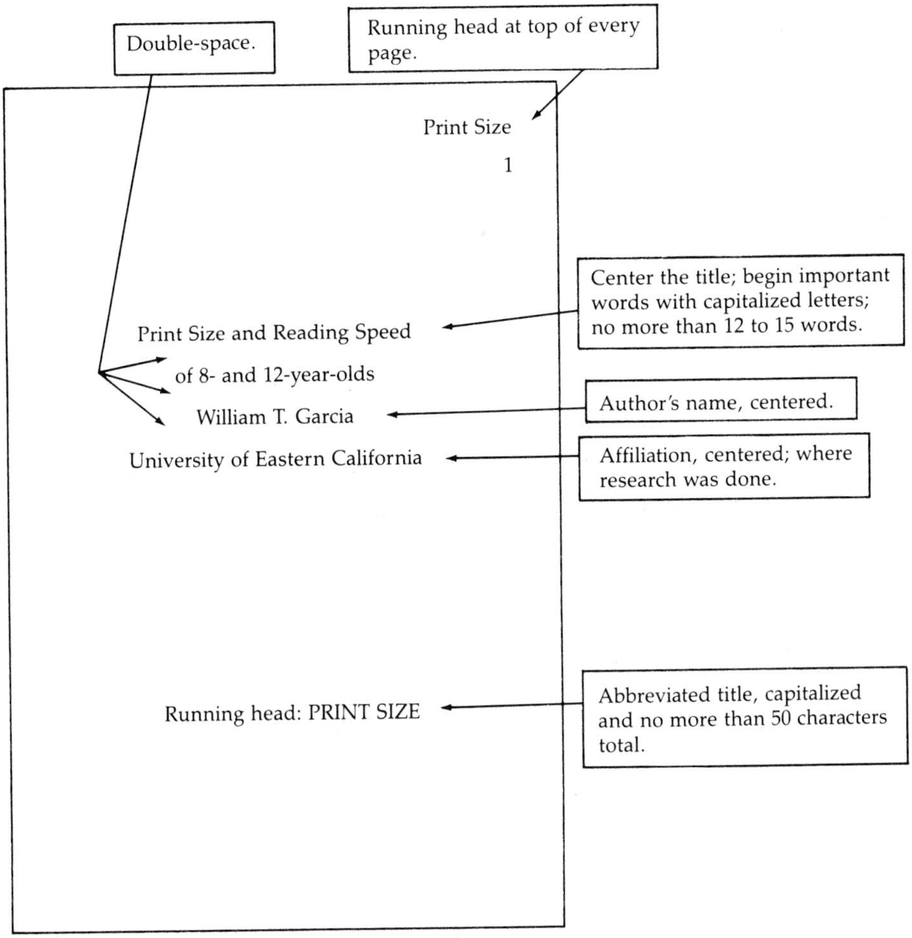

Double-space.

Running head at top of every page.

Print Size

1

Print Size and Reading Speed

of 8- and 12-year-olds

William T. Garcia

University of Eastern California

Center the title; begin important words with capitalized letters; no more than 12 to 15 words.

Author's name, centered.

Affiliation, centered; where research was done.

Running head: PRINT SIZE

Abbreviated title, capitalized and no more than 50 characters total.

Do not indent abstract.

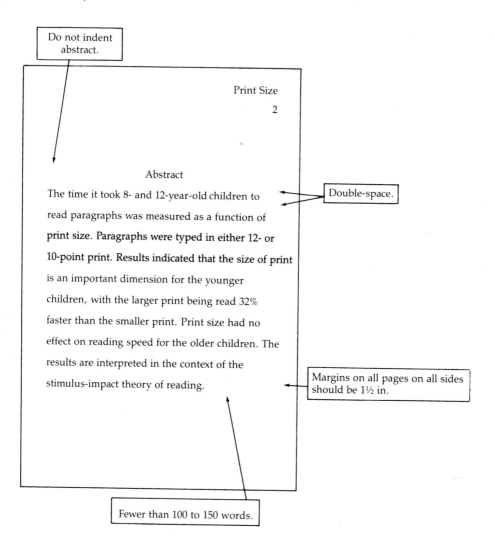

Print Size

2

Abstract

The time it took 8- and 12-year-old children to read paragraphs was measured as a function of print size. Paragraphs were typed in either 12- or 10-point print. Results indicated that the size of print is an important dimension for the younger children, with the larger print being read 32% faster than the smaller print. Print size had no effect on reading speed for the older children. The results are interpreted in the context of the stimulus-impact theory of reading.

Double-space.

Margins on all pages on all sides should be 1½ in.

Fewer than 100 to 150 words.

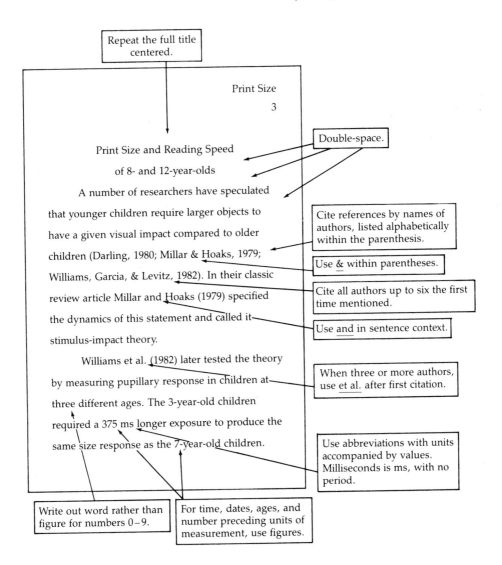

Repeat the full title centered.

Print Size

3

Print Size and Reading Speed

of 8- and 12-year-olds

A number of researchers have speculated that younger children require larger objects to have a given visual impact compared to older children (Darling, 1980; Millar & Hoaks, 1979; Williams, Garcia, & Levitz, 1982). In their classic review article Millar and Hoaks (1979) specified the dynamics of this statement and called it stimulus-impact theory.

Williams et al. (1982) later tested the theory by measuring pupillary response in children at three different ages. The 3-year-old children required a 375 ms longer exposure to produce the same size response as the 7-year-old children.

Double-space.

Cite references by names of authors, listed alphabetically within the parenthesis.

Use & within parentheses.

Cite all authors up to six the first time mentioned.

Use and in sentence context.

When three or more authors, use et al. after first citation.

Use abbreviations with units accompanied by values. Milliseconds is ms, with no period.

Write out word rather than figure for numbers 0–9.

For time, dates, ages, and number preceding units of measurement, use figures.

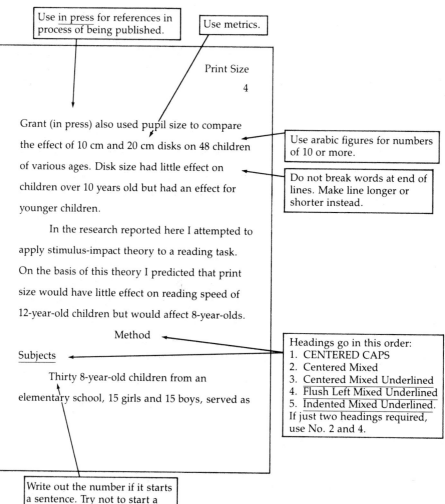

Use <u>in press</u> for references in process of being published.

Use metrics.

Print Size

4

Grant (in press) also used pupil size to compare the effect of 10 cm and 20 cm disks on 48 children of various ages. Disk size had little effect on children over 10 years old but had an effect for younger children.

In the research reported here I attempted to apply stimulus-impact theory to a reading task. On the basis of this theory I predicted that print size would have little effect on reading speed of 12-year-old children but would affect 8-year-olds.

Method

<u>Subjects</u>

Thirty 8-year-old children from an elementary school, 15 girls and 15 boys, served as

Use arabic figures for numbers of 10 or more.

Do not break words at end of lines. Make line longer or shorter instead.

Headings go in this order:
1. CENTERED CAPS
2. Centered Mixed
3. Centered Mixed Underlined
4. Flush Left Mixed Underlined
5. Indented Mixed Underlined.
If just two headings required, use No. 2 and 4.

Write out the number if it starts a sentence. Try not to start a sentence with a number.

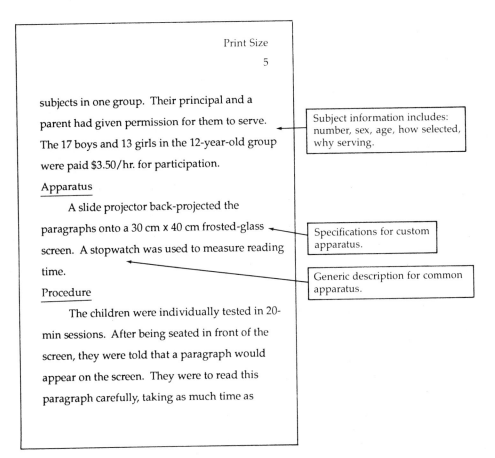

Print Size

5

subjects in one group. Their principal and a
parent had given permission for them to serve.
The 17 boys and 13 girls in the 12-year-old group
were paid $3.50/hr. for participation.

Apparatus

    A slide projector back-projected the
paragraphs onto a 30 cm x 40 cm frosted-glass
screen. A stopwatch was used to measure reading
time.

Procedure

    The children were individually tested in 20-
min sessions. After being seated in front of the
screen, they were told that a paragraph would
appear on the screen. They were to read this
paragraph carefully, taking as much time as

Subject information includes: number, sex, age, how selected, why serving.

Specifications for custom apparatus.

Generic description for common apparatus.

Print Size

6

necessary to understand the material. After reading a paragraph, each child was asked three questions, having single word answers, about the contents of the paragraph. After the questions were answered, another paragraph was presented until each child had read three paragraphs.

| Numbers under 10 are written as words. |

Each paragraph had been tested for readability and was at or below an 8-year age level. The questions had been found to be a good measure of comprehension.

| Numbers that represent time, ages, scores, or points on a scale are written as numerals. |

The experimenter manually timed the reading latency for each trial using a stopwatch. Scores were obtained for each of the 3 trials in

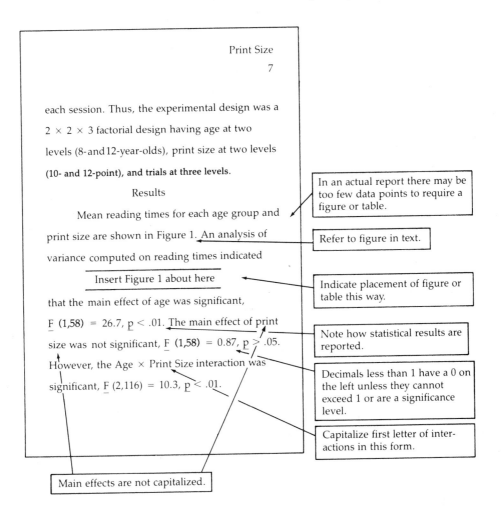

Print Size

7

each session. Thus, the experimental design was a 2 × 2 × 3 factorial design having age at two levels (8-and 12-year-olds), print size at two levels (10- and 12-point), and trials at three levels.

Results

Mean reading times for each age group and print size are shown in Figure 1. An analysis of variance computed on reading times indicated

Insert Figure 1 about here

that the main effect of age was significant, $F (1,58) = 26.7$, $p < .01$. The main effect of print size was not significant, $F (1,58) = 0.87$, $p > .05$. However, the Age × Print Size interaction was significant, $F (2,116) = 10.3$, $p < .01$.

In an actual report there may be too few data points to require a figure or table.

Refer to figure in text.

Indicate placement of figure or table this way.

Note how statistical results are reported.

Decimals less than 1 have a 0 on the left unless they cannot exceed 1 or are a significance level.

Capitalize first letter of inter-actions in this form.

Main effects are not capitalized.

Print Size

8

Average reading times for each of the three

trials are shown in Table 1. The main effect of

_____

Insert Table 1 about here

_____

trials failed to reach significance, $\underline{F}$ (2,24) =

1.53, $\underline{p}$ > .05.

Discussion

The present data are entirely consistent

with stimulus-impact theory. No difference in

reading time as a function of print size was found

for older children. However, for younger children

a print size difference caused a significant

difference in reading time. An interpretation of

these data within the framework of stimulus-

impact theory is that even the smaller print size

> This table is included only to illustrate the use of tables. In an actual report, using both a table and figure to present equivalent data is considered redundant.

Print Size

9

had maximum visual impact on the older children.
The younger children required a larger sized print
in order to perform at a high level.

The implication of these results is obvious
for publishers of childrens' reading material.
However, before recommendations can be
presented to these publishers, additional research
is needed to compare reading times for many
additional print sizes and for children at many age
levels.

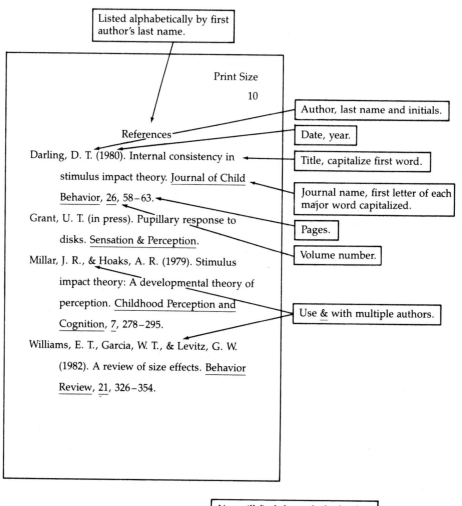

Listed alphabetically by first author's last name.

Print Size

10

References

Author, last name and initials.

Date, year.

Darling, D. T. (1980). Internal consistency in

Title, capitalize first word.

stimulus impact theory. Journal of Child

Behavior, 26, 58–63.

Journal name, first letter of each major word capitalized.

Grant, U. T. (in press). Pupillary response to

Pages.

disks. Sensation & Perception.

Volume number.

Millar, J. R., & Hoaks, A. R. (1979). Stimulus

impact theory: A developmental theory of

perception. Childhood Perception and

Cognition, 7, 278–295.

Use & with multiple authors.

Williams, E. T., Garcia, W. T., & Levitz, G. W.

(1982). A review of size effects. Behavior

Review, 21, 326–354.

You will find the style for books, magazines, and other references by looking at the end of each chapter in this book.

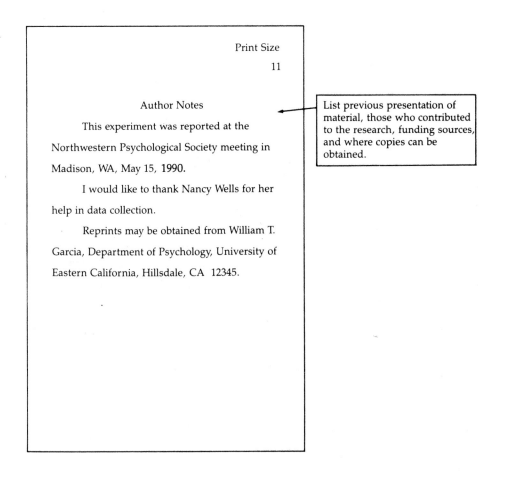

Print Size

11

Author Notes

This experiment was reported at the Northwestern Psychological Society meeting in Madison, WA, May 15, 1990.

I would like to thank Nancy Wells for her help in data collection.

Reprints may be obtained from William T. Garcia, Department of Psychology, University of Eastern California, Hillsdale, CA 12345.

List previous presentation of material, those who contributed to the research, funding sources, and where copies can be obtained.

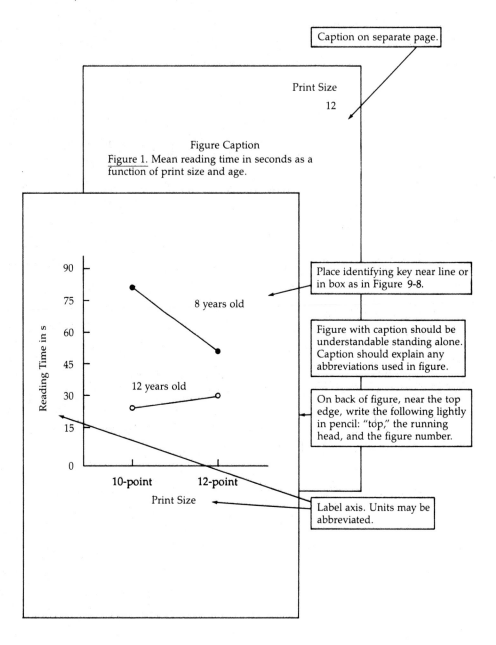

Caption on separate page.

Print Size

12

Figure Caption
Figure 1. Mean reading time in seconds as a
function of print size and age.

Place identifying key near line or
in box as in Figure 9-8.

Figure with caption should be
understandable standing alone.
Caption should explain any
abbreviations used in figure.

On back of figure, near the top
edge, write the following lightly
in pencil: "top," the running
head, and the figure number.

Label axis. Units may be
abbreviated.

8 years old

12 years old

90

75

60

45

30

15

0

Reading Time in s

10-point   12-point

Print Size

Print Size
13

Table 1

Mean Paragraph Reading Times in Seconds as a

Function of Age, Print Size, and Trials

Titles in mixed caps, left justified, and underlined.

Use only horizontal rule lines and draw with a pencil.

Print Size	Age	
	8 years	12 years
10-point		
Trial 1	84.2	31.2
Trial 2	83.4	27.7
Trial 3	81.0	24.7
12-point		
Trial 1	58.2	32.3
Trial 2	56.1	29.1
Trial 3	55.9	30.8

Stubheads should just be indented rather than taking a full column.

Summary

Because research is worthless unless other scientists know about it, experimenters must make their results known by writing a high-quality experimental report. This report should follow the guidelines recommended by the American Psychological Association in its *Publication Manual*. A report has standardized sections. Because many readers will decide whether to read a report on the basis of its **title,** it should be short but convey enough information to help the reader make this decision. The **authors** and the **institution** where the research was done follows the title. The **abstract,** a short (100 to 150 words) version of the complete report, ends the preliminaries.

In the body of the report, the **introduction** should review enough literature to give the reader an idea of the current state of the body of knowledge and should state the purpose of the experiment. The **method** section provides the information necessary to replicate the experiment. It is typically divided into three subsections: **subjects,** which describes the type and number of subjects and how they were recruited; **apparatus/material,** which gives others the information necessary to order or build the equipment and materials similar to those used; and **procedure,** which should give a detailed account of what happened to each subject. The **results** section summarizes the findings of the experiment using descriptive and inferential statistics along with tables and figures. The report writer then relates results back to the body of knowledge in the **discussion** section. The report concludes with an alphabetical list of the **references** cited in the paper.

To convey information as efficiently as possible while keeping the general writing style lively, it is no longer necessary to write experimental reports exclusively in third-person passive voice. Active verbs are now considered preferable, and occasional use of first person is acceptable. The introduction and method sections are typically written in past tense, while present tense is appropriate for the results and discussion sections. Because the report should be as concise as possible, you should avoid lazy writing and use the comments of other readers to make the report a high-quality product.

References

American Psychological Association (1983). *Publication manual of the American Psychological Association* (3rd ed.). Washington, D.C.: Author.

Garvey, W. D. & Griffith, B.C. (1971). Scientific communication: Its role in the conduct of research and creation of knowledge. *American Psychologist, 26,* 349–362.

11
How to Use Theory

Einstein told me how, since his boyhood, he thought about the man running after the light ray and the man closed in a falling elevator. The picture of the man running after the light ray led to special relativity theory. The picture of the man in a falling elevator led to general relativity theory.[*]

Holmes—"I have no data yet. It is a capital mistake to theorize before one has data. Insensibly one begins to twist facts to suit theories, instead of theories to suit facts."[†]

As disappointing as it may sound after having just read most of a book telling you how to do experiments, doing experiments is only part of doing science. Throughout the book, experiments have been referred to as building blocks used for constructing a scientific body of knowledge. Just as a randomly arranged pile of blocks is not a building, so a randomly arranged collection of experiments is not a science. In either case, we need a blueprint as well. In science, a blueprint is called a **theory.**

In fact, one reason experimental psychology is more fun than some of the other sciences is that experimental psychologists can be architects as well as builders. Other sciences have imposed a division of labor. For instance, most physicists are either theoretical physicists or experimental physicists, but not both. Experimental psychologists have traditionally done both jobs.

Types of Theories

Definitions of theory tend to be so general that they are not very instructive. However, if forced to define **theory,** I would say that a theory is a partially verified statement of a scientific relationship that cannot be directly observed. The qualification that a relationship not be observable stems from the fact that theoretical relationships are often between general categories of circumstances or behaviors rather than between specific instances. For example, the theoretical statement that viewing violence causes aggression is different from an experimental demonstration that children seeing a war

---

[*]Infeld, L. (1950). *Albert Einstein.* New York: Scribner's, p. 48.
[†]Doyle, Arthur Conan (1891). "A Scandal in Bohemia." *The adventures of Sherlock Holmes.* New York: Tom Doherty Associates, 1989, p. 4.

EXPERIMENTAL PSYCHOLOGISTS DO TWO JOBS.

movie choose to play with guns. Other theoretical statements may not be directly observable because they concern internal processes, such as the theory that some people remember words by forming mental pictures.

Theories can take many forms. In this chapter I will discuss three types of theories* and illustrate them by using the question "Does violence on television cause aggression?"

Descriptive Theories

A **descriptive theory** simply attaches names to events without necessarily explaining why or how the events have occurred. For example, Freud, as part of psychoanalytic theory, said that repression occurs when we unconsciously refuse to admit painful or disagreeable ideas to conscious thought. Although such a theory may help clinicians in their work, the mere naming does little to explain the conditions under which repression occurs or how it might be examined experimentally. In a similar way, for many years psychologists interested in motivation were enraptured with naming instincts. At first the concept of an instinct seemed to be useful, because it appeared that most animal behaviors could be classified as reflecting certain instincts (such as the feeding instinct or the mating instinct). However, eventually psychologists began to accumulate as many names for instincts as there were observable behaviors (such as the "running into a hole when attacked from the front" instinct), and the concept lost its usefulness.

Descriptive theories can be useful, however, if the names are attached to operationally definable classes of events rather than to individually observable events. For example, we might state that observing violence causes aggressive behavior. If we could operationally define violence and aggressive behavior as general classes of events, we might have a useful descriptive theory. But even this kind of descriptive theory is of limited value because it does not explain how the relationship works.

---

*The three types of theories discussed here are similar to those mentioned by Arnoult (1972) in his book *Scientific Method in Psychology,* although some of the names have been changed.

A DESCRIPTIVE THEORY

Analogical Theories

Analogical theories explain how relationships work by drawing an analogy between a psychological relationship and a physical model so that the physical analogue becomes a psychological model of behavior. For example, many of the theories that attempt to explain how humans process information use the computer as a physical analogue. Of course, nobody believes that the brain works exactly like a computer, but enough similarities exist for computer modeling to provide some useful analogical theories.

As an example of an analogical theory, let's take the physical properties of momentum as an analogue for the relationship between violence and aggression. As you may know, a physical object has momentum in proportion to its speed and mass; the faster it is traveling and the more massive it is, the more momentum it has. This momentum can be overcome by friction. Thus, an analogical theory relating violence and aggression might be stated this way: "The amount of aggression expressed by an observer is like the force exerted by a moving object, where the degree of violence observed is analogous to the mass of the object and the time of observing is analogous to the speed of the object. After exposure to violence, the aggressive tendencies will be high but will decrease over time in the same way that friction overcomes momentum."

This analogical theory is more useful than the descriptive theory proposed in the previous section because it explains some of the complexities of the relationship. We should also be able to test the theory based on our knowledge of how the physical model works. For example, we know that the longer a force is exerted on a physical object, the faster its speed and the greater its momentum. Thus, a longer time is needed for friction to overcome the momentum. By analogy, the longer a person observes violence, the longer it would take the aggressive tendencies to disappear.

Because of its explanatory power, an analogical theory is certainly more useful than a descriptive theory. However, analogical theories are also doomed

AN ANALOGICAL THEORY

to failure in the end, for at some point the properties of the physical analogue will no longer correspond to the properties of the human. For this reason, you can best use analogical theories as first approximations that help you identify the major variables and outline in a general way how the variables affect one another. But you will find that analogical theories are seldom powerful enough to help you specify the exact mathematical relationships among the variables.

Quantitative Theories

Quantitative theories do attempt to state relationships in mathematical terms. They specify not only the direction of relationships among categories of variables but also how these categories are quantitatively related. Few psychological theories have reached this level of sophistication. Only a few subareas in learning, memory, and information processing have attempted to use quantitative theories.

Quantitative theories have been limited in psychology because psychologists have more difficulty with variability than do physical scientists. For example, in physics the theory of gravity is a quantitative theory expressed in precise mathematical terms. Because gravity affects all physical objects in the same way, a physicist can assume that any variability in experimental results is simply a measurement error. In psychology, however, we cannot predict how all subjects will behave based on one subject's behavior, nor can we predict how the same subject will behave at any given time. Consequently, our quantitative theories must be able to accommodate variability. The best we can do is to predict how probable it is that a behavior will occur,* so we must express mathematical relationships in probabilistic terms (for example, the probability that a subject will learn this list of words in five trials is .8).

---

*In some areas, physical scientists deal with similar problems. The structure of atoms, for example, is expressed probabilistically.

A QUANTITATIVE THEORY

Psychologists also face the problem of deciding what scale to use in measuring behaviors. In the physical sciences, the units for measuring speed or mass are not controversial. In psychology, however, we have to find scales by which such concepts as violence or aggression can be measured. For example, consider the following quantitative theory: humans express a level of aggressiveness in direct proportion to the average level of violence they have observed. Because our proposed theory attempts to establish a mathematical relationship between the scales of violence and aggression, we must first determine how to measure them. As you can see, establishing scales for such concepts is no easy task.

As a result of these problems, most theories in psychology are still descriptive or analogical. However, as psychology becomes more sophisticated and we learn to handle the difficulties caused by variability and scaling, more psychological theories will become quantitative.

Properties of a Good Theory

How do you know a good theory when you see one? In the last section I implied that quantitative theories are better than analogical theories, which in turn are better than descriptive theories. Why is this true?

First, a theory must be able to **account for most of the data** already collected. There is no use proposing a theory if the data do not support it. (You can see why a thorough literature search is so important; it will allow you to eliminate some of the competing theories before collecting any data.) One or two items of disconfirming evidence, however, will usually not destroy a theory unless an alternative theory can account for all the evidence. We will consider shortly how experimental results affect theory.

A theory must also be **testable.** As we will discuss later in this chapter, science advances by doing research that eliminates some theories and leaves others as still possible. To be testable, then, means that the theory can potentially be disconfirmed. A theory is disconfirmed if the outcome of an experiment is not what the theory predicted it would be. If a theory is so universal that it can account for any experimental result, then disproving it is impossible. One reason a theory might not be testable is that the predicted results are expected to occur only some of the time in an unpredictable manner. For example, Freud's theory of repression is virtually untestable as it is usually stated. How could you disprove repression experimentally? Perhaps you could provide subjects with an experience they would rather forget. For instance, you might tempt subjects to cheat and then confront those who succumbed with their dreadful deed.* Sometime later you might have a close friend of each subject ask whether he or she had ever cheated. If no subjects report having cheated, you have support for the theory, because it shows that all subjects repressed the incident. However, if all subjects report having cheated, this result doesn't eliminate the theory, because the theory never claimed that all people repress a particular event, only that some people sometimes repress some events. Thus, your experiment would do little to dislodge the theory. A theory that is so general that no test can be proposed to discredit it is a worthless theory from a scientific point of view.

While a theory should not be so general that it can account for any behavior, it should also **not be too restrictive.** That is, the fewer directly observable events the theory can account for, the less valuable it is. In the most extreme case, a theory simply restates the relationship between observable events.† For example, the statement that "8-year-old children hit a punching bag more after watching a televised *Roadrunner* cartoon" is less useful than the statement that "Watching violence on television causes aggression in children." Even more useful is the statement that "observing violence causes people to be more aggressive." The more general our statements, the more valuable they are because they account for a larger set of observable events.

Finally, a good theory **predicts** the outcome of future experiments. Even descriptive theories specify the relationship between categories of events. Thus, the relationships between directly observable events that are members of these categories are predictable from the theory. Analogical and quantitative theories also allow you to predict the relationships between events, and these predictions are even more precise.

What Is a Theory Good For?

Why does science need theories? What are they good for? B. F. Skinner (1950) had a concise answer to this question; he said they are good for practically nothing. Skinner maintained that theories do more harm than good for three major reasons.

---

*Let's ignore for the moment whether this experiment would be considered ethical.
†Actually, such a statement would not fit our definition of a theory, but some investigators
  would call it a theory.

A GOOD THEORY ALLOWS YOU TO PREDICT...

First, he stated that our job as psychologists is to account for observable events and that, because theories are more abstract than the observable events, theories do not help us to account for events. Second, since theories seem to explain events that we haven't observed as well as those we have observed, they can lull us into believing that our research is complete when we still have much left to do. We are tempted to use theories to fill in the holes in our research without really knowing whether the answers the theories give us are true. Finally, Skinner pointed out that when we let a theory guide our research and then this theory is overthrown, we lose much of the research generated by the theory. He argued that good research is good research independent of any theory.

Skinner's position has some merit (we will return to some of his points at the end of the chapter), but most psychologists disagree with him and feel that theories are vital to research. What do they think theories are good for?

We have already discussed one of the major purposes of theory: it helps to **organize the data.** Studying data isolated from theory is about as interesting as reading the closing quotations from the New York Stock Exchange if you don't own any shares. By categorizing directly observable events and saying how the categories are related, a theory provides a meaningful way to organize our knowledge.

By organizing data, a theory also **suggests possible directions for future research.** If you randomly arranged half of the raw materials needed to build a house in front of you and someone asked you "What do you need next?" you would probably have a tough time answering the question. But if you had a blueprint and constructed as much of the house as possible, you have a way of determining what materials are missing. A theory provides a similar function for science. Even if the theory is somewhat vague or there are several competing theories, it can provide enough organization to indicate which variables we should investigate and which relationships we should look for.

Theory can also be valuable for **providing answers to applied problems.** For example, suppose you work for a television network, and somebody has proposed a new children's show. You want to know whether this show will make the children watching it more aggressive and, if so, how much more aggressive. You could take 100 children, expose them to a pilot show, and somehow measure their aggressiveness, but this procedure would be expensive and time-consuming. Furthermore, you would have to repeat the experiment every time another new show was proposed. However, if a theory existed specifying which dimensions make a television show violent and predicting how these dimensions affect children's aggressiveness, you could use the theory in place of direct observation, or at least you could use the theory to reduce the amount of data you needed to collect. The theory might tell you which dimensions need to be experimentally investigated.

Thus, theory can reduce the number of experiments we need to do in applied research. And in many cases a theory will give a close enough approximation to an experimental result that the theoretical prediction can be used in place of it.

Testing Theories

We discussed earlier that good theories must be testable. But how do we go about testing them? Obviously, we must do experiments, and somehow their results must tell us something about how well the theories account for the results.

In determining the impact of a particular experimental outcome on a theory, we must make an inference. There are two kinds of inferences: deductive and inductive. A **deductive** inference is a logical process in which a conclusion drawn from a set of premises contains no more information than the premises taken collectively. For example, if all mammals are animals and a horse is a mammal, then a horse is an animal. If the two premises are true, the conclusion must also be true. Likewise, if we know that the conclusion is not true, then we know that at least one of the premises is not true. Suppose, for example, our premises had been that all mammals are animals and a rock is a mammal. Then we would deduce that a rock is an animal. Because we know that a rock is not an animal, we know that one of the premises must be false. In an experimental context, the theory sets the premises and the experiment tests the truth of the conclusion. In principle, if the experiment finds the conclusion to be false, then the theory must also be false.

An **inductive** inference is a logical process in which the conclusion proposed contains more information than the observations on which it is based. For example, someone living in the jungle might say, "Every tree I have ever seen has leaves; therefore all trees have leaves." The truth of the conclusion is verifiable only if he has examined all trees in the world. When he travels beyond the jungle, every time he examines a tree and finds it to have leaves, he gains confidence in his conclusion through inductive infer-

ence. However, should he find an exception, a tree without leaves (for example, a pine tree), he could deductively disprove the set of premises. All trees have leaves and this pine is a tree; therefore it ought to have leaves, but it doesn't. If he were sure of the premise that the pine was a tree, then finding that the pine had no leaves would deductively disprove the premise that all trees have leaves. Again, in the experimental context, a result that is consistent with a theoretical prediction gives the theory inductive support, although this one result does not prove the theory. However, a result that is inconsistent with a theoretical prediction could deductively disprove the theory.

To illustrate this distinction between deductive and inductive inference, suppose we wanted to test the analogical theory mentioned earlier, that observing violence affects a person's aggressiveness the way momentum affects a physical object. The first step is to determine some consequences of this theory. Consequence A might be that subjects observing extremely violent situations become extremely aggressive. Consequence B might be that subjects exposed to violent situations for long periods of time are more aggressive than those exposed for only a short time. Consequence C might be that subjects exposed to violence for longer periods of time are aggressive for a longer time after exposure.

Because each of these consequences can be directly observed, we can test them by doing experiments. Suppose we do three appropriate experiments to test these consequences and find that Consequences A and B are true and C is false. What can we conclude about the theory?

Figure 11-1 illustrates the steps we have taken. From the theory at the top, we inferred three directly observable consequences. This inference was deductive: if the theory is true, then the consequences must be true. Next we did an experiment to test each consequence and found two of them to be true and the third to be false. Now we must make another inference as to the truth of the theory.

The two true consequences obviously support the theory, but they do so in an inductive way; that is, they increase our confidence in the theory, but they do not eliminate the possibility that the theory is false. The more

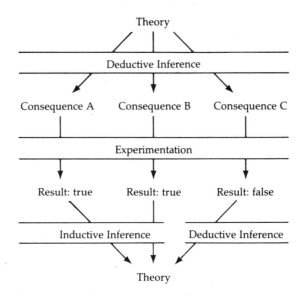

Figure 11-1. An illustration of the deductive and inductive links relating experimentation to theory.

consequences of the theory found to be true, the more probable that the theory is indeed true. However, using this process of inference, we can never be absolutely sure about the truth of a theory. You can see why I cringe when an investigator claims "My experiment *proves* that the theory is true." The inferential process simply does not allow such a statement to be made. A positive result can never prove a theory true. The investigator has a stronger claim (although still not quite accurate) if he or she says that a negative result proves the theory to be false. Why is this?

The basic rules of logic say that a theory can be disproven if a consequence is false. Because a consequence is deductively inferred from a theory, we know that if the theory is true, the consequence must be true. Thus, if we do an experiment showing that the consequence is false, we can deductively infer that the theory must also be false. From a logical point of view, then, we can disprove a theory. However, we have forgotten something we learned in Chapter 9. When a test statistic exceeds a critical value that is determined by the level of significance, we infer that the chances the samples came from the same population are small. Thus, a significant result tells us that the data samples probably came from different populations. Yet experimentally demonstrating that a consequence is false usually involves showing conditions to be equivalent rather than different, and, because we do not have statistical tests that do this, we have to be careful in concluding that the consequence is false.

To use an example, Consequence C of the momentum theory is that the longer a subject is exposed to violence, the longer the aggression will last. To test this consequence, suppose we do an experiment in which we expose one group of subjects to one hour of violent television, another group to two hours, and a third to four hours. We then measure how long each group's aggressiveness lasts and find no significant differences among the groups. Can we therefore declare the theory to be false? Not with absolute certainty, because the statistical test we used gave us only the probability that the differences we found could have been due to chance. The test cannot tell us how likely it is that the groups are equivalent.

Even if we could have shown the consequence to be false by testing in the proper direction (that is, by determining that the consequence is false because an effect is significant), we could still be in error. If we tested at the .05 level, for example, we could expect to be wrong one time in 20. So even in this case, the strong deductive links that could allow us to disprove a theory are weakened by the inductive inference we make when interpreting the experimental results.*

There are other reasons, besides the statistical one just mentioned, why the failure of a conclusion would not provide as strong a disproof of a theory as might be expected by deductive logic. For example, there could be some doubt about the adequacy of operational definitions used in the experiment, or about the control of extraneous variables, or about the levels of the independent variables chosen. So a single experiment is seldom considered to have disproven a theory until a number of contrary results have been found.

You don't have to analyze the logical basis for every experiment you do. However, it is important for you to understand in a general way how experimentation interacts with theory. This discussion should help you appreciate why it is necessary to do many experiments to gain confidence in or lose confidence in (not prove or disprove) any theory.

Does Theory Always Precede Data?

In our somewhat idealized discussion of the relationship between theories and experiments, we have been pretending that we first propose a theory and then do experiments to evaluate the theory. However, many investigators prefer to model themselves after Sherlock Holmes: only after collecting all possible clues (data) will they nail the culprit (theory). They feel that proposing a theory before collecting data is like deciding on the villain and then looking for clues related only to that person's guilt; both procedures are biased. We have already learned Skinner's opinion on this matter. Perhaps he stated it best when he wrote, "There are doubtless many men whose curiosity about nature is less than their curiosity about the accuracy of their guesses . . ." (Skinner, 1938, p. 44).

*For a more detailed discussion of these issues, see Chapters 12–14 of McGuigan's (1968) *Experimental Psychology: A Methodological Approach.*

Many investigators believe that research should be done because a problem exists. They collect data and then propose a theory to account for the data and solve the problem. This position certainly has some merit, because research motivated by theory as opposed to research motivated by a problem has some notable drawbacks. Perhaps the most serious drawback is that investigators often propose theories for easily solvable problems rather than for important ones. Because no science has the resources to investigate all problems, we must choose, and we obviously should choose important problems to work on. If, because of theories, we choose to investigate easy but rather unimportant problems instead of more difficult but important ones, we may be misusing our resources.* To counteract this trap, I have threatened at times to teach a course entitled *Psych 371—Things Psychology Knows Nothing About*. The purpose of this course would be to find important areas of human behavior that nobody is currently investigating and to propose how one might begin research in these areas.

A rational position probably lies somewhere between the theory-driven position and the problem-driven position. We should certainly be concerned with choosing important problems to work on, but we should not turn our backs on theories as excellent vehicles for organizing and directing research on these problems. In fact, most researchers do not take a radical position on the question of whether theorizing necessarily precedes data collection. The interaction of theory with data is a dynamic process. Usually some data must exist before a tentative theory can be proposed. Then, instead of simply throwing out the tentative theory should disconfirming results be found, researchers usually modify the theory so that the results can be accommodated. Thus, a theory is built and changes dynamically with experimentation, rather than merely being proposed and then summarily discarded if the outcome seems awry. It is this interplay of theory with data that advances science.

Summary

As scientists, psychologists not only do experiments but also use theories to build a scientific body of knowledge. A **theory,** which is defined as a partially verified statement of a scientific relationship that cannot be directly observed, can be of three types. A **descriptive theory** attaches names to events and is most useful when the names are attached to operationally

---

*Kuhn (1970) in his book *The Structure of Scientific Revolutions,* p. 37, argues, in fact, that once the scientific community has accepted a paradigm (a set of assumptions or a widely accepted model), scientists then work only on problems that can be assumed to have solutions within that paradigm. "To a great extent these are the only problems that the community will admit as scientific. . . . A paradigm can, for that matter, even insulate the community from those socially important problems that are not reducible to the puzzle form, because they cannot be stated in terms of the conceptual and instrumental tools the paradigm supplies."

definable classes of events. **Analogical theories** explain how relationships work by drawing an analogy between the psychological relationship and a physical model. **Quantitative theories** specify relationships in mathematical terms. Psychology has very few quantitative theories, since we are still learning how to account for variability and how to develop precise scales of measurement.

A good theory **accounts for most of the data,** is **testable,** is **not too restrictive,** and is able to **predict** the outcome of future experiments. Skinner felt that theories are practically useless because they do not help account for observable events, they lull us into believing unfinished research is complete, and they lead to research that becomes useless when the theory is overthrown. Most investigators disagree, however. They believe that theories are useful because they **help organize data, suggest possible directions for future research,** and **provide answers to applied problems.**

In testing theories, it is important to distinguish between **deductive inference,** in which the outcome is known with complete certainty, and **inductive inference,** in which the outcome is probabilistic. A theory leads deductively to certain consequences that can be experimentally tested. Those consequences found to be true increase our confidence in the theory through a process of inductive inference. The rules of logic say that a false consequence should cause us to deductively reject the theory, but since the inferential statistical tests used are inductive, rejecting a theory is also an inductive process.

Although investigators usually propose a theory before collecting data, many investigators feel that one should first have a problem, then collect data, and finally construct a theory. They argue that this order of events leads to research that investigates important problems rather than research that investigates easy but unimportant problems.

References

Arnoult, M. D. (1972). *Fundamentals of scientific method in psychology.* Dubuque, IA: William C. Brown.

Kuhn, T. S. (1970). *The structure of scientific revolutions* (2nd ed.). Chicago: University of Chicago Press.

McGuigan, F. J. (1968). *Experimental psychology: A methodological approach* (2nd ed.). Englewood Cliffs, NJ: Prentice-Hall.

Skinner, B. F. (1938). *The behavior of organisms.* New York: Appleton-Century-Crofts.

Skinner, B. F. (1950). Are theories of learning necessary? *Psychological Review, 57,* 193–216.

12

How to Tell When
You Are Ready to Begin

An error is a mistake only if repeated.   ANONYMOUS

You should now have all of the tools needed for beginning your experiment. However, you may have to ask yourself some questions to determine whether you have considered all the important issues before you can begin collecting data.

When I teach experimental methods, my students have to think up, design, and do an original experiment. Before they are allowed to start collecting data, they are required to present the proposed experiment to the class. It is the job of the class, and my job, to critique the experiment, trying to find flaws and determining whether the student experimenter has considered all necessary details before doing the research. This exercise serves several purposes. It helps develop a critical sense in the students listening to the presentation, an ability that all scientists must have. Preparing for the presentation also motivates the student experimenters to try to think about the many assumptions they have made and the small decisions that they may have avoided up to this point. Finally, this exercise allows all of us to help the experimenters by suggesting ways to improve the experiment.

The Have-a-Nice-Day Society

Prior to discussing some of the commonly unanswered questions that need to be considered before beginning an experiment, I would like to comment on the emotional response many of my students have to the presentations. Those making the presentations often consider this to be the most aversive and distressing part of the course. Part of the distress is just the act of making a presentation, any presentation, a skill that is seldom tapped in other college courses. But I suspect that most of the distress is due to having to defend their experiment before a potentially critical group of peers.

The first reaction of the student audience is to keep quiet; "I won't rock your boat if you don't rock mine." Even with my prodding, some students are reluctant to criticize their fellow students' ideas. We live in a have-a-nice-day society where the rules include extreme tolerance of the behaviors and opinions of others. Some people seem to believe that because we all have the right to express our views, the value of one opinion is equal to the

HOW TO KNOW WHEN YOU
ARE READY TO BEGIN YOUR
EXPERIMENT.

value of another. And criticizing other people's opinions is seen as a personal attack on them or on their right of free speech.

Judging from their comments on the student evaluations filled out at the end of the class, some students certainly do perceive my comments at the student presentations as personal and uncalled for. As much as I try to smile, keep my voice down, and project a helpful attitude, these students cannot seem to understand why their nice, friendly teacher has suddenly turned on them.

I hope that the preceding chapters in this book have, at least at an intellectual level, convinced you that, within science, one opinion is not as good as another. Opinions must be defendable. If the rules of science are violated, the results become suspect or useless. The rules of deductive and inductive logic, discussed in Chapter 11, *are* the basis for arguing that certain results support or refute a theory. The elimination of potential confounding variables, discussed in Chapter 1, *is* required to be able to build a case for causality—that is, to verify that the independent variable caused the change in the dependent variable. The random selection of an experimental sample of subjects, discussed in Chapter 1, *is* the basis on which results can be generalized to a larger population.

When the class, or the instructor, or colleagues criticize a research proposal, they are attempting to help the proposer follow the rules of science so that after the research is completed, the results can be defended and can be added to the scientific body of knowledge. Although criticism at the proposal stage can be irritating, once the research is completed it is devastating. After-the-fact criticism indicates not only that you made a mistake because you were not thoughtful enough, but that you wasted both your time and your subjects' time, and perhaps wasted other resources that could

A POTENTIALLY CRITICAL GROUP OF PEERS

have been used to advance the body of knowledge. The message here is not that science is a deadly serious enterprise in which mistakes bring great guilt, but that science has certain rules you must adhere to as a scientist. And you should use whatever resources are available, including the advice of others, to help you follow the rules and do good research.

Questions Before You Begin

The following questions are the ones I most frequently ask my students when they make their research proposals. You may already have answered them. Good for you! If not, be sure that you can before you begin collecting data.

How Many Subjects Do I Need?

It is often hard to figure out how many subjects you will need for your experiment. One of the most frequent mistakes students make is to use too few subjects, so that what appears to be a good result is not statistically significant. Of course, there may be some practical considerations, such as a limited subject pool, that restrict the number of subjects you are allowed to use. If so, you may just have to make do. Assuming that you may use as many subjects as you wish, there are statistical ways of determining the power of a statistical test and the approximate number of subjects needed. However, these tests are beyond the scope of this book and, in actuality, most experimenters do not use them.

You should also bear in mind that whereas too few subjects will not allow you to show statistical significance with a reasonable-sized experimental effect, too many subjects can show statistical significance even with an unimportant effect. In this case, not only is using too many subjects inefficient, it may be misleading.

Perhaps the best way to determine how many subjects to use is by studying the literature. Certainly, if you are replicating someone else's experiment and a statistically significant effect was reported, you will have a pretty good idea of subject numbers. Even if you are not doing a direct replication, you will probably be able to find similar experiments that have used the dependent variable you are proposing. The variability found in data generated from particular dependent variables such as reaction times or words recalled from a list tends to be relatively stable. In the unlikely event that you can find no similar experiments, you may have to do a pilot experiment to get some idea of the number of subjects you will need.

Should I Run Subjects Individually or in Groups?

Most new experimenters think first of bringing subjects in individually for an experiment. Sometimes there's no choice—for example, only one piece of equipment may be available for recording responses. In other cases, some subjects might affect the performance of others in the group, so subjects must be run individually. However, if you can run subjects in groups, you can collect data more efficiently.

When considering your options, you should ask yourself questions like these: Can I give groups of subjects a questionnaire rather than ask questions of individual subjects? Can I collect the necessary data by using slides or an overhead projector to display stimuli to a group, instead of using flip cards or a computer display with individual subjects? If you are presenting a consistent series of stimuli to subjects and recording only the accuracy of responses or the number of responses in a particular category, you can most likely use groups. If the order or timing of stimulus events depends on the responses made or if precise timing of the responses is necessary, then you should probably run subjects individually.

How Long Will My Experiment Take?

Calculating the length of the experiment poses questions at several levels. At the grossest level, how many hours, or days, or weeks of collecting data will be necessary? At a finer level, how long will a single experimental session take? If you are going to use individual trials, you cannot answer either of these questions without first determining the length of a trial and the number of trials. To figure out trial length, you must know the sequence of events that will occur during a trial and the time required by each event, including the intertrial interval (the time between trials). Then, by knowing how many trials will be presented, you can determine the total time taken to complete the trials. In some cases the number of trials may have to be estimated, as, for example, when subjects must achieve a performance criterion, such as two consecutive trials on which a list of words is correctly recalled.

You should also remember to include the time to do other tasks associated with the experiment. Usually the subjects will have to be given some instructions and be allowed to ask questions before starting. A set of practice trials may be included if some learning is anticipated and a relatively stable performance is desired. Subjects may need rest breaks to avoid fatigue during long or tedious experiments. A debriefing session at the end of the experiment may be required, particularly if subjects are serving in the experiment as part of a class requirement and are supposed to be learning about experiments. Finally, some "slop time" should be built in because subjects sometimes arrive late. Without this time, consecutive sessions will run progressively later and later. Figure 12-1 shows some of the steps required for determining the time expected for an experimental session.

You will then need to determine how many total subject-running hours you will be devoting to this experiment. Again, you should anticipate some unplanned time to run extra subjects, to replace those who failed to show up, or whose data were eliminated for failure to meet some criterion, or for whom the equipment malfunctioned. As for the total time needed to complete the experiment, remember that data collection is only part of the job. You will also need time to analyze the data, interpret them, and produce several drafts of the experimental report. And each of these tasks usually takes more time than anticipated.

Do I Need to Set Subject Restrictions?

In general, determining whether to set limitations on who may participate in your experiment depends on the population to which you want to generalize your findings. The limited pool of subjects from which you have to draw will probably have already reduced your ability to generalize to some extent. For example, if you use college students, you must consider that certain ages are definitely overrepresented and certain ones underrepresented. And you must take into account that, compared to the average population of the country, an average group of college students has a higher IQ, is in a higher socioeconomic bracket, has greater reading ability, and is less likely to have health problems. So you cannot legitimately generalize to the entire larger population.

However, for practical reasons you might wish to exclude some subjects from your experiment even though this further limits the generalizability of your results. For example, if you are studying language performance such as reading ability, identification of words, memory for words, or a number of related language tasks, you might limit your subjects to those whose first language is English. If you are studying visual perception, you might use subjects whose eyesight is corrected to 20/20 or who can pass a test for color blindness. If you are studying motor ability, such as in sports psychology, you might exclude subjects having physical impairments that would prevent them from contributing useful data. In some cases, you might use only men or only women, whereas in other cases, you might

One Trial

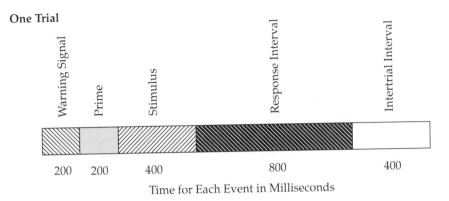

Total time for one trial = 200 + 200 + 400 + 800 + 400 = 2000 ms or 2 sec

With 10 blocks of 20 trials, 30-sec rest breaks, 5 minutes for instructions, and 5 minutes for debriefing:

One Session

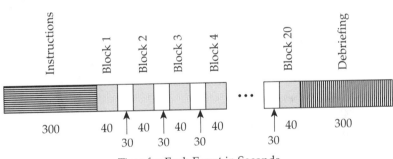

Total time for experiment = 300 sec + (20 trials x 40 sec) + (19 rest x 30 sec) + 300 sec = 1970 sec or 32 min 50 sec

Including some flexibility for late subjects, time to be seated, and so on, this experiment should be scheduled for 40 to 45 minutes.

Figure 12-1. An example of the calculations necessary for determining the time required for an experimental session. In this experiment each trial consists of a 200-msec warning signal, a 200-msec prime (prestimulus information), a 400-msec stimulus, an 800-msec response interval, and a 400-msec intertrial interval (time between trials).

have an equal number of men and women so that you can evaluate the effect of gender on performance. These are only some of the possible restrictions on subjects that you might wish to consider. Depending on the particular task to be performed in your experiment, other restrictions might be appropriate and should be carefully considered.

Should I Set Any A Priori Criteria for Eliminating Subjects?

As will be discussed in Chapter 13, there may be performance criteria that you wish to set prior to collecting data. For example, I often collect reaction-time data in my experiments. There are sometimes one or two subjects whose overall performance level is not comparable to that of the others. So I often set a criterion that data from any subject whose mean reaction time exceeds the mean reaction time of all subjects in the experiment by 300 milliseconds will be eliminated from the analysis. Such a criterion, along with the number of subjects thus eliminated, should be reported in the results section of the experimental report. And as noted in Chapter 13, subjects cannot be eliminated nor data thrown out for failure to support a predicted hypothesis.

The general purpose of setting a priori criteria is to eliminate subjects who are distinctly different from the others and who therefore add a large amount of variability to the data. They may be different because of motivational factors, personality factors, or personal limitations. Such differences might, certainly, be of interest to psychologists studying individual differences or abnormal behavior. But their behavior is usually not of much interest to most experimental psychologists whose concern is usually with establishing a science of the behavioral norm.

Can I Operationally Define All My Variables?

In Chapter 4, I discussed the necessity of being able to operationally define your independent and dependent variables and to state the required operations that need to be carried out to enable you to repeat your experiment. Although you should have determined operational definitions at an early stage of designing your experiment, sometimes experimenters fail to do this.

Because the independent variables are the variables of major interest to the experimenter, great care must be taken in specifying their definition. Suppose that you propose to do the experiment that sets the record for the one most often proposed by my students.* You would want to know the effects of listening to music on studying. Some variations of this basic experiment are the effects of rock versus classical music, of TV, of noise, and of

---

*This experiment is closely followed in popularity by experiments that test the effects of drug X (for instance, marijuana, alcohol, or cocaine) on the performance of task Y (such as driving, studying, or memorizing). If your instructor requires that you propose an experiment and you want to be impressively original, do not propose either of these experiments!

loud music versus soft music. Suppose the comparison is between rock and classical music. What is rock music? Heavy metal, punk rock, new wave, rock and roll? What is classical music? A Strauss waltz, Dvořak's *New World Symphony,* a Beethoven sonata, Tchaikovsky's *1812 Overture*? Even when you use classical music, the outcome of the experiment might be quite different if a quiet string quartet is played rather than a noisy overture complete with rolling tympany and cannons.

Likewise, if the comparison is between loud and soft music, the question is, how loud? An appropriate answer is not "I'll turn it up until it sounds loud," or even "I'll set the volume control of my tape player on 8." Another experimenter would not know what operations to follow to produce the same loudness. Ideally, you would have someone measure the sound with a meter and tell you the average sound-pressure level in decibels.

For the dependent variable, again an operational definition is required. What are you going to measure to see whether the music had an effect on studying? There are a number of possibilities. You could find out how many pages subjects were able to read within certain time limits. You could find out how many math problems were completed. You might give the subjects a quiz over the material studied. Or you could ask them how difficult they found studying to be under a particular condition. There are advantages and drawbacks to each of these measures, but some dependent variable will have to be operationally defined, because no proposal is complete until that is done.

Have I Arranged for Any Equipment or Materials Needed?

Many experiments require equipment and nearly all require some sort of materials to be prepared. Fortunately, today in many places computers are available that can be used to present stimuli with precise timing and to record and store responses. If you have access to such equipment and know how to use it, or can get help from someone who knows how, you will be able to carry out many experiments with a minimum of preparation. However, if computers are not readily available, or if your experiment cannot benefit from computers, you may have to carry out your experiment the old-fashioned way, using whatever equipment is on hand or constructing the equipment and materials yourself. In some cases, you may even have to plan your experiment around the resources that are available.

Among the materials that you may have to prepare are a set of instructions, response sheets on which to record data, and a debriefing script. You should generally write the instructions out ahead of time. Later you might well include them in an appendix in the experimental report. In any case, they should certainly be available if someone wanting to replicate your experiment requests them.

It is usually not a good idea to simply hand instructions to your subjects and expect them to be read properly. Some people's reading ability leaves a bit to be desired, particularly when the experimenter is hovering over

them waiting for them to finish. Experimenters often give the subjects the written instructions and then also read them aloud—slowly (after all, it's the first time the subjects have heard them, even though the experimenter may have read them many times). The last sentence of instructions is usually "Do you have any questions?" Even in experiments in which learning is not anticipated to be a problem, it is often useful to give subjects a few practice trials so that they know what to expect once the experiment starts. These practice trials can also be included toward the end of the instructions.

If your experiment is one in which data about individual responses are to be recorded (as opposed to questionnaires, for example), you will probably have to construct data sheets for recording these responses. If you are going to present various types of trials that represent different levels of the independent variable, the response sheets may also include this information. Especially if the trial types are to be randomly presented to the subject, you should have determined the random orders ahead of time by using a random number table or some other random device. If you attempt to create a random sequence while the experiment is under way, it will not really be random (see Chapter 1).

Finally, you should write a debriefing script so that you can inform the subjects at the end of the experiment about the purpose of the research. When subjects serve in an experiment as part of a class requirement, such a debriefing is usually necessary. Even if it is not, the debriefing is a good idea. Subjects will leave the experiment feeling more comfortable and not carry away misconceptions about what they just went through. In addition, they may be able to learn something about psychology from this experience and, at the very least, will feel better about their experience because somebody has taken the time to explain the purpose of the study and to thank them for their service.

Do I Know How I Will Analyze My Data?

Chapter 9 discusses how to interpret your experimental results using descriptive and inferential statistics, and Appendix A provides a guide to some commonly used statistical tests. If your experiment is relatively simple and small, these may be sufficient for you to be able to determine how to analyze your data. If your experiment is more complex, you may need some help from your instructor, a statistics book, or a statistical consultant to choose an appropriate way to analyze the results. Regardless of how you determine the best way, before you do the experiment you must know how the data will be analyzed. Statistical consultants tell horror stories about people coming to them with reams of data after an experiment is complete only to discover that the data are useless because they are unanalyzable! Don't you become a character in one of these stories. Know ahead of time what form your data will need to be in and how they can be analyzed.

How Will I Interpret the Possible Outcomes of My Experiment?

When you decide to do a particular experiment, you probably have some idea what the results might be. Unlike the starting assumption in statistics, called the *null hypothesis*, that there will be no effect of manipulating the independent variable, you probably actually expect that the differences in the levels of your independent variable will cause a difference in the dependent variable. Scientists are encouraged to be nonpartisan bystanders, not active participants rooting for a particular outcome. In fact, a good deal of the fun of science is predicting the outcome of experiments. Being a good predictor is part of the art of being a good scientist.* But be careful that you do not become so enamored of your predictions that you are tempted to lose objectivity and produce a biased experiment.

So, be prepared to interpret the results of your experiment regardless of the outcome. Some experiments, because of their design, are considered to be failures if certain outcomes occur. Scientists sometimes call outcomes such as these that support the null hypothesis a *negative result*. For example, suppose you did the experiment to determine whether rock versus classical music differentially affects a student's ability to study, and you find that the group listening to rock and the group listening to classical music are not statistically different in their performance. As discussed in Chapter 11, because our statistical tests are designed to test for differences not samenesses, you cannot really say that the performances of the groups were the same, only that you failed to show that they were different. Perhaps it would be interesting to know that rock music affects studying no differently than classical music, but the failure to find a difference could have been caused

---

*English professors would probably call this statement oxymoronic (but not, I hope, moronic).

by any of a number of factors aside from the lack of an actual difference: for example, using too few subjects or not having proper control of variables, which caused the variability of the data to be high, and so on. In some cases, where a series of experiments using similar experimental conditions produced statistically significant effects, you may be a bit more confident that your negative outcome is meaningful. But generally a negative outcome is uninteresting, except perhaps as a methodological example of what not to do.

One way to know whether you will be able to interpret the outcome of your experiment is to consider the various possible outcomes and determine whether you could predict them. As discussed in Chapter 11, a theory might help you to predict. Remember that a theory is simply a statement of a scientific relationship that cannot be directly observed, usually because it is more general than a statement of the specific outcome of any single experiment. So you may decide that your experiment fits within the context that a particular theory has been proposed to explain; thus, you predict the outcome of your experiment to be that predicted by the theory. You are in an even better situation if two or more theories have been proposed that make differing predictions. If one of these theories supports a positive result and the second a negative result, then interpreting your outcome will still be easier if the positive result occurs, for reasons discussed in the previous paragraph. However, the best of all possible worlds is when two theories each predict positive results, but in opposite directions. In this case, either outcome can be clearly interpreted.

A second way that a prediction can be made and supported is from prior research. Someone may have done an experiment that is similar to yours in some respects, but different in other respects. In this case, you might predict that you would find a similar outcome. If you do, you will have shown that the result can be repeated and that it can be generalized to your somewhat different experimental situation, and you are on your way to being able to make a more general theoretical statement. If your outcome is different from that reported in the earlier experiment, then you have discovered a limitation of the prior result, and, again, something has been learned.

A third justification for a prediction, particularly when no prior research or theorizing has been done in a particular area, is simply logical argument. For example, you might argue that it is logical for loud and unpredictable music to be distracting because it draws the student's attention away from the studying task in an obligatory way. You might also be able to logically predict some other effects from similar reasoning: for example, that the music might help if it masks a loud, even more unpredictable noise, or that the more familiar the student is with the music, the less performance will be degraded. While these predictions are initially based on logic, they could, if supported by experimental outcomes, gain theoretical status.

The reason you want to be able to predict the possible outcomes of your experiment is, basically, so that you will know ahead of time that when the experiment is completed, you will have contributed something important to science. If you cannot defend the various outcomes as supporting anything important, you will have added nothing useful. For example, if the outcome you predict would be expected by all the proposed theories and would eliminate no alternative theories, then your work would contribute nothing to the body of knowledge. As discussed in Chapter 11, advances in science are generally made by disconfirming theories, not by confirming theories, and you would not have disconfirmed any. The basic point is that if you believe a particular result could be important for advancing science, you should be able to defend this belief before doing the experiment. Otherwise there is no point in proceeding.

Now, Am I Ready?

If you have answered all of the questions posed here, you are probably ready to begin your experiment. As a final check, you should ask yourself whether you could, at this point, write all the sections of an experimental report except for the results. In fact, you could save yourself considerable time by doing this before collecting data. Graduate students in many experimental psychology programs are required to submit a formal prospectus prior to doing a thesis or dissertation. This document is essentially the final experimental report, except that the results section contains various predicted results rather than actual results and, obviously, contains no statistical analysis. One advantage of doing a prospectus is that most of the writing is completed early. In graduate schools, the procedure also helps protect the student to some extent because those on the student's faculty committee can indicate before the work is done whether they think the design contains any major flaws. For your purposes, the major advantage of trying to write most of the report is that you would have had to answer the questions in this chapter before writing it. Obviously, you cannot describe an experimental procedure until you have worked out all its details. You cannot write a literature review until you have searched the literature. You cannot predict the outcome of the experiment without knowing the theories that have been proposed or the results previously reported. Writing a prospectus is simply a good way of making sure that you have thoroughly thought through the experiment you are proposing to do.

At this point you should be ready for the excitement of collecting your own data. It can be fun, and a good intellectual exercise, to plan an experiment. Searching the literature requires some discipline and can be interesting. Finding the appropriate statistical tests may thrill some experimenters, but, to be honest, I do statistical tests just because they are part of the experimental process. The creative act of collecting data and testing your theories and predictions is worth the hard work of doing some of the steps that you may find less intrinsically interesting. I do receive satisfaction from moving science along, making a lasting, and potentially immortal, contribution to the body of knowledge. But for me—and I hope for you, too—

the most fun of being a scientist is the thrill of discovery, of looking for the first time at data nobody else has seen. And that, by itself, is what makes the whole enterprise worth the effort.

Summary

Before you are ready to conduct an experiment, there are many practical details that you should consider. A useful way to determine whether you have anticipated these details is to present your ideas to others—either orally, by means of a presentation, or in writing, through a prospectus. In determining the **number of subjects** needed you should find experiments similar to yours that have been reported in the literature and use similar numbers. In addition, you will decide whether to **run subjects individually or in groups.** To determine the **experimental time required** to complete the experiment you will have to determine the time taken for each trial, the number of trials, the time required for other activities, and the number of subjects in each condition. In determining whether to set **subject selection restrictions** you should consider to what population you will generalize your results. In order to avoid including experimental noise in the data you may also wish to determine **criteria for eliminating subjects** from the experiment. To have made adequate **operational definitions of variables** you should be able to specify precisely what operations are required to manipulate the independent variable(s) or measure the dependent variable(s). Arranging for needed **equipment or materials** often includes generating instructions, response sheets, and debriefing scripts. Finally, you should know how you will statistically **analyze the data** and **interpret the results.** This interpretation will be aided by existing theories, previously reported findings, or logical argument. If all of these issues have been considered before you begin your experiment, completing the experiment and reporting the results should run smoothly.

13
How to Be Fair with Subjects

Whatsoever ye would that men should do to you, do ye even so unto them.*

Our data show that the social structure of competition and reward is one of the sources of permissive behavior in experimentation with human subjects; the relatively unsuccessful scientist, striving for recognition, was most likely to be permissive....†

From an ethical point of view, we all stand on equal footing—whether we stand on two feet, or four, or none at all.‡

You may think that we have done all our preliminary work now and are ready to start experimenting. First, however, we should consider one more issue—the ethics of doing a psychology experiment. As experimenters, we can be unethical in at least two ways. We can mistreat the people or animals whose behavior we are measuring. We can also mistreat the body of knowledge that we are trying to establish—in other words, treat our science unfairly. This chapter will discuss treating our subjects fairly; Chapter 14 will discuss treating science fairly.

Society as a whole and the scientific community in particular have agreed on a set of rules by which we must do our research. Some of these rules are unwritten, such as the basic rules of courtesy. The assumption is that such rules are so obvious that everybody understands them. Other rules are written, such as the *Ethical Principles of Psychologists* (American Psychological Association, 1981) and the *Ethical Principles in the Conduct of Research with Human Participants* (American Psychological Association, 1982). These rules are continually revised as society's conception of the role of experimentation and the rights of an individual change. In this chapter, first I will consider the relationship between the person doing the experimenting and the one being experimented on, including some basic courtesies in the relationship. Then I will discuss how this relationship can affect the outcome of an experiment. Finally, I will discuss alternative experimenter-subject relationships.

---

*Matthew 7:12.
†Barber, B. (1976). The ethics of experimentation with human subjects. *Scientific American, 234,* no. 2, p. 30.
‡Singer, P. (1985). *In defense of animals.* New York: Basil Blackwell, p. 6.

Treating Human Subjects Fairly

Because our purpose in doing an experiment in psychology is to understand human behavior, we will usually be interacting with humans. Traditionally, psychologists have referred to the people who will provide the behavior as **subjects.** The early forefathers and foremothers of psychology probably liked this term because it sounded scientific. Unfortunately, the term implies that people are subject to the experimenter's will, or even worse, subjected to it! Back in the 1930s it was suggested that the term **experimentee** should be used in place of **subject,** but the suggestion never caught on (Rosen-zweig, 1970).

This discussion may seem pretty trivial to you—what's in a word? In this case, the word **subject** reflects the nature of the experimental relationship and as such suggests certain ethical considerations. Subjects are represented as passively reacting to the conditions of an experiment much like chemicals passively react when combined in the laboratory.

In the early history of experimental psychology, nobody worried about what to call the people who were experimented on because the experimenter and the subject were the same person. In those days, psychologists reported their own internal experiences as the dependent variable in their experiments. Believing that only time and training made it possible to become aware of these internal experiences, experimenters considered themselves their own best subjects.

Later in the history of psychology, many experimenters came to feel that verbal reports of internal events were inappropriate data for the science of psychology. Arguing that it is not possible to be objective and subjective at the same time, these experimenters started a revolution in psychology. Some psychologists, overreacting to the revolution, decided that only animal subjects were appropriate for psychology experiments. If you do not want a subject to make verbal reports, pick one who cannot talk! During this era, the rat became a prime subject for experimentation. Other inves-

tigators felt that although experimenters are too experienced to be experimented on, rats are rather unlike most humans. What was needed was a naive human. The naive human chosen was the college student. College students are the subjects in 70% to 85% of published research (Smart, 1966; Schultz, 1969) and as much as 90% of research conducted by university psychology departments (Jung, 1969).

In this latest view, the subject is supposed to be a naive, well-motivated observer who will react to experimental manipulations in an uncontaminated way. Yet, as we shall see, subjects are not uncontaminated observers. They usually have definite ideas about the experiment they are serving in, and they attempt to achieve specific goals that are often different from the experimenter's.

Humans (even college students) also have certain legal and moral rights. A physicist can take the block of wood from the inclined-plane experiment and drop it, hammer on it, swear at it, kiss it, or do any number of things with it. Although his colleagues may think he is pretty weird, they would not have him arrested or throw him out of the profession. Psychologists, however, must preserve their subjects' rights at all times.

The nature of the experimenter-subject relationship makes subjects particularly vulnerable because the experimenter usually has most of the power. For example, many subjects serve in experiments to satisfy part of a psychology class requirement. Under these circumstances, students may feel that their course grade will be affected if they fail to do as the experimenter asks. On the other hand, if subjects are paid for their services, they may feel that noncooperative behavior will earn them less money. Finally, if subjects volunteer for experiments because they believe they can advance the science of psychology, they may feel that society will benefit from their cooperation. In any of these cases, subjects see the experimenter as having the ultimate power to evaluate or manipulate their behavior.

In addition to these academic, monetary, or altruistic motives for cooperating with the experimenter, subjects may also share the commonly held opinion that psychologists have a mysterious bag of tricks for determining whether someone is cooperating. The first three sentences between a psy-

98-POUND SUBJECT

SUPER EXPERIMENTER

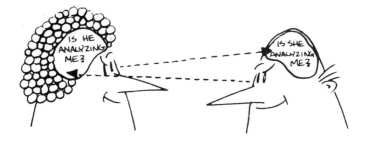

chologist and a stranger illustrate this belief: "What do you do for a living?" "I'm a psychologist." "Oh, are you analyzing me?" For some reason, many people believe that psychologists have X-ray vision and can look deep into their minds and find out what they are thinking. They believe they had better cooperate or the experimenter will get 'em! This belief, although it is sheer nonsense, again helps stack the experimenter-subject relationship in favor of the experimenter.

Rules of Courtesy

To unstack the relationship a little, experimental psychologists need to follow a code of behavior that treats their subjects with respect and dignity. As a new experimenter, you should hang a sign in your experimental room (an imaginary sign is OK) that says "Subjects are humans too!" Subjects deserve the same courtesies you would give anyone who offered to help you with a project. Some simple rules of courtesy you should follow are:

1. **Be present.** Too often experimenters forget that they had a subject signed up or fail to notify the subject if the equipment broke down or if the experiment is delayed or called off for some other reason. Once a subject signs up for an experiment, you should make every effort to fulfill your obligation to be present for the experiment.
2. **Be prompt.** A subject's time is valuable too. Don't waste it.
3. **Be prepared.** You should rehearse all phases of the experiment prior to meeting any subject. Not only is it discourteous to do otherwise, but if you stammer over the instructions, tinker with the equipment, and generally fumble and mumble your way through the experiment, subjects may become so confused or disgusted that they perform poorly.
4. **Be polite.** Unless the experiment calls for it, ask your subjects to do something; don't order them. Make liberal use of the words "please," "thank you," and "you're welcome."
5. **Be private.** Treat all information that a subject gives you within an experimental context as confidential. Be discreet not only about what the subject tells you but also about how he or she performs on the experimental task. Federally funded grants are specific about what information you may obtain from a subject, how you may use that information, and how to code and

store it. If possible, eliminate subjects' names from data sheets, and use a method that will prevent others from discovering the identity of individual subjects.

6. **Be professional.** You need not be so sober and stiff that your subjects feel uncomfortable, but do not be so casual and flippant that you convince your subjects that you don't care much about the experiment. They won't care either! Nor is an experiment the proper place to make dates, hustle golf partners, sell insurance, or use the experimenter-subject relationship for any purpose other than research.

These rules seem simple enough, but not all ethical issues concerning human subjects are so straightforward. More controversial issues, such as "What constitutes informed consent?" and "Should mental stress be permitted?" are discussed at length in *Ethical Principles in the Conduct of Research with Human Participants*. However, no publication can cover all possible ethical issues, so most research-oriented institutions now have human-experimentation committees made up of established researchers and sometimes physicians and other technical experts. These committees screen all research proposals that use human subjects. All federally funded and most institutionally funded human research must pass such a committee before it can be done.

Such review committees certainly help eliminate or improve many potentially unethical investigations. However, screening committees in the biomedical field have themselves been the subject of research, for it has been found that a significant minority of the people who serve on such committees are poor at balancing the risks and benefits of human research (Barber, 1976). A large majority of committee members surveyed had received no formal training of any kind in research ethics. So although these committees can be helpful, the primary responsibility for doing ethical research still lies with you, the experimenter.

The nature of the experimenter-subject relationship is important because it affects not only the subject's rights but also the experimental outcome. Although experimental psychologists like to pretend that subjects in psychology experiments are neutral creatures reacting in a sterile, controlled environment, most know that such is not the case. In the next section we'll consider in more detail how the experimental situation can influence the outcome of an experiment.

Demand Characteristics

When subjects show up for an experiment, they have little idea what they will be required to do, but they are usually interested in the experiment and want to know exactly what it is about. Experimenters in turn are often secretive about their intention, which prompts the subjects to try to determine what the experiment is really about from clues the experimenter gives them. The experiment then becomes a problem-solving game for the subjects.

These clues that influence subjects in the experimental situation have been called **demand characteristics** because they demand certain responses from subjects (Orne, 1962). Whereas the experimenter provides many such clues, subjects also bring demand characteristics with them to the experiment. If subjects have taken a psychology course, read about psychology experiments, or even been told about the experiment by a friend, they may bring such expectations as the following with them: The experimenter is going to shock me. The experimenter is trying to find out how intelligent I am. The experimenter is going to trick me into revealing something nasty about myself.

Sometimes these notions are so overpowering that a subject cannot be swayed from them. I once had a subject who was required to memorize a set of words presented to him through earphones. Shortly after starting the experiment, he tore off the headset and shouted "This thing is shocking me!" Thinking he might be right, I carefully measured for any current passing through the headset. The headset was well grounded. I tried to continue the experiment, but the subject still claimed that he was being shocked. He had made up his mind that I was going to shock him and would not believe otherwise. As a result, his data had to be discarded.

Other demand characteristics come from subtle cues that the subject picks up during the experiment. To minimize such cues, experimenters attempt to standardize all experimental procedures. An experimenter usually reads instructions to subjects from a written copy, for example, so that all subjects at least will have the same verbal demand characteristics. In some experiments, however, even the way the experimenter reads the instructions can affect the subject's performance. In one experiment, two sets of tape-recorded instructions were made by experimenters who were biased toward opposite experimental outcomes (Adair & Epstein, 1968). The experimenters found significant differences between the performances of subjects hearing different tapes. Although the experimenters read the same instructions, the subtle differences in their voices apparently produced results consistent with their biases.

Even animal subjects seem to be influenced by subtle cues given by the experimenter. In one of the more famous experiments on experimenter bias, student experimenters trained rats to run a maze (Rosenthal & Fode, 1973). Some of the experimenters were told that their rats had been specially bred to be bright, fast learners; the others were told that their rats were bred to be dull, slow learners. The supposedly bright rats learned to run the maze in fewer trials, even though they were in fact littermates of the supposedly dull rats. The usual reason given for this result is that the student experimenters must have treated the rats differently, playing with the "bright" rats more and handling them so that they became less fearful of being manipulated. However, other investigators have claimed that the results might be due to student experimenters cheating with their data (Barber & Silver, 1968). Whatever the reason, experimenter bias was reflected in the outcome of the experiment.

While my presentation of the concept of demand characteristics makes it sound pretty ominous, it may be less of a problem than I have suggested here. Several investigators (Weber & Cook, 1972) have reported that they found little evidence that experimental subjects typically try to confirm what they believe is the experimenter's hypothesis, which they have deduced from cues in the experiment. Instead, these investigators claim that subjects try to put their best foot forward; that is, they try to appear competent, normal, and likable. The subjects' concern with how they will be judged is far more important than their concern about fulfilling the experimenter's expectancies or confirming the hypothesis.

Barber (1976), in a book dealing with the pitfalls in human research, reports that many experiments claiming to demonstrate demand characteristics are themselves seriously weakened by other design flaws. He believes that much of the research supporting the concept has been poorly done. However, just because this research may be flawed, we cannot necessarily conclude that demand characteristics can be ignored as a potential problem in our experiments. Anything that we can do to minimize their potential effects should be done to improve our experiments. If subjects do detect the demand characteristics in an experiment, how might they respond?

Cooperative subjects   After human subjects determine in their own minds what the demand characteristics of the experiment are, they react according to their attitude toward the experiment (Adair, 1973). Most subjects tend to be **cooperative** and try to fulfill the perceived demands of the experimenter. Some subjects cooperate to an astounding degree. In one experiment testing cooperativeness, the experimenter gave the subject a stack of 2000 sheets of paper and asked him to compute the 224 addition problems on each page. Although this task was obviously impossible, the subject continued to add for five and one-half hours, at which point the experimenter gave up! In a second experiment, the experimenter instructed subjects to tear up each sheet into at least 32 pieces after completing the additions. Again subjects persisted in the task for several hours without appearing hostile.

To see how this desire to cooperate might be behind a subject's response to demand characteristics, consider the following experiment on group pressure: A subject is brought into a room with six other people. The subjects are asked to judge which of two lines is longer. The first few problems are easy and everybody agrees. Then two lines are presented, and our subject is sure that the top line is longer, but everybody else says the bottom line is longer. After a long pause, the subject finally agrees that the bottom line is longer. What happened in this experiment?

The experimenter designed the experiment to find out whether group pressure can cause someone to make an obviously incorrect response. The other "subjects" in the room were confederates or stooges trained by the experimenter to lie on the appropriate trial. Because the real subject gave in to the group pressure, the experimenter feels that the hypothesis has been confirmed. But let's read the mind of our subject* and see what really happened: "Well, here's another pair of lines. The top line is definitely longer. What a dumb experiment this is! Why waste our time having us do such an obviously easy task? And why are we doing it as a group? The experimenter must be trying to see if we can influence each other. Sure enough, everybody else is saying the bottom line is longer. They couldn't possibly really think that. Let's see, I could either give in to these shills and agree or hold my ground. I want to be a good subject so I can get out of here. Besides, I'm sure that a group of people can get someone to change his mind, so I might as well agree. Besides, the experimenter seems like a nice person and I don't want to mess up the experiment."

If our mind reading is correct, then our experimenter's conclusion was wrong. The subject, who is only trying to be cooperative, can cooperate us into drawing an incorrect conclusion!

Defensive subjects   Some subjects are less concerned with making the experimenter look good than with making themselves look good; let's call them **defensive subjects.** Such subjects search for demand characteristics in the same way that cooperative subjects do, but they use them differently. Usually a subject trying to perform as well as possible is an asset to an experiment. But in some experiments, particularly attitude-assessment experiments, these subjects can cause problems.

Suppose we are investigating the difference in the way Hispanics and Anglos view sex-role behavior in children. We post one sign-up sheet requesting volunteers who have Spanish surnames and speak Spanish as a first language and a second sheet requesting Anglos who meet neither of these criteria. Now we show each subject pictures of children in traditional sex roles (such as girls playing with dolls) and in nontraditional sex roles (such as boys playing with dolls). We then ask the subjects to rate the acceptability of each behavior. Suppose more Hispanics than Anglos report that they find the nontraditional behaviors acceptable. We might conclude that Hispanics are more liberal than Anglos. On the other hand, another interpretation is possible. The members of each group of subjects are aware that they were selected on the basis of ethnic origin. Suppose the Hispanics were more concerned with upholding the pride of their ethnic group than were the Anglos. In this case, they may have bent over backward to keep from looking like socially unacceptable chauvinists. In other words, they appropriately perceived the demand characteristics of the experiment and attempted to defend their ethnic group.

In an actual experiment that demonstrated the defensive subject's reaction to demand characteristics, experimenters asked subjects to tap a key with their right and then their left index finger (Rosenberg, 1969). Tapping rates are usually faster for the preferred finger, but one group of subjects was told that graduate students at Yale and Michigan had been found to

---

*See, psychologists *do* have mystical powers.

tap the key at similar rates with each finger. A second group was not given this information. The difference between tapping rates for the two fingers was significantly smaller for the first group. Again the subjects perceived the not-so-subtle demand characteristics of the experiment and tried to make themselves look as good as possible.

Noncooperative subjects Some subjects are neither cooperative nor defensive but downright **noncooperative!** The result of such behavior has been picturesquely called the "screw-you effect" (Masling, 1966). The noncooperative subject attempts to determine the demand characteristics of an experiment and then behave in such a way as to contradict the experimenter's hypothesis. Such subjects act out of any number of motives. They may be participating to fulfill a course requirement and resent being coerced. Or they may be opposed to the whole idea of studying human behavior scientifically. Or perhaps they are simply turned off by the experimenter. Whatever the reason, such subjects can be a real nuisance in an experiment. One way to eliminate noncooperative subjects is to set some minimal standard of performance so that you may exclude any subject's data that fall below this standard. This standard should be determined prior to the experiment and noted when the experiment is reported. Even this procedure will not eliminate the data of all noncooperative subjects, however. Sometimes the best we can do is attempt to give the subjects a positive impression of our experiment and hope that they will be cooperative.

How to Minimize Demand Characteristics

Although we cannot completely eliminate demand characteristics from an experiment, every attempt should be made to minimize those demand characteristics that might become confounding variables. It is important to know whether a change in a subject's behavior is due to the experimenter's manipulation of the independent variable or to the subject's perceived demand characteristics. Confounding caused by demand characteristics can be minimized in several ways.

Automation Demand characteristics can be controlled by **automating** as much of the experiment as possible. We have already discussed the use of tape-recorded instructions as one type of automation. Experimenters are often rather poor at reading instructions anyway, particularly after reading them aloud 20 or 120 times. You can also ask a person who is unaware of the expected outcome of the experiment to record the instructions if you want to minimize experimenter bias caused by voice inflections.

I have also used videotaped instructions in some of my own experiments. Videotape is particularly effective because it combines visual and aural modes during instruction. If experimental trials involve complicated sequences of events, sample trials can be presented at a slow enough rate for subjects to follow, thereby eliminating the need for the experimenter to go back and explain earlier portions of the instructions.

In some laboratories, computers are used to play all or part of the experimenter's role in an experiment. Some investigators program the computer so that a subject never sees a human experimenter. The subject shows up at the appointed time. A sign instructs the subject to be seated at the computer terminal and to press a button. The computer then displays the instructions. The subject indicates his or her understanding of the instructions, and the experiment proceeds. The general idea behind this approach is that if subjects are not the passive automatons we once thought they were, we can turn experimenters into automatons instead. However, some researchers object to this procedure on the grounds that the artificiality of the situation not only causes the subject to feel dehumanized but also decreases the generalizability of the results. This procedure also requires that subjects be able to read and understand the instructions, which makes it unsuitable for some subjects, such as children and rats (and college sophomores?).

Blind and double blind A second way of minimizing demand characteristics transmitted by the experimenter is to make the experimenter **blind** to the level of the independent variable being presented. For example, I once did an experiment to determine if it was possible to "feel" colors with the fingers. Subjects were blindfolded and given three cards, two red and one blue. On each trial they were required to put the two cards that were alike in one stack and the one that was different in another. I was concerned that I might unintentionally signal subjects when they were correct by changing my breathing rate, coughing, or grunting when they had the cards correctly arranged. Some of my ESP-believing friends even suggested that I might send subjects ESP messages when they were correct! To avoid such signaling, I sat behind a screen so that I could not observe the subjects. I was thus "blind" to the color they were feeling. In fact, this procedure is sometimes called **double blind,** because neither the subject nor the experimenter is aware of the experimental levels.

Unfortunately, experimenters cannot always be blind to the manipulation of the independent variable. For example, an experimenter who wants to measure the response time to either a single light or one of four lights and who has no way of automating the experiment will obviously know which condition is being presented. Nonetheless, for those experiments most likely to be affected by experimenter bias, you should make every effort to use a blind procedure.

Multiple experimenters A third way to deal with experimenter-caused demand characteristics is to use **multiple experimenters.** In this case you do not control the experimenter variable but allow it to vary by using random assignment of the available experimenters. Such a procedure increases the generality of your result and decreases the chances that a single, blatantly biased experimenter will influence the outcome.

Are Demand Characteristics a Problem in Your Experiment?

Even when you have attempted to minimize demand characteristics, they can creep into your experiment. Here are some procedures for detecting them.

Postexperiment questioning   For a number of years after the revolution against subjective verbal reports, experimenters seldom questioned subjects about their impressions following the experiment. Fortunately, today many experimenters routinely seek this information. Such information can be valuable not only for uncovering demand characteristics but also for suggesting new hypotheses that can later be tested in a formal experiment.

Postexperiment questioning can take many forms, from the experimenter asking an offhand question to a well-structured written questionnaire. If you want to be sure to uncover demand characteristics, you should plan your questions ahead of time.

In planning your questions, make sure that the questions do not have demand characteristics built into them. For example, in the group-pressure experiment discussed earlier, a biased question would be "You weren't aware that the other subjects weren't real subjects, were you?" The question itself demands that the subject say "no." If subjects say "yes," they therefore admit that they were not the naive cooperative subjects they agreed to be. They also put themselves in the position of telling the experimenter that the experiment was a waste of time because their data cannot be used.

You should also plan your questions so that they go from general, open-ended questions to specific, probing questions. For example, in one experiment designed to determine whether humans could be conditioned without being aware of it, subjects were asked to talk about any topic they wished and to continue until asked to stop (Krasner, 1958). Whenever subjects said a plural noun, the experimenter nodded, said "good" or "uh huh," and was generally reinforcing. As subjects continued to talk, they used plural nouns more frequently. As evidence that the subjects were unaware of the conditioning, the experimenters asked the postexperiment question "Did you notice that the experimenter was doing anything peculiar as you talked?" The subjects reported that they had not. Other investigators, not convinced by this experiment, did a similar experiment but followed the original question with progressively more specific questions, such as "Did you notice that the experimenter would respond when you said certain words?" Although the subjects had trouble verbalizing it, most of them were aware that "the experimenter was happier when I talked about certain things, like listing parts to cars." The subjects who mentioned this awareness were the same ones who had shown the effect of conditioning. Thus, to determine whether subjects are influenced by demand characteristics, we should ask questions related to specific demand characteristics as well as ask more general questions.

Nonexperiments Another way to determine whether demand characteristics could have affected the experimental outcome is to compare a **nonexperiment** control group with an experimental group (Adair, 1973). The nonexperiment control group is not exposed to manipulation of the independent variable at all. They are simply told about the experiment, given the instructions, shown any apparatus, and then asked to describe how they think they would perform if put into that situation. If their prediction is similar to the outcome of the experimental group, they may have been able to detect demand characteristics. These characteristics, rather than the independent variable, could have caused the outcome of the experiment. If their prediction is different from the experimental outcome, demand characteristics probably did not cause the observed behavior.

For example, Mitchell and Richman (1980) were suspicious of a finding that supported a "quasi-pictorial" memory representation of mental images. In a typical experiment, subjects are asked to memorize a visual stimulus, generate a mental image of it, and then "scan" from one point on the image to another. The usual finding is that there is a direct linear relationship between scan time and physical distance on the stimulus. Mitchell and Richman thought that demand characteristics were possible with this procedure, so they conducted a nonexperiment in which subjects were simply asked to predict their scan times. These subjects produced scatterplots that were indistinguishable from those found in the previous experimental work. For this reason, the researchers could not rule out the possibility that the original findings were also caused by demand characteristics.

Simulation control groups You might also have subjects **simulate** their performance by pretending they have been exposed to a certain level of the independent variable and showing you how they believe they would react. For example, in a hypnotism experiment you might ask members of a simulation control group to pretend they are hypnotized. If their behavior is indistinguishable from that of the real subjects who are hypnotized, the performance of the hypnotized subjects may be due to nothing more than suggestibility and demand characteristics.

Alternative Experimenter-Subject Relationships

In the beginning of this chapter was the naive subject. And the naive subject was pleasing in the sight of the experimenter. But not all naive subjects are good; most are not even naive. So far we have been considering ways of keeping the subject as naive as possible, or at least discovering when the subject cannot be considered naive. We have another alternative, however. We can give in to the fact that subjects are not naive and make use of their problem-solving ability.

Deception and role-playing One way to use this problem-solving ability is to give subjects false cues so that their interpretation of the demand characteristics is incorrect. This procedure of **deception** is a controversial topic in psychology on both moral and methodological grounds.

The moral argument for deceiving subjects goes something like this: Although we may temporarily mislead subjects, we are justified because we are contributing to the advancement of science. Certain experiments must depend on a certain amount of deception. For example, how can we find out whether a bystander will come to the aid of someone in trouble unless we deceive the bystander into believing that the person is really in trouble? Eliminating all deception in psychology experiments would mean eliminating most of social psychology and much of personality research. Besides, we always tell the subjects the truth at the end of the experiment.

The moral argument against deception goes something like this: You can use a term like "misleading" if you wish, but that is just a nice way of saying "lying." There is enough dishonesty in the world without being dishonest in the name of science. How many of these "scientifically justifiable" experiments have caused great leaps forward in science? Not many! We can devise alternative ways of doing many of the experiments anyway, such as having subjects role-play. It is naive to think that debriefing subjects at the end of the experiment wipes out all effects of the deception. At the least, such an experience will make them wary of anything they are told in future experiments and perhaps lead them to distrust all psychologists. The costs of deception are just not worth it.

The role-playing argument is testable. Some experimenters have tried to use both deception and role-playing under the same conditions and then compared the results. In **role-playing** the experimenter asks subjects to imagine that they are in a particular situation and to respond as they think they would in a similar real-world situation. If you are interested in bargaining behavior, for example, you might ask one subject to imagine that he is a labor leader, another subject to pretend that she is the president of a company, and a third to act like an arbitrator. You then operate under the assumption that their responses in some way resemble those of people in the same real-world situation.

Unfortunately, although some experiments do report equivalent results from deception and role-playing (Greenberg, 1967), many others do not (Orne, 1970). It is also difficult to specify the conditions under which similar results can be expected from the two methods. In many respects role-playing experiments are much like the simulation control mentioned in the previous section. Perhaps role-playing simply reflects the demand characteristics of the experiment, rather than allowing us to predict what behavior would occur in a real-world situation.

Naturalistic observation   I already mentioned this final alternative to the standard experimenter-subject relationship in Chapter 1. **Naturalistic observation** depends on the experimenter's being an unobtrusive observer. Rather than having subjects pretend to be in a bargaining role, for example, the experimenter might go to an actual bargaining situation and observe behavior. We have already discussed the problems associated with this method. Experimenters usually have little control over the variables in the situation. They often have to wait for them to occur naturally, and even then they cannot control potential confounding variables or draw causal conclusions from the correlational data.

In this section, we have discussed the problems of treating subjects as naive, uncontaminated observers. At the least, we should be aware of the problem-solving nature of subjects and design our experiments so that the effects of subjects' problem-solving attempts can be evaluated. Where possible, these attempts should work for us rather than against us.

I will give the American Psychological Association the final word (paraphrased) on the investigator's responsibilities for treatment of human participants. Here are the principles (American Psychological Association, 1981), the investigator would do well to follow:

1. Evaluate the ethical acceptability of the experiment.
2. Determine whether participants are at risk.
3. Retain responsibility for ethical procedures.
4. Disclose risks to participants and obtain informed consent.
5. Determine whether deception is justified and necessary.
6. Respect freedom of participants to decline participation.
7. Protect participants from discomfort, harm, and danger.
8. Give postexperimental debriefings.
9. Remove any undesirable consequences of participation.
10. Keep individual research information confidential.

If you follow these basic principles and, when in doubt, seek the advice of experienced investigators, you will probably never have problems with the ethics of human subjects. Perhaps the best advice concerns your attitude. The subjects are doing us a favor. Without their willingness to participate, the science of human behavior comes to an abrupt halt. Treat your human subjects with the proper appreciation.

Treating Animal Subjects Fairly

Although their numbers are decreasing, some experimental psychologists use animal subjects in their research. If you have been reading the newspapers and watching the news, you're surely aware of how controversial the use of animals in research is. Radical animal-liberation groups have broken into laboratories, stolen animals, and destroyed equipment (Cunningham, 1985). As I write this, my local newspaper has a headline, "Proposals on Animal Research Rattle Cages: New Rules Would Cost $2 Billion, Scientific Groups Say." In a recent issue of the *APA Monitor*, the official newspaper of the American Psychological Association, the headline on the front page was "New Animal Care Rules Greeted with Grumbles." What is going on here? What is the source of this controversy?

It is true that a huge number of animals are used in this country for all types of research. The number has probably decreased in recent years, but it has been estimated that in the United States, in one year alone, 85,000 primates, 500,000 dogs, 200,000 cats, 700,000 rabbits, 46,000 pigs, 23,000 sheep, 1.7 million birds, 45 million rodents, 15–20 million frogs, and 200,000 turtles, snakes, and lizards were used for one form of research or another (Staff, 1973). Keep in mind that many laboratory animals may be living relatively normal lives. For example, the pig who is being fed a particular diet in an agricultural feeding experiment is probably not suffering much. In psychology only about 7% of all studies involve animals, and few of these studies subject the animals to painful or harmful conditions (Gallup & Suarez, 1985). Before we discuss some of the ethical issues, let's consider the question of why psychologists use animal subjects for research.

Simpler Behaviors

If we view human behavior from an evolutionary perspective, we can hypothesize that some of the most basic human behavior patterns are also present in the lower animals, because certain behavioral abilities occurred early in evolutionary history. Thus, animal research is based on the assumption that we can investigate certain universal **basic behaviors** using lower-order animals. We know that, over time, the animals up the evolutionary line kept basic behaviors but also acquired more complex behaviors that tended to override the basic behavior patterns. Thus, if we are interested in studying basic behaviors, it may be not only possible but preferable to use animals that display the basic behaviors unconfounded by the more sophisticated patterns of behavior shown by higher-order animals. However, we must be careful when we attempt to generalize the behavior of an animal to humans. Humans are obviously much more complex than rats, and no reputable investigator suggests that rat behavior is exactly the same as human behavior. Although some less reputable interpreters of animal research have been known to overgeneralize findings out of ignorance or simplemindedness, such occasional misuses of animal data do not invalidate the original premise behind using animals.

Control

In addition to theoretical reasons for using animals in research, there are a number of practical reasons. For one thing, animals are available nearly all the time. For some reason, college students insist on taking weekends and holidays off. Animals can also be used for experiments that take place over a long period. It is also possible and legal to **control** the conditions under which animals exist, both in and out of the experiment. Thus, animal experimenters can investigate such interesting variables as overcrowding, sensory deprivation, wake-sleep cycles, and environmental stressors.

We can control both the heredity and the environment of animals—a task made easier by the fast reproduction and multiple births common to lower animals. In human research, heredity is seldom a controlled or constrained variable, whereas in animal research, it often is. It is not true that "anything goes" with animals, however. We will discuss animal ethics shortly.

Uniqueness

Some animals also have **unique characteristics** that make them more appropriate for certain types of research. For example, fruit flies not only reproduce quickly but also have large simple chromosomes. Squid have much larger nerve cells than humans and so lend themselves to investigation of nervous-system structure. Similarly, many animals have a larger portion of the central nervous system devoted to the sense of smell or the sense of balance than we do. In such cases, humans are simply not the best subjects for research.

Irreversible Effects

Finally, lower animals are often used when the research could have **irreversible effects** on the structure or function of the animal. Ablation research can be done only with animals, because it requires that a portion of the nervous system be purposely destroyed to observe behavioral consequences. Similarly, humans cannot be used in experiments requiring that electrodes be implanted into the central nervous system. In many cases this type of research also requires that the animal be destroyed and a histology* performed to locate the specific structural changes.

***Histology** usually involves examining the tissue of the nervous system to see what has been destroyed or where the electrodes were placed. The brain is stained and sliced into very thin pieces for microscopic examination.

Manipulations such as keeping animals socially isolated can also cause irreversible effects. One famous example of this procedure was the work in which infant monkeys were separated from their mothers shortly after birth and then presented with various artificial mothers to determine what the important mothering dimensions were (Harlow, 1958). People frown on using human babies for such research, and some people likewise frown on using animal babies.

It is this last reason for using animals that is most controversial because the animals can suffer and die. There are approximately 1800 animal-rights and animal-welfare groups in the United States, and about half of the American people believe that animals should not be used in research (Staff, 1983). Peter Singer, a philosopher of ethics who wrote a book entitled *Animal Liberation*, goes so far as to say, "The practice of experimenting on nonhuman animals as it exists today throughout the world reveals the brutal consequences of speciesism. Experiments are performed on animals that inflict severe pain without the remotest prospect of significant benefits for humans or any other animals" (Singer, 1976, p. 31).

The strong advocates for animal rights are perfectly serious about this issue. They would probably not find my cartoons in this section humorous because the cartoons illustrate a major reason for the problem: animals cannot come to their own defense. Their point is that while animals cannot speak, they can suffer. To quote another advocate, "Today, animals are by far the most oppressed section of the community: their exploitation is as great an evil as were Black slavery, child labour and the degradation of women at the beginning of the last century. It is the great moral blind spot of our age" (Ryder, 1979, p. 14). The most extreme of the animal-rights advocates are abolitionists such as the co-founder of People for the Ethical Treatment of Animals, who says she is "working for the day when there will be no animals in cages" (Havemann, 1989).

What is the response of researchers whose laboratories are being marched on and, in some cases, wrecked? They have begun to form groups of their own to state their case (McDonald, 1983). Their argument is that the research that does sometimes cause animals to suffer and die has an eventual benefit for humans. They emphasize the major breakthroughs that have improved

the human condition (Miller, 1985). For example, animal research has led to significant advances in the treatment of mental disorders and pain control. It is sometimes difficult to anticipate the exact nature of future benefits, particularly for basic research. Nevertheless, many researchers feel that the costs in terms of animal suffering are more than offset by the potential benefits.

Many animal researchers would point out that since 1966, when Congress passed the Animal Welfare Act, the United States Department of Agriculture has had a stringent set of rules for ensuring the welfare of research animals. Amendments in 1985 broadened the law to require that research facilities establish animal-care committees and provide environments for nonhuman primates that promote their psychological health. The most recently proposed amendments would require that dogs be housed in cages four times larger than currently specified and that they be released for exercise and socialization for 30 minutes a day. Researchers argue that these latest proposed requirements and the increased paperwork associated with them would greatly add to the cost of doing research.

Most animal advocates occupy a middle ground between the two extreme positions and are willing to approach the issue from an informed and reasonable perspective. The issue will certainly not disappear. There is even a journal now devoted to this topic, *Humane Innovations and Alternatives in Animal Experimentation*, published by Psychologists for the Ethical Treatment of Animals.

In establishing a rational position on this issue, it might be useful to consider the stance of the American Psychological Association (1981) in this paraphrase of its ethical principles on the care and use of animals:

> In striving to advance science and human welfare, the investigator ensures the health and welfare of animals by (1) obeying all laws and regulations, (2) having a trained, experienced psychologist supervise all procedures, (3) ensuring the instruction and competence of all individuals interacting with animals, (4) minimizing the discomfort, illness, and pain of animals when alternative procedures are unavailable and the goal is justified, and (5) terminating an animal's life rapidly and painlessly when appropriate.

If you wish to read further on this topic, a more detailed set of guidelines based on this statement has also been published (American Psychological Association, 1986).

In the end, you will have to decide for yourself about the ethics of using animals in research. In making your decision, you will have to go back to the very foundations of your beliefs about the relationship of humans and animals. If you are like most people, you will find it difficult to reach an entirely consistent position: Do you eat hamburgers? Would you agree to have your dog or other pet in a medical experiment? Would you condone the sacrifice of 100 dogs to find a cure that would save the life of your child? Do you buy ant and roach spray? Are you willing to adopt all the cats at the local animal shelter? From your answers to these questions, can you determine where you stand and come up with a consistent philosophy?

The issue is not clear-cut. Like most of us, you may simply have to weigh each case and try to determine whether the benefits exceed the costs. Some psychological experiments, by their very nature, will subject animals to stress and pain. In such situations, you should be convinced that the potential scientific gains are worth the costs before starting your research, and you should be able to defend your decision. Although most institutions do have committees composed of experts to screen animal research, you should consider these committees as imposing only minimum standards. You must satisfy what should be a more stringent standard of ethics—your own.

Summary

This chapter discusses the ethical and methodological issues of treating human and animal subjects fairly. Because most of the power in the experimenter-subject relationship lies with the experimenter, it is important that the experimenter follow certain basic rules of courtesy. The experimenter must be present, prompt, prepared, polite, private, and professional. Although we have assumed in the past that human subjects are naive observers in the experiment, they are in reality problem solvers who are sensitive to the **demand characteristics,** or hidden clues, of the experimental situation. How subjects react to these demand characteristics depends on whether they are **cooperative, defensive,** or **noncooperative** in the experiment. We can minimize the demand characteristics by **automating** much of the experiment, by using a **blind** or **double-blind** design so that the experimenter is unaware of the specific conditions the subjects are responding to, or by using **multiple experimenters.** If unwanted demand characteristics are present in an experiment, we can sometimes detect them through **post-experiment questioning** of the subject or by using **nonexperiment** or **simulation** control groups. An alternative to assuming that subjects are naive is to use their problem-solving natures and give them false demand characteristics to deceive them about the actual purpose of the experiment. Alternatives to deception are to ask subject to **role-play** or to observe them in a **naturalistic** setting.

Psychologists also use animal subjects in experiments because animals exhibit some of the same basic behavior patterns that humans do in a form unconfounded by more complex behaviors. They also provide an opportunity for greater environmental and genetic control. Some animals possess certain unique characteristics that make them superior for certain types of research. While it is sometimes necessary for animal subjects to sustain **irreversible effects** from an experimental procedure, we should adopt a code of ethics that maximizes the care given to them and minimizes their suffering.

References

Adair, J. G. (1973). *The human subject.* Boston: Little, Brown. See Chapter 2 for a complete discussion of subject attitudes.

Adair, J. G., & Epstein, J. (1968). Verbal cues in the mediation of experimenter bias. *Psychological Reports, 22,* 1045–1053.

American Psychological Association (1981). *Ethical principles of psychologists.* Washington, DC: Author.

American Psychological Association (1982). *Ethical principles in the conduct of research with human participants.* Washington, DC: Author.

American Psychological Association (1986). Guidelines for ethical conduct in the care and use of animals. *Journal of the Experimental Analysis of Behavior, 45,* 127–132.

Barber, B. (1976). The ethics of experimentation with human subjects. *Scientific American, 234,* 25–31.

Barber, T. X. (1976). *Pitfalls in human research.* New York: Pergamon Press.

Barber, T. X., & Silver, J. J. (1968). Fact, fiction, and the experimenter bias effect. *Psychological Bulletin Monograph Supplement, 70,* 1–29.

Cunningham, S. (1985, June). Animals stolen, facility damaged in lab break-in. *APA Monitor,* pp. 1, 2.

Gallup, G. G., & Suarez, S. D. (1985). Alternatives to the use of animals in psychological research. *American Psychologist, 40,* 1104–1111.

Greenberg, M. S. (1967). Role playing: An alternative to deception? *Journal of Personality and Social Psychology, 7,* 152–157.

Harlow, H. F. (1958). The nature of love. *American Psychologist, 13,* 673–685.

Havemann, J. (1989, July 13). Proposals on animal research rattle cages. *Albuquerque Journal,* p. E4.

Jung, J. (1969). Current practices and problems in use of college students for psychological research. *Canadian Psychologist, 10,* 280–290.

Krasner, L. (1958). Studies of the conditioning of verbal behavior. *Psychological Bulletin, 55,* 148–170.

Masling, J. (1966). Role-related behavior of the subject and psychologist and its effects upon psychological data. In D. Levine (Ed.), *Nebraska symposium on motivation.* Lincoln: University of Nebraska Press.

McDonald, K. (1983, June 15). New group to tell public of benefits of animals in research. *Chronicle of Higher Education,* p. 7.

Miller, N. E. (1985). The value of behavioral research on animals. *American Psychologist, 40,* 423–440.

Mitchell, D. B., & Richman, C. L. (1980). Confirmed reservations: Mental travel. *Journal of Experimental Psychology: Human Perception and Performance, 6,* 58–66.

Orne, M. T. (1962). On the social psychology of the psychological experiment: With particular reference to demand characteristics and their implications. *American Psychologist, 17,* 776–783.

Orne, M. T. (1970). Hypnosis, motivation and the ecological validity of the psychological experiment. In W. J. Arnold & M. M. Page (Eds.), *Nebraska symposium on motivation.* Lincoln: University of Nebraska Press.

Rosenberg, M. J. (1969). The conditions and consequences of evaluation apprehension. In R. Rosenthal & R. L. Rosnow (Eds.), *Artifact in behavioral research.* New York: Academic Press.

Rosenthal, R., & Fode, K. L. (1973). The effect of experimenter bias on the performance of the albino rat. *Behavioral Science, 8,* 183–189.

Rosenzweig, S. E. G. (1970). Boring and the Zeitgeist: Eruditione gesta beavit. *Journal of Psychology, 75,* 59–71.

Ryder, R. D. (1979). The struggle against speciesism. In D. Paterson & R. D. Ryder (Eds.), *Animal rights—a symposium.* London: Centaur Press, p. 14.

Schultz, D. P. (1969). The human subject in psychological research. *Psychological Bulletin, 72,* 214–228.

Singer, P. (1976). *Animal liberation.* London: Jonathan Cape.

Smart, R. (1966). Subject selection bias in psychological research. *Canadian Psychologist, 7,* 115–121.

Staff (1973, July 18). *Christian Science Monitor.*

Staff (1983, June 15). *Chronicle of Higher Education,* p. 7.

Weber, S. J., & Cook, T. D. (1972). Subject effects in laboratory research: An examination of subject roles, demand characteristics, and valid inference. *Psychological Bulletin, 77,* 273–295.

14

How to Be Fair With Science

Science is willingness to accept facts even when they are opposed to wishes.*

To obtain a certain result, one must wish to obtain such a particular result: If you want a particular result you will obtain it.   LYSENKO[†]

Fraud in science is not just a matter of rotten apples in the barrel. It has something to do with the barrel itself.   NICHOLAS WADE[‡]

Research is a collegial activity that requires its practitioners to trust the integrity of their colleagues.   ARNOLD S. RELMAN[§]

In this chapter our discussion of ethics continues, but here we will think about treating science fairly. In some respects, science has fewer defenses than a subject does. Animal subjects squirm and yell and sometimes die when mistreated. Human subjects squirm and yell and sometimes sue when mistreated. Science can't even squirm and yell. If you mistreat it long enough, however, your fellow scientists might eventually squirm and yell.

You might wonder how you can be unfair to an inanimate thing like science. In one sense, science *can* be considered animate in that it is a moving, changing, and, we hope, expanding body of knowledge. New research constantly replaces or builds on old findings and theories. Anything you do that retards the expansion of science or causes it to expand in the wrong direction can be considered scientifically unethical.

Science has a few safeguards built into it to ensure that the body of knowledge will continue to expand in a proper direction. For example, before you are allowed to report the outcome of an experiment in the scientific literature, a group of scientists who have been selected for their research accomplishments review it. This review establishes whether the research appears to follow the rules of experimentation discussed in this book. Furthermore, the reviewers attempt to determine whether your contribution is sufficient to warrant using the limited number of pages available

---

*Skinner, B. F. (1953). *Science and human behavior.* New York: Free Press, p. 12.
[†]Lerner, I. M. (1968). *Heredity, evolution, and society.* San Francisco: Freeman, p. 284.
[‡]McDonald, K. (1983, June 15). Fraud in scientific research: Is it the work of "psychopaths"? *Chronicle of Higher Education*, p. 7.
[§]McDonald, K. (1983, June 15). Fraud in scientific research: Is it the work of "psychopaths"? *Chronicle of Higher Education*, p. 7.

in the journals. In this way the reviewers and editors of our journals attempt to screen research so that only competent and relevant findings are added to the body of knowledge.* Although this reviewing process is not perfect, most psychologists feel that it accomplishes this important screening function rather well.

While the review system is designed to exclude research that was poorly done or that fails to make a large enough contribution, it is not designed to determine whether an investigator who may be capable of doing good research has lied about his or her research. People who know the rules and say that they have followed them when in fact they have not cheat science. Such behavior is usually geared toward making personal gains of some sort: "They weren't going to promote me unless I had five publications"; "I had to make our product look good"; or "I had to have a positive result on the experiment to get a passing grade."

For the purposes of this discussion, I will define cheating as reporting that something happened in an experiment when it did not happen or, conversely, failing to report something that did happen. My use of the term **cheating** does not necessarily imply that the behavior is unacceptable, because, by this definition, some forms of cheating are considered acceptable. The general criterion we will establish for determining whether an action is acceptable is "Does the action lead to an efficient expansion of our scientific body of knowledge?" If the answer is "no," the action is unacceptable.

We can further subdivide unacceptable cheating into moderate cheating and blatant cheating. Although the distinction is not always clear-cut, moderate cheating is any behavior that leads to verbal reprimands by fellow scientists, whereas blatant cheating is any behavior so harmful to the body of knowledge or to the scientific process that a person's privileges as a scientist are taken away.

Blatant Cheating

Fabricating

One form of blatant cheating is to **fabricate results.** Some "experimenters" know that the easiest way to run an experiment is not to run it at all. They do not have to bother with such mundane matters as buying equipment, signing up subjects, or learning to do statistics. All they have to do is learn to write up experiments (fabricators better read Chapter 9). They also better learn a different profession because they will not be psychologists for long.

As a student, you may be tempted to fabricate because an assignment is due and you have not completed it. Don't do it! Late assignments cause lowered grades, but contrived results cause class dismissals and terrible

---

*Note here that I am using the term **relevant** differently than many people use it. I mean relevant to science, not relevant to faddish topics. Sometimes topics that are relevant in the latter sense are the least relevant in the former sense.

letters of recommendation. Professional scientists are totally intolerant of such behavior.

Back in the early 1900s, a biologist named Kammerer attempted to demonstrate that acquired characteristics could be inherited (Ley, 1955)—a concept quite different from Darwinian evolution. He claimed that he had kept generations of fire salamanders on black soil. He reported not only that the salamanders, which are normally black with yellow spots, showed increasingly smaller spots over generations, but also that this reduction was passed on by inheritance. A second researcher, who doubted these claims, added the time required to bring forth the number of generations Kammerer reported and found that the total time was considerably longer than Kammerer had been at work. Other scientists also began to demand explanations until, after seven years, two leading scientists were allowed to examine some specimens. They found injections of India ink. Kammerer admitted that his results "had plainly been 'improved' post mortem with India ink." He then promptly committed suicide.

The most dastardly deed in science is to add noise to the body of knowledge. If you do bad research, people can and will ignore it, but if you pretend that you have done good research when you have not, you will retard the expansion of the body of knowledge. Others will come along and attempt to build their research on yours, only to discover eventually that something is wrong. They must then waste their time fixing the foundation and possibly rebuilding the whole structure. The longer such cheating goes undetected, the greater the eventual waste of science's resources.

If undetected, the cheating of science can also lead to the cheating of society. In the late 1930s, for example, a Russian named Lysenko also supported the notion that acquired characteristics could be inherited (Lerner, 1968). He was so adamant about this theory that he falsified a great deal of data. Lysenkoites claimed that they had brought about such miraculous results as transforming wheat into rye, barley, oats, and even cornflowers; beets into cabbage; pine into fir; a tree of the hornbeam group into forest walnut (using doctored photographs as evidence); and even the hatching of cuckoos·from eggs laid by warblers (Lerner, 1968).

Lysenko's grossly unethical behavior hurt not only science but society as well. He was personally responsible for the dismissal, exile, and execution of a number of Russian geneticists. He convinced Stalin and later Khrushchev that his theories were correct and that they should be applied on a large scale in agricultural programs (Medvedev, 1969). When later devastating agricultural failures were attributed in part to Lysenko's methods, Lysenko fell, Khrushchev fell (though not only for this reason), and Russian society suffered.

When I wrote this section for the first edition of this book, I had to look back into history to find examples of scientific fraud. Unfortunately, finding examples of fraud is much easier today. In several professional and local newspapers I recently found the following headlines: "Allegations of Plagiarism of Scientific Manuscript Raise Concerns About 'Intellectual Theft,' "

"Indictment, Congress Sends Message on Fraud," "Nobel Honoree Faces Misconduct Charges," and "Harvard Professor Resigns" (due to fraud).

Is blatant cheating a new phenomenon or is there simply more interest today in discovering it? Apparently even the old-time scientists were not without guilt. The geneticist Mendel was accused almost half a century ago of being somewhat less than truthful (Fisher, 1936). Even Isaac Newton apparently reported correlations to a degree of precision well beyond his ability to measure (Westfall, 1973).

More recently a researcher at the Sloan-Kettering Institute admitted fudging data by painting the skin of two mice to make it appear that the skin had been successfully grafted without an immune response (Culliton, 1974). A physician at the Harvard University medical school also recently admitted falsifying data in a research experiment (Staff, 1982).

Closer to psychology, a prominent ESP researcher discovered that his laboratory manager had fudged data. A suspicious research assistant had concealed himself and observed the manager changing data to support ESP findings.

The most famous case in psychology concerned Sir Cyril Burt, an eminent British psychologist who had been knighted by King George VI. His research with identical twins was one of the major pillars supporting the argument that IQ is largely inherited. After his death, researchers discovered that the correlations he reported for identical twins remained the same to the third decimal place over many years as more twins were added to the study. This seemed a highly unlikely coincidence. Fraud allegations were made in the London *Sunday Times*, and the controversy continues. On one side are researchers who argue that Burt's data should be considered fraudulent and probably fabricated (McAskie, 1978). Others argue that the case for fraud is weak and that a more probable explanation is simply carelessness (Jensen, 1978). It is also unfortunate that this heated debate is fueled by the politics of elitism versus egalitarianism.

How can we guard science against the possibility of dishonesty by researchers? Basically, we cannot. However, some suggestions have been made that might minimize the possibility. The Association of American Universities recommends that institutions should establish explicit policies about standards and have administrators to carry out the policies (Staff, 1983). Procedures for dealing with deviations should also be specified, and these should protect the confidentiality of the accusers as well as the accused.

One suggestion that has been made is to establish data archives for the raw data* from research (Bryant & Wortman, 1978). Apparently one problem encountered by investigators attempting to validate Burt's research was his incredibly sloppy data storage. The raw test sheets on the twin studies were among papers stuffed into half a dozen tea chests and later destroyed! The data from research could be stored by individual researchers or possibly sent to a centralized location. In this way, research data would be available to the public, which is often not the case. For instance, a graduate student requesting raw data from 37 published authors received only 24% compliance (Wolins, 1962).

The archiving requirement has the following additional benefits: Researchers would probably be more careful in their original data analysis; others could add to the body of knowledge by examining issues not originally addressed; and longitudinal studies in which data are compared over a number of years are possible.

The costs of such a system include the cost of the bureaucratic structure to administer it, the time and money required to duplicate the data or conform to a standardized format, and perhaps the cost to science of a recognized loss of trust in the integrity of scientists. Some feel that the costs of this solution are too great when the problem is relatively small. They believe that the checks and balances provided by the replication process are sufficient to detect most fraud and make the problem of blatant cheating an anomaly rather than a common practice.

Some data do indicate that blatant cheating is relatively rare. For example, from 1982 to 1988 the National Institutes of Health, which supports the research of 50,000 scientists, had handled reports of only 15–20 allegations of wrongdoing. On the other hand, among scientists at a major research university who responded to a survey, one third said they had suspected a colleague of plagiarism or falsifying data, but fewer than half took action to verify or report their suspicions (Hostetler, 1988). At this time it appears that unless scientists take more formal steps to find and eliminate scientific misconduct, Congress will impose such steps through legislation. This possibility disturbs the many scientists who believe that regulation by those not trained or experienced in science could lead to undesirable consequences.

---

*The individual measurements of your dependent variable prior to combining them for statistical analysis are your **raw data**. Unlike meat, raw data do not spoil—they just take up room.

Regardless of formal requirements, you should keep data for a minimum of five years. Investigators often request data from each other, and with computers, storage and retrieval of raw data are easy. If you make a habit of storing raw data, you are helping to protect science, and you are protecting yourself against false accusations as well.

Falsifying Credentials

If you were to walk up to a friend and say, "Would you stand on your head for me?" the response would probably be "Why?" However, if you were to walk up to another friend and say, "I'm doing an experiment. Would you stand on your head for me?" your friend's response is more likely to be "How long?" This difference arises from the fact that our society grants scientists a number of privileges not given to the average citizen. We allow scientists, particularly behavioral scientists, the freedom to experiment because, as a society, we feel that the gains usually outweigh the costs. We also grant scientists a certain amount of prestige and generally respond to them somewhat compliantly.

Scientists not only are allowed to manipulate the lives of those around them, but sometimes are supported in this effort by our tax money. However, we are also capable of taking away these privileges if we believe that the gains no longer outweigh the costs. Requiring professional credentials of experimenters is one way we police ourselves. Consequently, to prove to other scientists that you are a qualified investigator, you must present them with your professional record, usually in the form of a vita or résumé. A résumé is a piece of paper that shows who you are professionally: it lists your educational degrees, your job experience, and your published papers and articles. You use it to get into graduate school, to become professionally certified, or to get a job. Perhaps it should go without saying that this document must be totally accurate. I will say it anyway—*falsifying credentials* is blatant cheating.

Early in my career, I saw a very talented student attempt to get into graduate school using a falsified vita. He had a fine record and great letters of recommendation from his professors, but he listed several papers and articles on his vita that did not exist. When his professors discovered his deception, the student no longer had either a fine record or letters of recommendation, nor is he an experimental psychologist today. Because the agreement between scientists and society is fragile, this type of dishonesty upsets the delicate balance and cannot be tolerated.

I hope that this discussion of blatant cheating was a waste of your time and that you would not have considered doing it in the first place. Yet I believe that such topics must be mentioned early in an experimenter's training. Doing psychology experiments can be fun, but the real purpose of experimentation is building science. Those who are not willing to follow the rules that make this process an orderly one do not belong in science.

Moderate Cheating

Those actions that most investigators find unacceptable but that lead to frowning and scolding rather than banishment can be considered moderate cheating. These actions can take place during the design of an experiment, during the experiment itself, during data analysis, or in experimental reporting.

Experimental Design

In the previous chapter, we discussed experimenter bias as communicated through demand characteristics. If you design your experiment so that the demand characteristics themselves could cause a desired change in the dependent variable and do not attempt to minimize these demand characteristics or even discover them, you are, in a sense, cheating. You can also confound an experiment if you claim to have made a particular variable into a control variable when, in fact, this variable systematically changed with your independent variable. In some nonlaboratory experiments such confounding is difficult to control, but in many cases we can legitimately call this situation cheating.

For example, suppose a college instructor wants to find out if the rate at which he lectures in his introductory psychology class has an effect on his students' attentiveness. He designs the following experiment. On some days he will attempt to speak at a slow pace, on other days he will speak at a moderate pace, and on others at a fast pace. He will measure attentiveness by recording the level of background noise and by videotaping selected students. Such an experiment would be easy to bias.* A biased instructor could change not only his pace but also the degree of liveliness with which he talks about the topic or perhaps the places in the room from which he lectures. Such nonverbal cues could easily confound the independent variable, whether or not the confounding was intended by the instructor.

---

*I know. I was the instructor in this experiment (Grobe, Pettibone, & Martin, 1973)!

One way to minimize the chance of cheating is to design the experiment so that colleagues with little investment in any given outcome rate each lecture in terms of the possible confounding variables. The experimenter could then collect data only from those lectures with equivalent ratings. Moderate cheating in the form of experimenter bias would not necessarily occur in the first design, of course, but the second design would be more convincing because such bias would be less likely to occur.

Collecting Data

You can also cheat when collecting your data, especially if you must use human judgment to determine what response the subject has made. In the experiment just discussed, for example, the experimenter wants to classify the subject's behavior as attentive or inattentive to record the percentage of time spent in attentive versus inattentive listening. Suppose one student sits scribbling with her pencil on a piece of paper. Is she taking notes or doodling? Another student has his eyes closed. Is he concentrating or sleeping? We can classify the behaviors differently depending upon our bias. If the experimenter who holds the bias is also doing the classifying, the potential problems are obvious.

To avoid this form of cheating, the experimenter might construct a standard checklist of attentive and inattentive behaviors and have several judges observe the tapes and independently classify the subjects' behaviors. It is even possible to keep judges blind to the pace the instructor had used for the tape being observed. Such precautions decrease the possibility of cheating, either intentional or unintentional.

Bias can sometimes occur even in experiments in which measurement of responses seems straightforward. An experiment was carried out in which subjects moved a stick to line up a marker with a moving target. After every ten-second interval, the experimenter quickly read a pointer on a voltmeter dial and reset it. (The farther the marker was from the target, the more quickly the pointer moved across the dial.) This task was difficult because

WHICH STUDENT IS THE ATTENTIVE ONE?

the needle seldom fell directly on an index line. The experimenter could easily have made biased judgments about the location of the pointer on the dial. In this experiment, experimenters had to read the dial over 15,000 times, giving rise to the possibility that small inconsistencies in reading the instrument would eventually bias experimental results. Thus, whenever biased experimenters must use judgment to interpret a subject's response, they should devise procedures to ensure that the judgment will be made accurately.

Data Analysis

You must also avoid cheating in analyzing your data. As we discussed in Chapter 9, statistical tests are usually computed to determine whether a particular result is likely to be a real effect or whether it is due to chance. These statistical tests can be used only when certain assumptions can be approximated. Using the test when the test assumptions are grossly violated is cheating.

For example, the most frequently used statistical tests require that the underlying distribution be approximately normal, a symmetrical bell shape. While a small violation of this assumption usually does not totally invalidate such a test, some investigators continue to use one of these tests when their distributions in no way resemble a normal distribution. As an experimenter, it is up to you to know what assumptions your statistical test requires and how likely it is that you will make an error if you fail to meet one or more of these assumptions.

When analyzing your data, you may discover that while most of the subjects seem to be showing the predicted experimental effect, several do not show the effect. At this point, you can do nothing about these renegade subjects.* Obviously, if you could throw out data from all the subjects who fail to show an expected result, you would never do an experiment that

---

*Unless you are specifically interested in investigating individual differences.

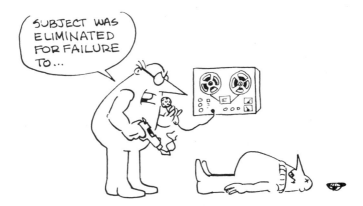

failed to support your predictions! For this reason, you must be careful about eliminating subjects from an analysis based on their performance on the dependent variable. And you should never eliminate them based on their differential responses to the levels of the independent variable.

You can eliminate subjects for failing to meet some overall performance level on the dependent variable only if you determine this performance level before collecting the data, if you can logically defend it, and if you specify the performance level in your experimental report. As an illustration, suppose you were interested in the effects of noise on a subject's ability to perform a typing task. Before starting the experiment, you might decide to exclude data from all subjects who fail to type at least ten words per minute in the absence of noise. Your logic might be that these subjects are such poor typists to begin with that even if noise has a detrimental effect on typing, they would not show the effect. Or you might argue that you are interested in the effect of noise on experienced typists and that a speed of less than ten words per minute indicates that the subject is not an experienced typist. However, if you do not have a logical argument for eliminating subjects based on a predetermined dependent-variable performance level, you should not do it.

You are much safer in eliminating subjects on a basis other than performance on your dependent variable. Again, however, such criteria should be set prior to the experiment and should be specified when you report the results. For example, you might be having subjects search through an array of letters to report which letter is printed in red ink. In this case, you might exclude subjects who cannot pass an acuity test or a color-blindness test prior to the experiment.

Reporting Results

Suppose you have analyzed your experiment and are now ready to report the results. Usually you will want to put some of your results into a graph. (We discussed some rules to follow in making a graph in Chapter 10.) People

have written books on how to lie by **distorting graphs** (Campbell, 1974; Huff, 1954). For example, an experimenter could blow up one of the graph's axes to make a tiny effect look like a gigantic effect or possibly distort the scale on one axis so that the function being displayed changes shape. If you are a creative person, you can find all sorts of ways to make crummy results look good. Obviously, such behavior does nothing to advance science and so is considered cheating.

One other form of moderate cheating is **piecemeal reporting** of experimental results. Whereas research must progress one experiment at a time, you should not report research in this way. Several decades ago the typical journal article in psychology reported the results of a single experiment. In recent years, however, the field of psychology has grown by such leaps and bounds that there has been a literature explosion. So many people are doing so many experiments that the process of keeping current with experimental advances is nearly impossible. For this reason, few journals will accept a report of a single experiment unless it makes an unusually large contribution by itself.

Usually, you should report the results of your experimental research program as an integrated series of experiments. With this procedure, the growth of knowledge becomes much more efficient and orderly and readers are spared the task of reorienting themselves to the research, rereading introduction and procedure sections with each experiment, and integrating fragmented research into a coherent structure. In today's "publish or perish" world, an investigator can be tempted to do piecemeal reporting to accumulate publications. However, in the end, such behavior does nothing to improve either the investigator's reputation or the body of scientific knowledge.

Accepted Cheating

Although the term **accepted cheating** sounds self-contradictory, it is sometimes necessary to "lie" to the reader of a research report to communicate efficiently. Research is usually a sloppy process, yet when you read an experimental report it sounds as if the investigator proceeded in a systematic, orderly fashion at all times.* Don't believe it! Rarely does a researcher's mind work in the totally logical manner reflected in the report. Experimenters make many decisions based on hunches or gut-level intuitions. They make false starts based on bad guesses. They do experiments the right way for the wrong reasons or the wrong way for the right reasons.

Unfortunately, many students become turned off to experimental psychology because they think it is dry and unexciting, when in most cases it is actually an exciting, disorderly, haphazard treasure hunt. You know little about experimentation until you try your first experiment.[†]

The most obvious reason for cleaning up an experimental report is to save time and space. While it might be fun to read about all your colleague's mistakes, you do not have the time and journals do not have the space to allow you the luxury. The experimental report is designed to convey information efficiently, not entertain the reader.[‡]

Leaving Things Out

One way of cleaning up your experimental report is to **leave out experiments and analyses.**[§] Suppose you had a bad day when you designed the third experiment in a series, you had a bad intuition, or you were temporarily confused. Nobody else is interested in the condition of your life, your viscera, or your head. So you blew the experiment. I don't want to read about it. You don't want to write about it. So don't. Science loses nothing, I lose nothing, and you save face. Be sure, however, that you are not tempted to leave out a perfectly good experiment because the results do not support your favorite hypothesis. Doing this is not accepted cheating!

Not only is it acceptable to leave out whole experiments if they add nothing to the report, but at times it is also proper to ignore the details of some data analyses. Perhaps there were a number of ways to analyze your data, and you did them all. Although you should probably report that you did the analyses, you need give details of only those that are most representative and convey the most information.[§§]

Reorganizing

Especially when doing exploratory research, you may find that the outcome of an experiment shows that it should not have been the first experiment in the series. You may find it desirable to back up and do some preliminary

---

*A charmingly written article on the sometimes haphazard process of research is B. F. Skinner's (1959) "A Case History in Scientific Method."
[†]It's kind of like making love: reading about it is a poor substitute for doing it.
[‡]A lot of textbook writers think this, too. They never have any fun!
[§]Or else put them in a footnote. Nobody reads footnotes.
[§§]Note that I am not endorsing the practice of conducting a multitude of tests and then picking and choosing only those that yield significant results. In this case, you are distorting the level of significance (Chapter 9).

experiments. In such cases, you need not tell the reader that "owing to misjudgment and lack of foresight on the experimenter's part, the following experiments are out of order." You may report them in the most logical order, whether or not this order matches the order in which you did them. Data are data, and you should report them as efficiently as possible, as long as bending the truth does not bend the science.

Reformulating

Finally, an accepted method of cheating in an experimental report is to **reformulate the theory** underlying an experiment. Occasionally you do an experiment for some reason and later discover a better reason for having done it. Or perhaps you discover that somebody else has done an experiment that casts a different light on one you are conducting. In this case, you have to determine how your contribution to the body of knowledge best fits with the new information. Unfortunately, there will be times when your theory does not fit at all and you will have to go back to the drawing board. Often, however, you will be able to fit your experiment into the revised theory by changing your emphasis or reinterpreting your results. In reporting your results, you need not burden the reader with obsolete theory. Again, your major ethical consideration should be whether you are adding to the body of knowledge in an efficient manner.

In this chapter we have by no means exhausted all the ethical questions that you will face as an experimenter. In some cases, you will find it difficult to decide whether a particular action is fair to science. When a problem comes up, you may wish to discuss it with colleagues, who may be able to raise points and suggest alternatives that you have not considered. In the end, though, the decision is yours. If you apply the principle that ethical actions are those that aid in the efficient growth of the body of knowledge, you will never be a blatant cheater and seldom be a moderate cheater.

Summary

Because science is a growing body of knowledge, any action that retards the efficient expansion of that body of knowledge is unethical. We can be less than totally truthful with science in a number of ways. We can blatantly cheat by **fabricating results** or by **falsifying our credentials.** We can also **cheat in more moderate ways**—by failing to control confounding variables in the design of an experiment, for example, or by misclassifying responses and misreading instruments during collection of our data. During data analysis, failing to meet test assumptions and inappropriately eliminating subjects are forms of moderate cheating. **Cheating in experimental reporting** includes distorting graphs and reporting a series of experiments as piecemeal reports. For the sake of efficiency, it is acceptable to write up experimental reports in a form that does not exactly parallel the experiment.

For example, we can leave out experiments and analyses from a report if they do not add to the report, or we can reorder experiments and reformulate theory if these actions increase the efficiency of the experimental report.

References

Bryant, F. B., & Wortman, P. M. (1978). Secondary analysis: The case for data archives. *American Psychologist, 33*, 381–387.

Campbell, S. K. (1974). *Flaws and fallacies in statistical thinking.* Englewood Cliffs, NJ: Prentice-Hall.

Culliton, B. J. (1974). The Sloan-Kettering affair (II): An uneasy resolution. *Science, 184*, 1154–1157.

Fisher, R. A. (1936). Has Mendel's work been rediscovered? *Annals of Science, 1*, 115.

Grobe, R. P., Pettibone, T. J., & Martin, D. W. (1973). Effectiveness of lecture pace on noise level in a university classroom. *Journal of Educational Research, 67*, 73–75.

Hostetler, A. J. (1988, June). Indictment, congress send message on fraud. *The APA Monitor*, p. 5

Huff, D. (1954). *How to lie with statistics.* New York: Norton.

Jensen, A. R. (1978). Sir Cyril Burt in perspective. *American Psychologist, 33*, 499–503.

Lerner, I. M. (1968). *Heredity, evolution, and society.* San Francisco: Freeman.

Ley, W. (1955). *Salamanders and other wonders.* New York: Viking Press.

McAskie, M. (1978). Carelessness or fraud in Sir Cyril Burt's kinship data? A critique of Jensen's analysis. *American Psychologist, 33*, 496–498.

Medvedev, Z. A. (1969). *The rise and fall of T. D. Lysenko* (I. M. Lerner, trans.). New York: Columbia University Press.

Skinner, B. F. (1959). A case history in scientific method. In S. Koch (Ed.), *Psychology: A study of a science.* New York: McGraw-Hill.

Staff (1982, January 6). Harvard physician admits fabricating data. *Chronicle of Higher Education, 23*, p. 3.

Staff (1983, April 27). AAU statement on preventing and probing research fraud. *Chronicle of Higher Education, 26*, p. 8.

Westfall, R. S. (1973). Newton and the fudge factor. *Science, 179*, 751–758.

Wolins, L. (1962). Responsibility for raw data. *American Psychologist, 17*, 657–658.

Epilog

Congratulations on having wended your way through my thoughts on doing psychology experiments. May my words and pictures have helped hold your interest rather than obstruct your progress. There is a delicate balance between informality and precision, a balance that varies from one reader to another. I hope my prose was not too unbalanced for you.

Obviously, this book has not instantly transformed you into a full-blown experimental psychologist, but I trust it has given you enough information so that you can attempt some simple experiments on your own. You will find that doing experiments is a lot more fun than reading about doing experiments. So now go have some fun!

Appendix A:
How to Do Basic Statistics

If you are a calculatophobic (see Chapter 2), this appendix is written for you. You should be able to use this simplified "cookbook" version of statistics if you have learned only basic algebra. In the preface to the first edition, I claimed that this book was not a statistics book; and the minor concession I am making in this appendix does not contradict that statement. Some teachers and students who used the first edition felt the need for a brief description of basic descriptive statistics and inferential statistical tests. Here I will tell you how to do a few of these. I will not tell you why you are doing what you are doing, however, and generally I will tell you only a little bit about the conditions for choosing what to do.

It has been my observation that writing words about numbers usually confuses things. Instead, I have attempted to show you what to do with the numbers by means of a worked example. If you arrange the numbers from your data the way the numbers are arranged in the example and follow the same steps, you should have few problems.

I will first mention some characteristics of numbers. Then I will give you a short glossary of statistical symbols. Finally, I will provide you with worked examples of each statistical operation.

Characteristics of Numbers

Numbers can be used in a variety of ways. Some ways convey a lot of information (it is 28 miles to the fair) and some only a little (the first baseman is number 28). Some statements and statistical operations are possible with some numbers (the theater, which is 14 miles away, is half as far as the fair). These same statements are ludicrous with others (the second baseman is number 14; for this reason he is only half the first baseman). So, before you can do a statistical operation on numbers, you must determine whether that operation makes sense for the type of numbers you are using.

Nominal Scale

Numbers that are simply used to name something are said to be on a **nominal scale.** Nominal scale data have no quantitative properties. The only legitimate statistical operation you can do with nominal data is to count the number of instances that each number occurs: how many players are there with the number 28?

Ordinal Scale

Numbers that can be ordered or ranked are said to lie on an **ordinal scale.** The racecar driver who was champion the previous year is allowed to put the number 1 on his or her car. The driver who was second in the point standings is number 2, and so on. We know from these ordinal scale numbers that driver 1 performed better than driver 2, but we do not know by how much. Drivers 1 and 2 may have been 500 points apart, whereas drivers 2 and 3 may have been only 2 points apart.

Interval Scale

If the intervals between numbers are meaningful, the numbers lie on an **interval scale.** Temperature measured on a Fahrenheit scale is interval. It is 10° between 50° and 60°. It is also 10° between 60° and 70°.

Ratio Scale

If you can make a ratio out of two numbers and that ratio is meaningful, you have a **ratio scale.** Thus, while you cannot say that a temperature of 20° is twice as hot as 10°, you can say that 20 miles is twice as far as 10 miles. The big difference between an interval and a ratio scale is that the latter has an absolute zero point. On the Fahrenheit scale, "zero degrees" has no particular meaning other than the fact it is 32 arbitrary degrees below the freezing point of water. For quantities like distance, weight, and volume, zero units is a meaningful concept.

One question you must answer before you perform a statistical operation is "What number scale am I dealing with?" Table A-1 lists the operations we will be discussing in this appendix and the scales they require.

Operations that can be carried out on numbers from lower-order scales such as nominal can also be used with numbers from higher-order scales such as ratio. For this reason, the shaded area in the table indicates that all the operations can legitimately be performed with interval or ratio data, but only three of them can be used with nominal data.

Symbols Used in Statistical Formulas

X = a datum or score
N = the total number of scores
Σ = sum or add the scores
X^2 = square X; multiply it by itself
X^3 = cube X; multiply it by itself twice
$\sqrt{X}$ = square root of X; what number multiplied by itself equals X?
$|x|$ = absolute value of X; the number disregarding its sign

Table A-1.
The Data Satisfy the Properties of Which Number Scale?

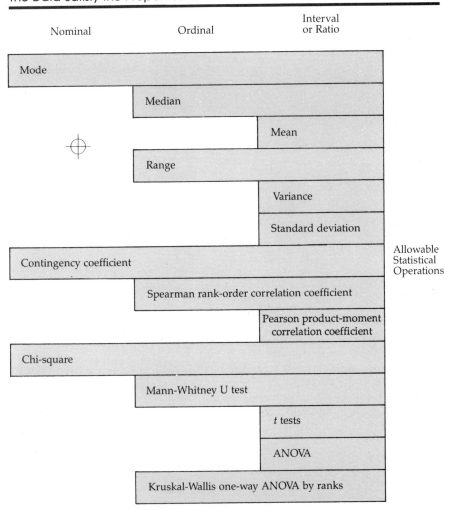

Nominal	Ordinal	Interval or Ratio	
Mode			
	Median		
		Mean	
	Range		
		Variance	
		Standard deviation	
Contingency coefficient			Allowable Statistical Operations
	Spearman rank-order correlation coefficient		
		Pearson product-moment correlation coefficient	
Chi-square			
	Mann-Whitney U test		
		t tests	
		ANOVA	
	Kruskal-Wallis one-way ANOVA by ranks		

Descriptive Statistics

Measures of Central Tendency

Mode

The **mode** is the most frequently occurring score. Count the number of times each score occurs and pick the score with the most occurrences. The mode in the example in the next section is 2 because this number occurs twice.

Median

The **median** is the middle score. The scores should first be ordered by size. For an odd number of scores, the median is the middle one. For an even number of scores, the median lies halfway between the two middle scores. In the following example the median is 2.5 because the middle two scores are 2 and 3.

Mean

$$\text{Mean} = M = \overline{X} = \frac{\Sigma X}{N}$$

Example

$$
\begin{array}{l}
X \\
1 \\
2 \\
2 \\
3 \\
4 \\
\underline{5} \\
\Sigma X = 17 \\
N = 6
\end{array}
$$

$$\overline{X} = \frac{17}{6} = 2.8$$

Measures of Dispersion

Range

The **range** is the largest score minus the smallest score. In the previous example:

$$\text{Range} = 5 - 1 = 4$$

Variance

$$\text{Variance} = S^2 = \frac{\Sigma(X - \overline{X})^2}{N}$$

Example

	X	X*	X − X̄	(X − X̄)²
	1	3	−2	4
	2	3	−1	1
6 scores	3	3	0	0
so	3	3	0	0
N = 6	4	3	1	1
	5	3	2	4
	ΣX = 18			Σ(X − X̄)² = 10

*Mean $= \overline{X} = \dfrac{18}{6} = 3.$

$$\frac{\Sigma(X - \overline{X})^2}{N} = \frac{10}{6} = 1.67$$

Standard Deviation

$$\text{Standard deviation} = SD = \sigma = \sqrt{S^2} = \sqrt{\frac{\Sigma(X - \overline{X})^2}{N}}$$

In the previous example:

$$SD = \sqrt{1.67} = 1.29$$

Measures of Association

Contingency Coefficient

The **contingency coefficient** (C) is a measure of the strength of association between two sets of numbers when nominal scale data are being considered. A chi-square (χ^2) test must first be done (see p. 257). Suppose that a chi-square test was conducted on a two-variable experiment and you wish to know the strength of association between these two nominal-scale variables. Also suppose that χ^2 was found to be 15, with a total number of observations of $N = 100$. Then the contingency coefficient is

$$C = \sqrt{\frac{\chi^2}{N + \chi^2}} = \sqrt{\frac{15}{100 + 15}} = \sqrt{.130} = .36$$

No further testing for the statistical significance of the association is necessary as the chi-square test has already been computed to test for significance.

Spearman Rank-Order Correlation Coefficient

A **Spearman rank-order correlation coefficient** (rho) is used to measure the strength of association between two ordinal scale variables. In this case, two scores or ranks are obtained for each subject and the difference d is determined.

Example

Subject	Rank on first measure	Rank on second measure	d	d^2	
Bill	4	4	0	0	
Jane	1	2	−1	1	
Bob	5	5	0	0	$N = 5$
Pete	2	3	−1	1	
Mary	3	1	+2	4	
				$\Sigma d^2 = 6$	

$$rho = 1 - \frac{6\Sigma d^2}{N^3 - N} = 1 - \frac{6(6)}{125 - 5} = 1 - \frac{36}{120}$$

$$= 1 - .3 = .7$$

To determine whether the obtained *rho* is likely to have occurred because of chance variation rather than to an actual association, we must consult the table of critical values for *rho* in Appendix B (Table B-1). We see that with N of 5, *rho* must equal or exceed 1 to be significant. It does not. We can also see from the table that the larger the number of subjects, the better our chances of finding a statistically significant effect, given that there is an association present.

Pearson Product-Moment Correlation Coefficient

A **Pearson product-moment correlation coefficient** (r) can be used to measure the strength of association between two interval or ratio scale variables. In the following example, X represents the score on one variable and Y the score on a second variable.

Example

Subject	X	X²	Y	Y²	XY	
Tom	9	81	8	64	72	
Sue	4	16	4	16	16	
Jill	4	16	6	36	24	
Dave	2	4	4	16	8	$N = 8$
Ken	1	1	3	9	3	
Jo	3	9	2	4	6	
Juan	7	49	8	64	56	
Al	5	25	5	25	25	
	$\Sigma X = 35$	$\Sigma X^2 = 201$	$\Sigma Y = 40$	$\Sigma Y^2 = 234$	$\Sigma XY = 210$	

$$r = \frac{N\Sigma XY - \Sigma X \Sigma Y}{\sqrt{N\Sigma X^2 - (\Sigma X)^2}\sqrt{N\Sigma Y^2 - (\Sigma Y)^2}} = \frac{8(210) - (35)(40)}{\sqrt{8(201) - 35^2}\sqrt{8(234) - 40^2}}$$

$$= \frac{1680 - 1400}{\sqrt{1608 - 1225}\sqrt{1872 - 1600}} = \frac{280}{\sqrt{383}\sqrt{272}} = \frac{280}{(19.57)(16.49)}$$

$$= \frac{280}{322.7} = .868$$

To test whether an r of this size is statistically significant with eight pairs scores, refer to Table B-2 in Appendix B listing critical values of r. To use this table, you must determine a quantity called the **degrees of freedom** *(df)*. For this test the degrees of freedom is $N - 2$. So in the example, $df =$

6. Because r of .868 exceeds the listed value of .834, it is statistically significant at the $p < .01$ level. That is, we would expect this strength of association to occur in a sample less than one time in 100 due to chance selection from a single population.

Inferential Statistical Tests

Chi-Square

The **chi-square (χ^2) test** is used to determine whether the observed frequency of occurrence of scores is statistically different from the expected frequency.

Example

	Number of subjects predicting heads after a string of tails	Number of subjects predicting tails after a string of tails
Observed	60	40
Expected	50	50
$O - E$	$+10$	-10
$(O - E)^2$	100	100
$\dfrac{(O - E)^2}{E}$	2	2

$$\chi^2 = \Sigma \frac{(O - E)^2}{E} = 2 + 2 = 4$$

The expected frequency can be the frequency based on a set of previous observations or based on a theoretical prediction. Usually the theoretical prediction is that the observed frequency will be that expected by chance. For instance, in the previous example the expectation is that the subjects' predictions will show no bias (no gambler's fallacy); half of the time heads will be predicted and half of the time, tails.

The final step in doing an inferential statistical test is to compare the final result of your computation to a table of critical values. You will find a table for chi-square values in Appendix B (Table B-3). To find the appropriate number in the table, you must first determine the number of degrees of freedom as follows:

df = The number of $O - E$ being considered, minus 1, which in this case equals $2 - 1 = 1$

In the table we find that with $df = 1$, χ^2 must exceed 3.84 to be significant at the $p < .05$ level of significance. Thus, the data in our example are statistically different from chance at the .05 level. If we had been testing at the

$p < .01$ level, $\chi^2 = 4$ would not have exceeded 6.64, and the test would have failed to reach significance.

t Test for Uncorrelated Measures

There are two forms of the t test—one for uncorrelated and one for correlated measures. The t test for uncorrelated measures is used to determine the probability that an observed difference between two independent groups of subjects occurred by chance. The underlying distributions are assumed to be normal.

Example

	Group 1		
X_1	$\overline{X}_1$	$X_1 - \overline{X}_1$	$(X_1 - \overline{X}_1)^2$
9	7	2	4
8	7	1	1
7	7	0	0
7	7	0	0
4	7	-3	9
$\Sigma X_1 = 35$			$\Sigma(X_1 - \overline{X}_1)^2 = 14$

$N_1 = 5$

$$M_1 = \overline{X}_1 = \frac{\Sigma X_1}{N_1} = \frac{35}{5} = 7$$

$$\sigma_1 = \sqrt{\frac{\Sigma(X_1 - \overline{X}_1)^2}{N_1}} = \sqrt{\frac{14}{5}} = \sqrt{2.8} = 1.67$$

Example

	Group 2		
X_2	$\overline{X}_2$	$X_2 - \overline{X}_2$	$(X_2 - \overline{X}_2)^2$
5	3	2	4
4	3	1	1
3	3	0	0
2	3	-1	1
1	3	-2	4
$\Sigma X_2 = 15$			$\Sigma(X_2 - \overline{X}_2)^2 = 10$

$N_2 = 5$

$$M_2 = \overline{X}_2 = \frac{\Sigma X_2}{N_2} = \frac{15}{5} = 3$$

$$\sigma_2 = \sqrt{\frac{\Sigma(X_2 - \overline{X}_2)^2}{N_2}} = \sqrt{\frac{10}{5}} = \sqrt{2} = 1.41$$

$$t = \frac{M_1 - M_2}{\sqrt{\left(\frac{\sigma_1}{\sqrt{N_1 - 1}}\right)^2 + \left(\frac{\sigma_2}{\sqrt{N_2 - 1}}\right)^2}} = \frac{7 - 3}{\sqrt{\left(\frac{1.67}{\sqrt{5 - 1}}\right)^2 + \left(\frac{1.41}{\sqrt{5 - 1}}\right)^2}}$$

$$= \frac{4}{\sqrt{\left(\frac{1.67}{2}\right)^2 + \left(\frac{1.41}{2}\right)^2}} = \frac{4}{\sqrt{.697 + .497}} = \frac{4}{\sqrt{1.194}} = \frac{4}{1.09} = 3.67$$

The degrees of freedom for an uncorrelated t test is:

$$df = N_1 + N_2 - 2$$
$$= 5 + 5 - 2 = 8$$

Table B-4 in Appendix B indicates that, with 8 df, t must exceed 3.355 for the difference to be significant at $p < .01$. Thus, our value of 3.67 is significant at that level.

t Test for Correlated Measures

The t test for correlated measures is used to determine the probability that an observed difference (D) between two conditions for the same or matched subjects occurred by chance.

$$t = \frac{\overline{X}_D}{\dfrac{\sigma_D}{\sqrt{N - 1}}}$$

Example

Subject	Condition 1	Condition 2	Difference (D)	$\overline{X}_D$*	$X_D - \overline{X}_D$	$(X_D - \overline{X}_D)^2$
1	9	6	3	3	0	0
2	8	5	3	3	0	0
3	7	5	2	3	-1	1
4	8	4	4	3	1	1
5	8	5	3	3	0	0
$N = 5$	$\Sigma X_1 = 40$	$\Sigma X_2 = 25$	$\Sigma D = 15$			$\Sigma(X_D - \overline{X}_D)^2 = 2$

$$^*M_D = \overline{X}_D = \frac{\Sigma D}{N} = \frac{15}{5} = 3$$

$$\sigma_D = \sqrt{\frac{\Sigma(X_D - \overline{X}_D)^2}{N}} = \sqrt{\frac{2}{5}} = \sqrt{.4} = .632$$

$$t = \frac{\overline{X}_D}{\dfrac{\sigma_D}{\sqrt{N-1}}} = \frac{3}{\dfrac{.632}{\sqrt{5-1}}} = \frac{3}{\dfrac{.632}{2}} = \frac{3}{.316} = 9.49$$

The degrees of freedom for correlated measures is

$$df = N - 1 = 5 - 1 = 4$$

Table B-4 is used for either form of the t test. In this example, t must exceed 4.604 to be significant at the $p < .01$ level. It does, so it is.

Mann-Whitney *U* Test

The Mann-Whitney U test is used under the same general conditions as an uncorrelated t test but only when the assumptions of normal distributions or an interval scale cannot be met.

$$U = N_1 N_2 + \frac{N_1(N_1 + 1)}{2} - R_1$$

or

$$U = N_1 N_2 + \frac{N_2(N_2 + 1)}{2} - R_2$$

whichever is smaller

where

N_1 = the number of subjects in the smaller group
N_2 = the number of subjects in the larger group
R_1 = the sum of the ranks for the smaller group
R_2 = the sum of the ranks for the larger group

Example

Group 1		Group 2	
X_1	Rank	X_2	Rank
1	1	2	2
3	3.5	4	5
3	3.5	7	8
5	6	8	9.5

Example *(continued)*

	Group 1			Group 2	
	X_1	Rank		X_2	Rank
$N_1 = 10$	6	7	$N_2 = 10$	10	13.5
	8	9.5		13	16
	9	11.5		15	17
	9	11.5		16	18
	10	13.5		17	19
	12	15		18	20
		$R_1 = 82$			$R_2 = 128$

The rankings were determined by ordering all scores regardless of which group they came from. Where there were ties in rankings, an average was used.

$$U = N_1 N_2 + \frac{N_1(N_1 + 1)}{2} - R_1 = (10)(10) + \frac{10(10 + 1)}{2} - 82$$

$$= 100 + \frac{110}{2} - 82 = 73$$

or

$$U = (10)(10) + \frac{10(10 + 1)}{2} - 128 = 27$$

Because 27 is smaller, $U = 27$.

Two tables for determining the critical values of U can be found in Appendix B. If we wished to test for significance at the $p < .05$ level, we would use Table B-5. The value for U when $N_1 = 10$ and $N_2 = 10$ is 23. To be significant our value must be equal to or *smaller* than this critical value. Because 27 is not, it is not statistically significant at this level.

Note that the Mann-Whitney U test is different from the other tests in that to be significant the value must be smaller rather than larger than the value in the table. To find a table for values of N_1 smaller than 7, you will have to use a more advanced text than this one. For values of N_2 larger than 20, U must be converted to a z score using the formula

$$z = \frac{U - \dfrac{N_1 N_2}{2}}{\sqrt{\dfrac{(N_1)(N_2)(N_1 + N_2 + 1)}{12}}}$$

The z score can then be compared to the critical values listed in Table B-7 in Appendix B.

Analysis of Variance

Analysis of variance (ANOVA) can be used for interval or ratio data when the underlying distributions are approximately normal. ANOVA tests are available for either within-subject (repeated measures) or between-subjects (separate groups) designs and for designs with multiple independent variables. In this appendix, however, we will limit our consideration to a between-subjects design with one independent variable. In the following example the independent variable has three levels. However, the formulas given can also be used for designs having more than three groups.

Although the calculations for ANOVA appear to be complicated, the rationale behind the test is really relatively simple. Suppose you conduct an experiment in which you collect data from three groups of subjects. The experimental question is whether the three samples of subjects come from the same population and differ only by chance variation, or whether the samples come from different populations and differ due to the independent variable as well as to chance variation. ANOVA allows you to partition the variance found in the distribution containing all the scores you sampled. Part of the variance in this distribution is due to differences between groups, including variance due to the independent variable. A second part is due to chance variation between subjects within groups.

The final number calculated when doing ANOVA is called an **F value.** It is a ratio of the variance between groups to the variance within groups. If the groups sampled come from the same population and the independent variable has no effect, we would expect the ratio to be close to 1. That is, the between-group variance should be about the same size as the within-group variance. However, if the independent variable has an effect and the groups come from different populations, we would expect the between-group variance to be larger than the within-group variance. The F value would then be greater than 1. As the value of F gets larger, we would become increasingly confident that the differences among groups were due to the effects of the independent variable rather than to chance variation.

In the following example, we first calculate a quantity called the **total sum of squares** (SS_{TOT}) followed by a **sum of squares between groups** (SS_{bg}) and **within groups** (SS_{wg}). SS_{bg} and SS_{wg} are then divided by their appropriate degrees of freedom to get the mean squares between groups (MS_{bg}) and within groups (MS_{wg}). MS_{bg} is then divided by MS_{wg} to find the value of F.

You should be able to follow the example, but if you get into trouble, the following definitions might help:

T is the total sum of all scores for all groups.
T_j is the total sum of scores in group j.
N is the number of scores in all groups.
n_j is the number of scores in group j.
$\displaystyle\sum_{j=1}^{k}$ means to sum for all groups from 1 to k.
k is the number of groups.

Example

Group 1		Group 2		Group 3	
X_1	X_1^2	X_2	X_2^2	X_3	X_3^2
3	9	9	81	10	100
5	25	6	36	8	64
4	16	5	25	11	121
3	9	8	64	10	100
1	1	7	49	9	81
2	4	7	49	10	100
5	25	6	36	11	121
2	4	4	16	12	144
3	9	8	64	10	100
1	1	7	49	9	81
$T_1 = 29$	103	$T_2 = 67$	469	$T_3 = 100$	1012
$n_1 = 10$		$n_2 = 10$		$n_3 = 10$	

$N = 10 + 10 + 10 = 30$
$T = 29 + 67 + 100 = 196$
$k = 3$

$$SS_{TOT} = \Sigma X^2 - \frac{T^2}{N} = (103 + 469 + 1012) - \frac{(196)^2}{30}$$

$$= 1584 - \frac{38416}{30} = 1584 - 1281 = 303$$

$$SS_{bg} = \sum_{j=1}^{k} \frac{T_j^2}{n_j} - \frac{T^2}{N} = \frac{29^2}{10} + \frac{67^2}{10} + \frac{100^2}{10} - \frac{(196)^2}{30}$$

$$= \frac{841}{10} + \frac{4489}{10} + \frac{10000}{10} - 1281$$

$$= 84.1 + 448.9 + 1000 - 1281 = 1533 - 1281 = 252$$

$$SS_{wg} = SS_{TOT} - SS_{bg} = 303 - 252 = 51$$

$$df_{bg} = k - 1 = 3 - 1 = 2$$

$$df_{wg} = N - k = 30 - 3 = 27$$

$$MS_{bg} = \frac{SS_{bg}}{df_{bg}} = \frac{252}{2} = 126$$

$$MS_{wg} = \frac{SS_{wg}}{df_{wg}} = \frac{51}{27} = 1.89$$

$$F = \frac{MS_{bg}}{MS_{wg}} = \frac{126}{1.89} = 66.7$$

We can now compare this number with the critical values for F listed in Table B-8 in Appendix B. With 2 df in the numerator and 27 df in the denominator, F must equal or exceed 3.38 to be significant at $p < .05$ and equal or exceed 5.57 to be significant at $p < .01$. Since 66.7 far exceeds these critical values, the difference between the groups is highly significant. Note that the test could reach statistical significance owing to a difference between any two groups. To determine which means are statistically different from one another, further tests would have to be conducted. These tests are beyond the scope of this book. They can be found in the recommended texts at the end of Chapter 9.

Kruskal-Wallis One-Way ANOVA by Ranks

If the assumptions of an interval or ratio scale or normal distributions cannot be met, a Kruskal-Wallis ANOVA can be used to test for differences between two or more independent groups. Only an ordinal scale is necessary.

In the following example:

K = the number of groups
n_j = the number of scores per group
N = the total number of scores
R_j = the sum of ranks for group j
t = the number of ties for each score

Example

Group 1		Group 2		Group 3	
X_1	Rank	X_2	Rank	X_3	Rank
8	15	2	2.5	6	11
4	5.5	5	8.5	5	8.5
7	13	2	2.5	4	5.5
5	8.5	3	4	5	8.5
7	13	1	1	7	13
	$R_1 = 55.0$		$R_2 = 18.5$		$R_3 = 46.5$

$K = 3$
$n_j = 5$
$N = 15$

Rank all the scores to get the ranks for each group.

Score	Rank	Average for Ties	t
1	1	1	
2	2 ⎫		
2	3 ⎭	2.5	2
3	4	4	
4	5 ⎫		
4	6 ⎭	5.5	2
5	7 ⎫		
5	8		
5	9	8.5	4
5	10 ⎭		
6	11	11	
7	12 ⎫		
7	13	13	3
7	14 ⎭		
8	15	15	

Now place the ranks from this table next to the individual scores for each group in the previous table and sum them to get R_1, R_2, R_3.

$$H = \frac{12}{N(N + 1)} \sum_{j=1}^{k} \frac{R_j^2}{n_j} - 3(N + 1)$$

$$= \frac{12}{15(15 + 1)} \left[\frac{(55)^2}{5} + \frac{(18.5)^2}{5} + \frac{(46.5)^2}{5} \right] - 3(15 + 1)$$

$$= \frac{12}{15(16)} \left[\frac{3025}{5} + \frac{342.25}{5} + \frac{2162.25}{5} \right] - 3(16)$$

$$= \frac{12}{240} \left[\frac{5529.5}{5} \right] - 48$$

$$= .05(1105.9) - 48 = 55.295 - 48 = 7.295$$

The correction for ties is to divide H by $1 - \dfrac{\Sigma(t^3 - t)}{N^3 - N}$.

$$1 - \frac{(2^3 - 2) + (2^3 - 2) + (4^3 - 4) + (3^3 - 3)}{15^3 - 15}$$

$$1 - \frac{(8-2) + (8-2) + (64-4) + (27-3)}{3375 - 15}$$

$$1 - \frac{96}{3360} = 1 - .029 = .971$$

$$H = \frac{7.295}{.971} = 7.51$$

According to Table B-9 in Appendix B, for group sizes of five, five, and five, the probability of having an H as large as 7.51 is less than .049. Thus, the difference between groups is statistically significant at the $p < .05$ level. Because this value is smaller than the 7.98 required for the $p < .01$ level, the difference is not significant at that level.

If the groups contain more than five subjects, H is distributed like chi-square. To determine the critical value in that case, refer to Table B-3 with $k - 1$ degrees of freedom.

Conclusion

This appendix should allow you to compute some very basic statistical operations. However, if you go much beyond a basic course in experimentation, you will need to do at least three additional things. First, you will need to learn to use more complex tests for designs having multiple independent variables and mixtures of within-subject and between-subjects variables. Second, you will need to learn to use packaged computer programs to save time and effort. Third, and probably most important, you must go beyond a cookbook approach to statistics. As a researcher you should understand why you do what you do.

An understanding of the concepts underlying statistical operations not only allows you to choose the most powerful way to analyze your data, but also allows you to design research so that the data can be effectively analyzed. Statistical consultants tell horror stories about inexperienced researchers who dump volumes of data on their desks and ask, "How do I analyze this?" In some cases the data defy analysis.

The point is that design and statistical analysis are integrally linked. If you plan to design your research, you should also understand the concepts underlying the statistical operations that should be used to analyze the outcome.

Appendix B:
Statistical Tables

Table B-1.
Critical Values of *rho* (Spearman Rank-Order Correlation Coefficient).

N	$p = .0500$	$p = .0100$
5	1.000	—
6	.886	1.000
7	.786	.929
8	.738	.881
9	.683	.833
10	.648	.794
12	.591	.777
14	.544	.715
16	.506	.665
18	.475	.625
20	.450	.591
22	.428	.562
24	.409	.537
26	.392	.515
28	.377	.496
30	.364	.478

Computed from Olds, E. G., Distribution of the sum of squares of rank differences for small numbers of individuals, *Annals of Mathematical Statistics*, 1938, 9, 133–148, and the 5% significance levels for sums of squares of rank differences and a correction, *Annals of Mathematical Statistics*, 1949, 20, 117–118. Table B-1 is taken from *Elementary Statistics*, Underwood et al., Appleton-Century-Crofts.

Table B-2.

Critical Values of r (Pearson Product-Moment Correlation Coefficient).

df	Level of significance for two-tailed test		
	.10	.05	.01
1	.988	.997	.9999
2	.900	.950	.990
3	.805	.878	.959
4	.729	.811	.917
5	.669	.754	.874
6	.622	.707	.834
7	.582	.666	.798
8	.549	.632	.765
9	.521	.602	.735
10	.497	.576	.708
11	.476	.553	.684
12	.458	.532	.661
13	.441	.514	.641
14	.426	.497	.623
15	.412	.482	.606
16	.400	.468	.590
17	.389	.456	.575
18	.378	.444	.561
19	.369	.433	.549
20	.360	.423	.537
25	.323	.381	.487
30	.296	.349	.449
35	.275	.325	.418
40	.257	.304	.393
45	.243	.288	.372
50	.231	.273	.354
60	.211	.250	.325
70	.195	.232	.303
80	.183	.217	.283
90	.173	.205	.267
100	.164	.195	.254

Adapted from R. A. Fisher, *Statistical Methods for Research Workers*. 14th Edition. Copyright 1973. Hafner Press.

Table B-3.
Critical Values of Chi-Square.

df	p = .05	p = .01
1	3.84	6.64
2	5.99	9.21
3	7.82	11.34
4	9.49	13.28
5	11.07	15.09
6	12.59	16.81
7	14.07	18.48
8	15.51	20.09
9	16.92	21.67
10	18.31	23.21
11	19.68	24.72
12	21.03	26.22
13	22.36	27.69
14	23.68	29.14
15	25.00	30.58
16	26.30	32.00
17	27.59	33.41
18	28.87	34.80
19	30.14	36.19
20	31.41	37.57
21	32.67	38.93
22	33.92	40.29
23	35.17	41.64
24	36.42	42.98
25	37.65	44.31
26	38.88	45.64
27	40.11	46.96
28	41.34	48.28
29	42.56	49.59
30	43.77	50.89

Table B-3 is taken from Table 4 of Fisher & Yates, *Statistical Tables for Biological, Agricultural and Medical Research*, published by Longman Group Ltd., London (previously published by Oliver and Boyd Ltd., Edinburgh). By permission of the authors and publishers.

Table B-4.
Critical Values of *t*.

df	p = .10	p = .05	p = .02	p = .01
1	6.314	12.706	31.821	63.657
2	2.920	4.303	6.965	9.925
3	2.353	3.182	4.541	5.841
4	2.132	2.776	3.747	4.604
5	2.015	2.571	3.365	4.032
6	1.943	2.447	3.143	3.707
7	1.895	2.365	2.998	3.499
8	1.860	2.306	2.896	3.355
9	1.833	2.262	2.821	3.250
10	1.812	2.228	2.764	3.169
11	1.796	2.201	2.718	3.106
12	1.782	2.179	2.681	3.055
13	1.771	2.160	2.650	3.012
14	1.761	2.145	2.624	2.977
15	1.753	2.131	2.602	2.947
16	1.746	2.120	2.583	2.921
17	1.740	2.110	2.567	2.898
18	1.734	2.101	2.552	2.878
19	1.729	2.093	2.539	2.861
20	1.725	2.086	2.528	2.845
21	1.721	2.080	2.518	2.831
22	1.717	2.074	2.508	2.819
23	1.714	2.069	2.500	2.807
24	1.711	2.064	2.492	2.797
25	1.708	2.060	2.485	2.787
26	1.706	2.056	2.479	2.779
27	1.703	2.052	2.473	2.771
28	1.701	2.048	2.467	2.763
29	1.699	2.045	2.462	2.756
30	1.697	2.042	2.457	2.750
60	1.671	2.000	2.390	2.660
∞	1.645	1.960	2.326	2.576

Table B-4 is taken from Table 3 of Fisher & Yates, *Statistical Tables for Biological, Agricultural and Medical Research*, published by Longman Group Ltd., London (previously published by Oliver and Boyd Ltd., Edinburgh). By permission of the authors and publishers.

Table B-5.
Critical Values of the Mann-Whitney U Test at the $p < .05$ Level.

| N_2 | \multicolumn{14}{c}{N_1} |
	7	8	9	10	11	12	13	14	15	16	17	18	19	20
3	1	2	2	3	3	4	4	5	5	6	6	7	7	8
4	3	4	4	5	6	7	8	9	10	11	11	12	13	13
5	5	6	7	8	9	11	12	13	14	15	17	18	19	20
6	6	8	10	11	13	14	16	17	19	21	22	24	25	27
7	8	10	12	14	16	18	20	22	24	26	28	30	32	34
8	10	13	15	17	19	22	24	26	29	31	34	36	38	41
9	12	15	17	20	23	26	28	31	34	37	39	42	45	48
10	14	17	20	23	26	29	33	36	39	42	45	48	52	55
11	16	19	23	26	30	33	37	40	44	47	51	55	58	62
12	18	22	26	29	33	37	41	45	49	53	57	61	65	69
13	20	24	28	33	37	41	45	50	54	59	63	67	72	76
14	22	26	31	36	40	45	50	55	59	64	67	74	78	83
15	24	29	34	39	44	49	54	59	64	70	75	80	85	90
16	26	31	37	42	47	53	59	64	70	75	81	86	92	98
17	28	34	39	45	51	57	63	67	75	81	87	93	99	105
18	30	36	42	48	55	61	67	74	80	86	93	99	106	112
19	32	38	45	52	58	65	72	78	85	92	99	106	113	119
20	34	41	48	55	62	69	76	83	90	98	105	112	119	127

Adapted and abridged from Tables 1, 3, 5, and 7 of Auble, D., Extended tables for the Mann-Whitney statistics, *Bulletin of the Institute of Educational Research at Indiana University*, 1953, 1(2).

Table B-6.
Critical Values of the Mann-Whitney U Test at the $p < .01$ Level.

| N_2 | \multicolumn{14}{c}{N_1} |
	7	8	9	10	11	12	13	14	15	16	17	18	19	20
3	—	—	0	0	0	1	1	1	2	2	2	2	3	3
4	0	1	1	2	2	3	3	4	5	5	6	6	7	8
5	1	2	3	4	5	6	7	7	8	9	10	11	12	13
6	3	4	5	6	7	9	10	11	12	13	15	16	17	18
7	4	6	7	9	10	12	13	15	16	18	19	21	22	24
8	6	7	9	11	13	15	17	18	20	22	24	26	28	30
9	7	9	11	13	16	18	20	22	24	27	29	31	33	36
10	9	11	13	16	18	21	24	26	29	31	34	37	39	42
11	10	13	16	18	21	24	27	30	33	36	39	42	45	48
12	12	15	18	21	24	27	31	34	37	41	44	47	51	54
13	13	17	20	24	27	31	34	38	42	45	49	53	56	60
14	15	18	22	26	30	34	38	42	46	50	54	58	63	67
15	16	20	24	29	33	37	42	46	51	55	60	64	69	73
16	18	22	27	31	36	41	45	50	55	60	65	70	74	79
17	19	24	29	34	39	44	49	54	60	65	70	75	81	86
18	21	26	31	37	42	47	53	58	64	70	75	81	87	92
19	22	28	33	39	45	51	56	63	69	74	81	87	93	99
20	24	30	36	42	48	54	60	67	73	79	86	92	99	105

Adapted and abridged from Tables 1, 3, 5, and 7 of Auble, D., Extended tables for the Mann-Whitney statistics, *Bulletin of the Institute of Educational Research at Indiana University*, 1953, 1(2).

Table B-7.
Probabilities Associated With Various z-Scores.

The body of the table gives one-tailed probabilities under H_o of z. The left marginal column gives various values of z to one decimal place. The top row gives various values to the second decimal place. Thus, for example, the one-tailed p of $z \geq .11$ or $z \leq -.11$ is $p = .4562$.

z	.00	.01	.02	.03	.04	.05	.06	.07	.08	.09
.0	.5000	.4960	.4920	.4880	.4840	.4801	.4761	.4721	.4681	.4641
.1	.4602	.4562	.4522	.4483	.4443	.4404	.4364	.4325	.4286	.4247
.2	.4207	.4168	.4129	.4090	.4052	.4013	.3974	.3936	.3897	.3859
.3	.3821	.3783	.3745	.3707	.3669	.3632	.3594	.3557	.3520	.3483
.4	.3446	.3409	.3372	.3336	.3300	.3264	.3228	.3192	.3156	.3121
.5	.3085	.3050	.3015	.2981	.2946	.2912	.2877	.2843	.2810	.2776
.6	.2743	.2709	.2676	.2643	.2611	.2578	.2546	.2514	.2483	.2451
.7	.2420	.2389	.2358	.2327	.2296	.2266	.2236	.2206	.2177	.2148
.8	.2119	.2090	.2061	.2033	.2005	.1977	.1949	.1922	.1894	.1867
.9	.1841	.1814	.1788	.1762	.1736	.1711	.1685	.1660	.1635	.1611
1.0	.1587	.1562	.1539	.1515	.1492	.1469	.1446	.1423	.1401	.1379
1.1	.1357	.1335	.1314	.1292	.1271	.1251	.1230	.1210	.1190	.1170
1.2	.1151	.1131	.1112	.1093	.1075	.1056	.1038	.1020	.1003	.0985
1.3	.0968	.0951	.0934	.0918	.0901	.0885	.0869	.0853	.0838	.0823
1.4	.0808	.0793	.0778	.0764	.0749	.0735	.0721	.0708	.0694	.0681
1.5	.0668	.0655	.0643	.0630	.0618	.0606	.0594	.0582	.0571	.0559
1.6	.0548	.0537	.0526	.0516	.0505	.0495	.0485	.0475	.0465	.0455
1.7	.0446	.0436	.0427	.0418	.0409	.0401	.0392	.0384	.0375	.0367
1.8	.0359	.0351	.0344	.0336	.0329	.0322	.0314	.0307	.0301	.0294
1.9	.0287	.0281	.0274	.0268	.0262	.0256	.0250	.0244	.0239	.0233
2.0	.0228	.0222	.0217	.0212	.0207	.0202	.0197	.0192	.0188	.0183
2.1	.0179	.0174	.0170	.0166	.0162	.0158	.0154	.0150	.0146	.0143
2.2	.0139	.0136	.0132	.0129	.0125	.0122	.0119	.0116	.0113	.0110
2.3	.0107	.0104	.0102	.0099	.0096	.0094	.0091	.0089	.0087	.0084
2.4	.0082	.0080	.0078	.0075	.0073	.0071	.0069	.0068	.0066	.0064
2.5	.0062	.0060	.0059	.0057	.0055	.0054	.0052	.0051	.0049	.0048
2.6	.0047	.0045	.0044	.0043	.0041	.0040	.0039	.0038	.0037	.0036
2.7	.0035	.0034	.0033	.0032	.0031	.0030	.0029	.0028	.0027	.0026
2.8	.0026	.0025	.0024	.0023	.0023	.0022	.0021	.0021	.0020	.0019
2.9	.0019	.0018	.0018	.0017	.0016	.0016	.0015	.0015	.0014	.0014
3.0	.0013	.0013	.0013	.0012	.0012	.0011	.0011	.0011	.0010	.0010
3.1	.0010	.0009	.0009	.0009	.0008	.0008	.0008	.0008	.0007	.0007
3.2	.0007									
3.3	.0005									
3.4	.0003									
3.5	.00023									
3.6	.00016									
3.7	.00011									
3.8	.00007									
3.9	.00005									
4.0	.00003									

Reproduced by permission from Siegel, S., *Nonparametric Statistics for the Behavioral Sciences*. New York: McGraw-Hill Book Company, Inc., 1956 (p. 247).

Table B-8.
Critical Values of *F*. (Top Number in Each Cell Is for Testing at .05 Level; Bottom Number for Testing at .01 Level.)

Degrees of freedom for denominator

					Degrees of freedom for numerator					
	1	2	3	4	5	6	8	12	24	∞
1	161.45	199.50	215.72	224.57	230.17	233.97	238.89	243.91	249.04	254.32
	4032.10	4999.03	5403.49	5625.14	5764.08	5859.39	5981.34	6105.83	6234.16	6366.48
2	18.51	19.00	19.16	19.25	19.30	19.33	19.37	19.41	19.45	19.50
	98.49	99.01	99.17	99.25	99.30	99.33	99.36	99.42	99.46	99.50
3	10.13	9.55	9.28	9.12	9.01	8.94	8.84	8.74	8.64	8.53
	34.12	30.81	29.46	28.71	28.24	27.91	27.49	27.05	26.60	26.12
4	7.71	6.94	6.59	6.39	6.26	6.16	6.04	5.91	5.77	5.63
	21.20	18.00	16.69	15.98	15.52	15.21	14.80	14.37	13.93	13.46
5	6.61	5.79	5.41	5.19	5.05	4.95	4.82	4.68	4.53	4.36
	16.26	13.27	12.06	11.39	10.97	10.67	10.27	9.89	9.47	9.02
6	5.99	5.14	4.76	4.53	4.39	4.28	4.15	4.00	3.84	3.67
	13.74	10.92	9.78	9.15	8.75	8.47	8.10	7.72	7.31	6.88
7	5.59	4.74	4.35	4.12	3.97	3.87	3.73	3.57	3.41	3.23
	12.25	9.55	8.45	7.85	7.46	7.19	6.84	6.47	6.07	5.65
8	5.32	4.46	4.07	3.84	3.69	3.58	3.44	3.28	3.12	2.93
	11.26	8.65	7.59	7.01	6.63	6.37	6.03	5.67	5.28	4.86
9	5.12	4.26	3.86	3.63	3.48	3.37	3.23	3.07	2.90	2.71
	10.56	8.02	6.99	6.42	6.06	5.80	5.47	5.11	4.73	4.31
10	4.96	4.10	3.71	3.48	3.33	3.22	3.07	2.91	2.74	2.54
	10.04	7.56	6.55	5.99	5.64	5.39	5.06	4.71	4.33	3.91
11	4.84	3.98	3.59	3.36	3.20	3.09	2.95	2.79	2.61	2.40
	9.65	7.20	6.22	5.67	5.32	5.07	4.74	4.40	4.02	3.60
12	4.75	3.88	3.49	3.26	3.11	3.00	2.85	2.69	2.50	2.30
	9.33	6.93	5.93	5.41	5.06	4.82	4.50	4.16	3.78	3.36
14	4.60	3.74	3.34	3.11	2.96	2.85	2.70	2.53	2.35	2.13
	8.86	6.51	5.56	5.03	4.69	4.46	4.14	3.80	3.43	3.00
16	4.49	3.63	3.24	3.01	2.85	2.74	2.59	2.42	2.24	2.01
	8.53	6.23	5.29	4.77	4.44	4.20	3.89	3.55	3.18	2.75
18	4.41	3.55	3.16	2.93	2.77	2.66	2.51	2.34	2.15	1.92
	8.28	6.01	5.09	4.58	4.25	4.01	3.71	3.37	3.01	2.57
20	4.35	3.49	3.10	2.87	2.71	2.60	2.45	2.28	2.08	1.84
	8.10	5.85	4.94	4.43	4.10	3.87	3.56	3.23	2.86	2.42
25	4.24	3.38	2.99	2.76	2.60	2.49	2.34	2.16	1.96	1.71
	7.77	5.57	4.68	4.18	3.86	3.63	3.32	2.99	2.62	2.17
30	4.17	3.32	2.92	2.69	2.53	2.42	2.27	2.09	1.89	1.62

(continued)

Table B-8. *(continued)*

	\multicolumn{10}{c}{Degrees of freedom for numerator}
	1	2	3	4	5	6	8	12	24	∞
	7.56	5.39	4.51	4.02	3.70	3.47	3.17	2.84	2.47	2.01
40	4.08	3.23	2.84	2.61	2.45	2.34	2.18	2.00	1.79	1.52
	7.31	5.18	4.31	3.83	3.51	3.29	2.99	2.66	2.29	1.82
50	4.03	3.18	2.79	2.56	2.40	2.29	2.13	1.95	1.74	1.44
	7.17	5.06	4.20	3.72	3.41	3.19	2.89	2.56	2.18	1.68
60	4.00	3.15	2.76	2.52	2.37	2.25	2.10	1.92	1.70	1.39
	7.08	4.98	4.13	3.65	3.34	3.12	2.82	2.50	2.12	1.60
70	3.98	3.13	2.74	2.50	2.35	2.23	2.07	1.89	1.67	1.35
	7.01	4.92	4.07	3.60	3.29	3.07	2.78	2.45	2.07	1.53
80	3.96	3.11	2.72	2.49	2.33	2.21	2.06	1.88	1.65	1.31
	6.98	4.88	4.04	3.56	3.26	3.04	2.74	2.42	2.03	1.47
90	3.95	3.10	2.71	2.47	2.32	2.20	2.04	1.86	1.64	1.28
	6.92	4.85	4.01	3.53	3.23	3.01	2.72	2.39	2.00	1.43
100	3.94	3.09	2.70	2.46	2.30	2.19	2.03	1.85	1.63	1.26
	6.90	4.82	3.98	3.51	3.21	2.99	2.69	2.37	1.98	1.39
200	3.89	3.04	2.65	2.42	2.26	2.14	1.98	1.80	1.57	1.14
	6.97	4.71	3.88	3.41	3.11	2.89	2.60	2.28	1.88	1.21
∞	3.84	2.99	2.60	2.37	2.21	2.09	1.94	1.75	1.52	
	6.64	4.60	3.78	3.32	3.02	2.80	2.51	2.18	1.79	

Degrees of freedom for denominator

Adapted from Table F of H. E. Garrett, *Statistics in Psychology and Education*, 5th Edition, Copyright 1958, David McKay Co., Inc.

Table B-9.
Critical Values for H (Kruskal-Wallis One-Way ANOVA by Ranks).

Sample sizes					Sample sizes				
n_1	n_2	n_3	H	p	n_1	n_2	n_3	H	p
2	1	1	2.7000	.500	4	3	2	6.4444	.008
								6.3000	.011
2	2	1	3.6000	.200				5.4444	.046
2	2	2	4.5714	.067				5.4000	.051
			3.7143	.200				4.5111	.098
								4.4444	.102
3	1	1	3.2000	.300					
3	2	1	4.2857	.100	4	3	3	6.7455	.010
			3.8571	.133				6.7091	.013
								5.7909	.046
3	2	2	5.3572	.029				5.7273	.050
			4.7143	.048				4.7091	.092
			4.5000	.067				4.7000	.101
			4.4643	.105					
					4	4	1	6.6667	.010
3	3	1	5.1429	.043				6.1667	.022
			4.5714	.100				4.9667	.048
			4.0000	.129				4.8667	.054
								4.1667	.082
3	3	2	6.2500	.011				4.0667	.102
			5.3611	.032					
			5.1389	.061	4	4	2	7.0364	.006
			4.5556	.100				6.8727	.011
			4.2500	.121				5.4545	.046
								5.2364	.052
3	3	3	7.2000	.004				4.5545	.098
			6.4889	.011				4.4455	.103
			5.6889	.029					
			5.6000	.050	4	4	3	7.1439	.010
			5.0667	.086				7.1364	.011
			4.6222	.100				5.5985	.049
								5.5758	.051
4	1	1	3.5714	.200				4.5455	.099
4	2	1	4.8214	.057				4.4773	.102
			4.5000	.076					
			4.0179	.114	4	4	4	7.6538	.008
								7.5385	.011
4	2	2	6.0000	.014				5.6923	.049
			5.3333	.033				5.6538	.054
			5.1250	.052				4.6539	.097
			4.4583	.100				4.5001	.104
			4.1667	.105					
					5	1	1	3.8571	.143
4	3	1	5.8333	.021	5	2	1	5.2500	.036
			5.2083	.050				5.0000	.048
			5.0000	.057				4.4500	.071
			4.0556	.093				4.2000	.095
			3.8889	.129				4.0500	.119

(*continued*)

Table B-9. *(continued)*

Sample sizes					Sample sizes				
n_1	n_2	n_3	H	p	n_1	n_2	n_3	H	p
5	2	2	6.5333	.008	5	4	4	7.7604	.009
			6.1333	.013				7.7440	.011
			5.1600	.034				5.6571	.049
			5.0400	.056				5.6176	.050
			4.3733	.090				4.6187	.100
			4.2933	.122				4.5527	.102
5	3	1	6.4000	.012	5	5	1	7.3091	.009
			4.9600	.048				6.8364	.011
			4.8711	.052				5.1273	.046
			4.0178	.095				4.9091	.053
			3.8400	.123				4.1091	.086
5	3	2	6.9091	.009				4.0364	.105
			6.8218	.010	5	5	2	7.3385	.010
			5.2509	.049				7.2692	.010
			5.1055	.052				5.3385	.047
			4.6509	.091				5.2462	.051
			4.4945	.101				4.6231	.097
5	3	3	7.0788	.009				4.5077	.100
			6.9818	.011	5	5	3	7.5780	.010
			5.6485	.049				7.5429	.010
			5.5152	.051				5.7055	.046
			4.5333	.097				5.6264	.051
			4.4121	.109				4.5451	.100
5	4	1	6.9545	.008				4.5363	.102
			6.8400	.011	5	5	4	7.8229	.010
			4.9855	.044				7.7914	.010
			4.8600	.056				5.6657	.049
			3.9873	.098				5.6429	.050
			3.9600	.102				4.5229	.099
5	4	2	7.2045	.009				4.5200	.101
			7.1182	.010	5	5	5	8.0000	.009
			5.2727	.049				7.9800	.010
			5.2682	.050				5.7800	.049
			4.5409	.098				5.6600	.051
			4.5182	.101				4.5600	.100
5	4	3	7.4449	.010				4.5000	.102
			7.3949	.011					
			5.6564	.049					
			5.6308	.050					
			4.5487	.099					
			4.5231	.103					

Adapted and abridged from Kruskal, W. H., and Wallis, W. A. Use of ranks in one-criterion variance analysis. *Journal of American Statistical Association*, 1952, *47*, 614–617, with the kind permission of the authors and the publisher. (The corrections to this table given by the authors in Errata, *Journal of the American Statistical Association*, 1953, *48*, 910, have been incorporated.)

Glossary

ABBA counterbalancing—A technique for minimizing the effect of a linear confounding variable in an experiment having one independent variable with two levels, A and B. Level A is presented first, followed by two presentations of level B and a final presentation of A.

abscissa—The horizontal axis of a graph upon which the levels of an independent variable are often represented. Also called *x* **axis.**

analysis of variance—A parametric test of statistical inference used for analyzing data from a factorial experiment or a multilevel single-variable experiment.

asymptote—The imaginary line that a negatively accelerated function approaches as it flattens out.

bar graph—A means of illustrating the frequency of qualitative data using spaced vertical bars. Qualitative class intervals are plotted on the abscissa, with frequency represented on the ordinate and the frequency of each class represented by the height of the bar over that class interval.

baseline experiment—A type of single-variable experiment that can show effects using data from a single subject. A steady-state baseline rate of responding is established, and then an experimental manipulation is made and a transition state established. Finally, the manipulation is removed and the baseline recovered. Also called a small-N baseline design.

basic research—Research whose goal is to understand the basic mechanisms of science. Although such research can lead to the solution of applied problems, the goal is simply to enhance the body of knowledge. Also called **pure research.**

between-subjects design—An experimental research strategy in which each research participant provides data for only one level of the independent variable(s).

bimodal distribution—A frequency distribution having two humps, each of which has a maximum value.

blind experiment—An experiment in which subjects are unaware of the levels of the independent variable to which they are being exposed.

case history—A nonexperimental means of collecting data that contains detailed accounts of the behaviors of a single person or event.

ceiling effect—The truncation of data at the top of a distribution due to a limit on the highest score possible.

chi-square test—A nonparametric test of statistical inference that is used to determine whether the observed frequency of occurrence of scores is statistically different from the expected frequency.

complete counterbalancing—An experimental design in which the order of the levels of the independent variable is such that across subjects every level of the independent variable occurs an equal number of times and also follows every other level an equal number of times.

composite dependent variable—A measure of behavior that combines the results of several dependent variables into one measure of overall performance.

confounding variable—A variable whose levels are correlated with the levels of the independent variable so that any change in behavior could be due either to the levels of the independent variable or to those of the confounding variable.

construct validity—The strength of the link between the term used to refer to a class of behaviors (for example, aggression) and the behavior being manipulated or measured (for example, number of threatening statements).

contingency coefficient—A measure of the strength of association between two sets of nominal-scale numbers.

control group—In a between-subjects design the subjects who are treated in a way comparable to the experimental group(s) except for not being exposed to the experimental manipulation.

control variable—A circumstance of the experiment that the experimenter sets at a particular level and prevents from varying.

converging-series design—A sequence of experiments that are conducted to progressively eliminate competing theoretical hypotheses.

correlation—A relationship between two variables that is of a particular direction and a particular strength.

counterbalancing—A way of ordering the presentation of levels of the independent variable so as to minimize or eliminate the effects of sequential confounding variables.

critical incident—In applied research, a single instance that is considered to be diagnostic of a possible relationship between independent and dependent variables.

curvilinear function—A function that departs from a straight line and contains components that can be fit by various mathematical formulas for curved lines.

deductive inference—A means of reaching a logical conclusion from a set of premises (for example, A is a B, B is a C, therefore A is a C).

demand characteristics—Characteristics of an experiment that lead a subject to behave in a certain way, usually in support of the experimental hypothesis, independent of the levels of the independent variable.

descriptive statistics—Ways of reducing data sets so that only certain properties are described (for example, central tendency or dispersion of a distribution).

double-blind experiment—An experiment in which neither the subject nor the experimenter knows the particular level of the independent variable being presented.

experimental group—The subjects in a between-subjects experiment exposed to the treatment condition.

external validity—The generalizability of an experimental result to a particular real-world population, situation, or setting different from that represented in the experiment.

factorial design—An experimental design containing more than one independent variable in which every level of each independent variable is combined with every other level.

floor effect—The truncation of data at the bottom of a distribution due to a limit on the lowest score possible.

frequency distribution—A plot on the number of scores occurring for each score value or for two or more limited ranges of score values.

functional experiment—An experiment having three or more levels of an independent variable so that a functional relationship between the independent and dependent variables can be shown.

histogram—A means of illustrating the frequency of quantitative data using contiguous vertical bars. Quantitative class intervals are plotted on the abscissa with their frequency represented on the ordinate and the frequency of each class represented by the height of the bar over that class interval.

hypothesis—A statement about the possible relationship between two or more variables.

independent variable—A circumstance having two or more levels manipulated by the experimenter so that effects on the dependent variable can be observed.

inductive inference—A form of reasoning whereby a number of individual observations that represent a general class of observations is used to generalize to the entire class, thereby arriving at general principles.

inferential statistic—A statistical test that allows one to infer the likelihood that an observed result is due to chance alone.

interaction—The dependence of the size or direction of the relationship between an independent and dependent variable on the level of other independent variables.

internal validity—The certainty of the assertion that it was the manipulation of the independent variable that caused the change in the dependent variable.

interrupted time-series design—A quasi-experimental design in which a single group is observed multiple times both before and after an experimental manipulation.

interval scale—Measurements in which the intervals between numbers are a constant unit; $1 = n - (n - 1)$ (for example, Fahrenheit temperature).

level of significance—The statistical probability scientists require in order to say that an observed sample characteristic is due to chance rather than to being a characteristic of the underlying population. This probability is usually $p < .05$ or $p < .01$.

linear function—A function that forms a straight line.

literature search—The process of examining the formal scientific body of knowledge for written material relevant to a particular area of research.

main effect—In a factorial design the relationship between the levels of one independent variable and a dependent variable averaged across the levels of other independent variables.

Mann-Whitney U test—A nonparametric test of statistical inference used for testing the difference between two groups of subjects using rank-order information.

matched-groups design—A method of assigning subjects in between-subjects designs whereby sets of subjects are first formed by matching them on a variable that is highly correlated to the dependent variable and then subjects from each set are randomly assigned to groups.

mean—A measure of central tendency of a distribution that is calculated by adding all the scores and then dividing the total by the number of scores.

median—A measure of central tendency of a distribution that is calculated by ordering all the scores and selecting the middle score.

mode—A measure of central tendency of a distribution that is the most frequent score.

monotonic function—A function that increases throughout its range or decreases throughout its range.

naturalistic observation—A type of research in which behavior is studied within its natural setting.

negative function—A relationship in which increasing values of one variable are associated with decreasing values of a second variable.

negatively accelerated function—A function in which the rate of increase or decrease of one variable decreases as a second variable increases. Such functions are characterized by steep initial slopes that progressively become flatter.

nominal scale—A measurement scale without quantitative properties in which numbers are used as names (for instance, a runner with the number 342 pinned to her shirt).

nondifferential transfer—The situation in an experiment in which, when the two levels of the independent variable are A and B, the effect on behavior is the same whether A follows B or B follows A. Also called **symmetrical transfer.**

nonequivalent control-group design—A quasi-experimental design that uses a control group that is constituted in a manner different from that of the experimental group.

nonexperimental design—A research design that, unlike an experimental or quasi-experimental design, does not have protection from threats to internal validity. The results of such research are therefore impossible to defend.

nonexperiment control group—Subjects used to assess the demand characteristics of an experiment who are not actually exposed to the levels of the independent variable but are told of the experimental conditions and asked how they would respond.

nonmonotonic function—A function that changes from negative to positive slope or positive to negative slope in at least one place.

nonparametric test—A test of statistical inference that does not require any assumptions about the underlying population distributions, such as that they are normally distributed.

normal distribution—A frequency distribution, defined by a particular mathematical function, that is bell-shaped, unimodal, and symmetrical and has the same mean, median, and mode.

one-group posttest-only design—A nonexperimental design in which a single group of subjects is exposed to only one level of an independent variable.

one-group pretest-posttest design—A nonexperimental design in which a single group is tested, exposed to only one level of an independent variable, and then retested.

operational definition—The definition of a concept by means of specifying the operations required to manipulate or measure the concept.

ordinal scale—A measurement scale in which the order of the numbers is meaningful but intervals between or ratios of the numbers are not (for example, 9 is greater than 8).

ordinate—The vertical axis of a graph upon which the levels of a dependent variable are usually represented. Also called **y axis.**

parametric test—A test of statistical inference in which an assumption is made about the underlying population distribution; usually the assumption is that it is normal.

partial counterbalancing—A way of ordering the presentation of levels of the independent variable to minimize some of the effects of sequential confounding variables.

percent savings—A composite dependent variable in which the number of trials to relearn a task is subtracted from the number of trials to originally learn the task, and the result is divided by the number of trials to originally learn and then multiplied by 100 to determine the percentage of trials saved by having learned the task previously.

pilot experiment—A small-scale experiment that might not satisfy all the requirements of experimentation but is conducted to pretest the levels and procedures to be used in the final experiment.

positive function—A relationship in which increasing values of one variable are associated with increasing values of a second variable.

positively accelerated function—A function in which the rate of increase or decrease of one variable increases as a second variable increases. Such functions are characterized by shallow initial slopes that progressively become steeper.

posttest-only design with nonequivalent groups—A nonexperimental design in which one group is exposed to one level of an independent variable and a second group, chosen by a different selection mechanism, is exposed to a second level.

proceedings—The published reports of papers that were presented at a professional research conference.

proxy pretest—A test whose results are correlated with the posttest and is used to demonstrate partial equivalence of groups in quasi-experimental designs having nonequivalent groups.

psychohistory — Psychobiographies, usually of well-known individuals, that attempt to explain behavior patterns by examining critical events in their lives.

Psychological Abstracts—A journal published by the American Psychological Association that prints abstracts from articles contained in most psychological research journals.

pure research—Research whose goal is to understand the basic mechanisms of science. Although such research can lead to the solution of applied problems, the goal is simply to enhance the body of knowledge. Also called **basic research.**

quasi-experimental designs—Research designs that do not satisfy the subject randomization requirements of experimentation but that have designs allowing many of the threats to internal validity to be assessed.

randomization—A method of selection that operates by chance such that every item has an equal chance of being selected.

random variable—An experimental circumstance whose level is determined by chance rather than being controlled by the experimenter.

range—The difference between the smallest value and the largest value in a set of numbers.

ratio scale—A measurement scale in which the ratios of the numbers are meaningful (for example, 4 centimeters is twice as long as 2 centimeters).

reliability—The degree to which a measurement can be successfully repeated.

repeated-measures design—An experimental design in which each subject is exposed to all levels of the independent variable(s). Also called **within-subject design.**

response-surface methodology—A technique used to estimate the effects of a combination of many independent variables without having to conduct a complete factorial experiment combining all levels of all variables.

scatterplot—A means of graphing data points in which the position of each point is determined by its value corresponding to the variables on each axis.

Science Citation Index—A publication that lists scientific articles that have cited the article in question.

separate-groups design—An experimental design in which each group of subjects is exposed to only one level of the independent variable(s). Also called **between-subjects design.**

simulation control group—Subjects who are asked to pretend that they have been exposed to an experimental manipulation and to simulate the expected behavior so that the demand characteristics of an experiment can be assessed.

skewed distribution—An asymmetrical distribution whose tail extends farther in one direction than the other.

small-N baseline design—A type of single-variable experiment that can show effects using data from a small number of subjects. A steady-state baseline rate of responding is established, and then an experimental manipulation is made and a transition state established. Finally, the manipulation is removed and the baseline recovered. Also called a **baseline experiment.**

Social Sciences Citation Index—A publication that lists research articles from the social sciences that have cited the article in question.

standard deviation—A measure of the dispersion of a frequency distribution in which each score is sub-

tracted from the mean and then squared and summed. The sum is then divided by the number of scores, and the square root taken.

statistical conclusion validity—The degree to which a statistically significant relationship between the independent and dependent variables indicates that there is a real relationship.

statistical regression—The tendency, when subjects are chosen on the basis of having scored very high or very low on a test, for their scores to move toward the mean on a second test.

symmetrical transfer—The situation in an experiment in which, when the two levels of the independent variable are A and B, the effect on behavior is the same whether B follows A or A follows B. Also called **nondifferential transfer.**

theory—A partially verified statement of a scientific relationship that cannot be directly observed.

treatment—The application of an experimental manipulation by the experimenter, usually as contrasted to the control condition or group not exposed to the treatment.

truncated distribution—A limitation on the range of a particular variable that results in a bounded frequency distribution (for example, a ceiling or floor effect).

t-**test**—A parametric test of statistical inference used for determining the probability that an observed difference between data samples representing two different levels of an independent variable occurred by chance.

validity—The degree to which something (for example, a measuring device or a concept) corresponds to a standard.

variance—A measure of the dispersion of a frequency distribution in which each score is subtracted from the mean and then squared and summed. The sum is then divided by the number of scores.

within-subject design—An experimental design in which each subject is exposed to all levels of the independent variable(s). Also called **repeated-measure design.**

x **axis**—The horizontal axis of a graph upon which the levels of an independent variable are often represented. Also called **abscissa.**

y **axis**—The vertical axis of a graph upon which the levels of a dependent variable are usually represented. Also called **ordinate.**

Index